GATEWAYS TO TH

MEHRAN KAMRAVA

Editor

Gateways to the World

Port Cities in the Persian Gulf

جـامـعـة جـورجـتـاون قـطـر

GEORGETOWN UNIVERSITY QATAR

Center *for* International *and* Regional Studies

HURST & COMPANY, LONDON

Published in Collaboration with
Center for International and Regional Studies,
Georgetown University–Qatar

First published in the United Kingdom in 2016 by
C. Hurst & Co. (Publishers) Ltd.,
41 Great Russell Street, London, WC1B 3PL
© Mehran Kamrava and the contributors, 2016
All rights reserved.
Printed in India

The right of Mehran Kamrava and the Contributors to be identified
as the author of this publication is asserted by them in accordance
with the Copyright, Designs and Patents Act, 1988.

A Cataloguing-in-Publication data record for this book
is available from the British Library.

978-1-84904-563-6 *paperback*

This book is printed using paper from registered sustainable
and managed sources.

www.hurstpublishers.com

In loving memory of Barb Gillis

CONTENTS

vii

CONTENTS

LIST OF ILLUSTRATIONS

LIST OF ILLUSTRATIONS

CONTRIBUTORS

Pooya Alaedini is Associate Professor of Social Planning in the Faculty of Social Sciences, University of Tehran. Over the past few years, he has acted as a consultant for several international development projects in the Middle East, Central Asia, and Africa. His publications include *From Shelter to Regeneration: Slum Upgrading and Housing Policies in I.R. Iran* as well as two earlier books in Persian on urban entrepreneurship in Tehran and post-disaster reconstruction in Iran, a dozen peer-reviewed articles in Persian and English, and two full-length reports produced for international organizations.

Marike Bontenbal is a Senior Policy Officer at the Netherlands National Commission for UNESCO in The Hague. An urban geographer with extensive experience in the Persian Gulf region, Bontenbal is the author of *Cities as Partners: The Challenge to Strengthen Urban Governance through North-South City Partnerships*. She has also published articles in journals such as the *Journal of Arabian Studies, Urban Studies, Environment and Urbanization, Habitat International,* and *Public Administration and Development*.

Remah Gharib is Assistant Professor in the School of Islamic Studies at Hamad Bin Khalifah University, where he coordinates the Urban Design and Architecture in Muslim Societies Programme. He holds a PhD in Architecture and Urban Design from the University of Nottingham, where he developed his knowledge of revitalization and management of historic quarters. His research focuses on aspects of public policy formulation and implementation. He is a collaborating editor for *ArchNet International Journal of Architectural Research*.

Mehrdad Javaheripour is Assistant Professor of Social Sciences at the Islamic Azad University, Central Branch, Tehran, where he focuses on urban sociology and social stratification. With more than twenty years of experience in

working for urban development consulting firms as well as the research arm of the Ministry of Housing and Urban Development in Iran, he has written a number of articles and reports on slum upgrading and was instrumental in the preparation of Iran's "National Document on Strategies for Enabling and Regularizing Informal Settlements."

Mehran Kamrava is Professor and Director of the Center for International and Regional Studies at Georgetown University's School of Foreign Service in Qatar. He is the author of a number of journal articles and books, including, most recently, *The Impossibility of Palestine*; *Qatar: Small State, Big Politics*; *The Modern Middle East: A Political History since the First World War*, 3rd edn; and *Iran's Intellectual Revolution*. His edited books include *Beyond the Arab Spring: The Evolving Ruling Bargain in the Middle East*; *The International Politics of the Persian Gulf*; *The Political Economy of the Persian Gulf*; and *The Nuclear Question in the Middle East*.

Ahmed Kanna teaches cultural anthropology, human geography, and urban sociology at the University of the Pacific. He is author of *Dubai, The City as Corporation*, and numerous articles that have appeared in *City*, *Cultural Anthropology*, *Jadaliyya*, *Journal of Urban Affairs*, and other journals. He is also the editor of *Rethinking Global Urbanism* (with Xiangming Chen) and *The Superlative City: Dubai and the Urban Condition in the Early 21st Century*. He currently works on urban theory, urban knowledge production, and global south urbanism, and lives in Oakland, California.

Arang Keshavarzian is Associate Professor of Middle Eastern and Islamic Studies at New York University. He is the author of *Bazaar and State in Iran: The Politics of the Tehran Marketplace*. His most recent journal article, "When Ties don't Bind: Smuggling Effects, Bazaars and Regulatory Regimes in Post-Revolutionary Iran," was co-authored with Narges Erami and published in *Economy and Society* in 2015.

Stephen J. Ramos is Assistant Professor in the College of Environment and Design at the University of Georgia. He is the author of *Dubai Amplified: The Engineering of a Port Geography*, co-editor of *Infrastructure Sustainability and Design*, and a founding editor of the journal *New Geographies*.

Ashraf M. Salama is Professor and Head of the School of Architecture at the University of Strathclyde, Glasgow, UK. He was the founding Head of Architecture and Urban Planning at Qatar University. His most recent books include *Spatial Design Education: New Directions for Pedagogy in Architecture* *and Beyond*; and *Demystifying Doha: On Architecture and Urbanism in an Emerging City* (with Florian Wiedmann). His latest co-edited book is *Architecture Beyond Criticism: Expert Judgment and Performance Evaluation.*

M. Evren Tok is Assistant Professor in the Faculty of Islamic Studies at Hamad Bin Khalifa University, where he also serves as Coordinator of the Public Policy in Islam Program. His most recent publications include *Qatar: Policy Making in a Transformative State* (with Lolwah Al Khater and Leslie A. Pal). He holds a PhD from Carleton University, Ottawa.

Florian Wiedmann is co-founder of ARRUS (an urban planning consultancy), and Lecturer in the Department of Architecture at the Frankfurt University of Applied Sciences in Germany. His most recent books include *Demystifying Doha: On Architecture and Urbanism in an Emerging City* (with Ashraf Salama), and *Post-oil Urbanism in the Gulf: New Evolutions in Governance and the Impact on Urban Morphologies.* He has also published in journals such as the *Journal of Urbanism.*

Mohammad Zebian is an Innovation Manager at Qatar Science and Technology Park and also a PhD candidate in Innovation Policy at Carleton University, Ottawa. His dissertation focuses on strengthening knowledge economies in the Gulf states.

ACKNOWLEDGMENTS

This volume emerged as one of the research initiatives undertaken by the Center for International and Regional Studies of Georgetown University School of Foreign Service. A number of specialists and scholars helped identify original research questions concerning the study of Persian Gulf port cities and shaped the intellectual discussions that went into crafting this volume. They included Ala Al-Hamarneh, Farah Al-Nakib, Zahra Babar, Samer Bagaeen, Matthew Buehler, Mohammad Reza Farzanegan, Remah Gharib, Nelida Fuccaro, Suzi Mirgani, Dwaa Osman, and Marcus Stephenson. Suzi Mirgani expertly read and provided extensive comments on the entire manuscript. My own two contributions here benefited also from Zahra Babar's keen insights. The incomparable staff of CIRS was instrumental in ensuring the success of two working groups in Doha in which the contributors brainstormed ideas concerning urbanism and port cities in the Persian Gulf and critiqued each other's works. Without their hard work the task of editing the volume would have been much harder. Other colleagues at Georgetown University, Qatar were equally instrumental in shaping our ideas and providing helpful advice and insight into the topic. Grateful acknowledgment goes also to the Qatar Foundation for its support of research and other scholarly endeavors.

1

INTRODUCTION

Mehran Kamrava

By all accounts, the growth of cities on the southern shores of the Persian Gulf has been phenomenal, all shooting forward from dusty little port towns and villages, dependent as late as the 1920s and the 1930s on pearling and fishing, into gleaming cities with global aspirations. As Sulayman Khalaf commented back in the mid-2000s, "oil-generated growth has literally demolished small mud-walled seaports and villages. In just four decades, they have been transformed into glittering commercial capitals and sprawling suburbs integrated within the global economy and culture. The speed, pattern, and policies of urban development have been similar across the Gulf."[1] Today, rightly or wrongly, a number of the cities consider themselves as "global cities," or at least aspire to be one. Collectively, not only have the Persian Gulf's port cities changed the geography and face of the region, but, more importantly, they have altered the region's role in relation to broader, global networks of trade

---

[1] Sulayman Khalaf, "The evolution of the Gulf city type, oil, and globalization," in John W. Fox, Nada Mourtada-Sabbah, and Mohammad al-Mutawa, eds, *Globalization and the Gulf* (London: Routledge, 2006), p. 247.

1

and commerce, service delivery, corporate decision-making, and the production of information.

This book explores how the urban face of the Persian Gulf is changing, and the processes and consequences of the changes that have occurred at an incredibly rapid pace. In a region long viewed by domestic and international actors as critically important to global networks of trade and commerce, in recent decades internal dynamics rooted in endogenous political forces have combined and colluded with external developments to shape the Persian Gulf's port cities. Some of these cities have capitalized on emerging trends in the global political economy in order to give themselves roles and profiles that would link them to networks far beyond the region. Others have been left behind, or have taken themselves out of the race, having instead developed a different rhythm of urban life internally and connections externally to other cities and transnational networks. The focus of this book revolves around these differential rates of engagement by the port cities of the Persian Gulf with internal and external dynamics and developments, the resulting emergence of different types of port cities, their roles, changing faces, and the broader consequences for the region and beyond. The Persian Gulf has long been a gateway to the world. This volume explores the roles and the rise and fall of its port cities in modern times.

Cities, Ports, and Global Cities

In recent years, the study of cities has drawn from social network analysis. As such, cities are seen as interconnected networks in which attention is paid to specific actors (nodes), flows (paths or exchanges), and relationships between them.[2] But this focus on flows and relationships need not be at the expense of attention to the internal dynamics within cities that also define or at least shape their forms, growth patterns, resources, and dominant features. In the Persian Gulf, regional forces and geostrategic dynamics, as well as the policies and priorities of state leaders, have been equally important in shaping the overall profile and form of cities within and their position in broader regional and global networks. The exploration of these internal and external dynamics that have shaped the contemporary port cities of the Persian Gulf, and examinations of how these dynamics came about, the ways in which they manifest themselves, and their consequences, form the focus of this book.

[2] Bruce Stanley, "Middle East city networks and the 'new urbanism,'" *Cities*, Vol. 22, No. 3 (2005), p. 190.

INTRODUCTION

Cities, of course, form one of the most elemental foundations of human society, and "come alive and develop personalities that represent the many people, objects, and technologies in continuous negotiations and symbiosis within them." They are also "the canvass upon which the collective history, relationships, and aspirations of [their] residents are painted."[3] Recent decades have seen greater levels of state intervention and planning in the making and remaking of the urban built environment. At the same time, modern changes in patterns of urban development have resulted in "pronounced disunions in urban life in general and in the built urban environment in particular."[4] As the contributions in this volume demonstrate, these steadily increasing levels of state involvement in urban planning, whether on a coordinated and larger scale or on an ad hoc basis, and the resulting discontinuities and disjunctures in urban form constitute one of the important and relatively universal hallmarks of the Persian Gulf's port cities.

Among cities, those located along coastlines and major rivers—port cities— tend to develop particular characteristics and specialized relationships with other cities and ports. Ports and port cities have evolved at the intersection of local and global forces.[5] Despite major structural transformations in the economic and functional nature of global trade, shipping, and logistics, ports and cities remain closely interconnected.[6] In fact, urban geographers are agreed that it would be mistaken to assume that cities and especially ports are "solitudes of unconnected actors and stakeholders."[7] The role and significance of port cities tend to be particularly sensitive to changes arising from larger contextual political, economic, and technical transformations unfolding around them, as well as endogenously-initiated changes to their own built environment.[8] This is all the

---

[3] James H. Spencer, *Globalization and Urbanization: The Global Urban Ecosystem* (Lanham, MD: Rowman & Littlefield, 2015), p. 17.

[4] Hooshang Amirahmadi and Mohamad R. Razavi, "Urban Development in the Muslim World: Encounter with Modernity and Implications for Planning," in Hooshang Amirahmadi and Salah S. El-Shakhs, eds, *Urban Development in the Muslim World* (New Brunswick, NJ: Transaction, 1993), p. 2.

[5] Carola Hein, et al., "Port cityscapes: dynamic perspectives on the port-city-waterfront interface," Special Paper Session at the Annual Meeting of the Association of American Geographers, Los Angeles, 12 April 2013, p. 810.

[6] Ibid., p. 806.

[7] Ibid., p. 805.

[8] Carola Hein, "Port Cityscapes: A Networked Analysis of the Built Environment," in Carola Hein, ed., *Port Cities: Dynamic Landscapes and Global Networks* (London: Routledge, 2011), pp. 19–20.

more important since, historically, port cities have played crucial roles as relay stations in globalization by constituting important hubs of trade and traffic.[9] Any serious analysis of port cities must therefore necessarily take an integrated approach to the complex interactions between a port city's built environment, metropolitan spatial form, urban planning actors, and economic and commercial land and sea networks.[10]

Urban historians generally divide the history of port cities into a number of discernible phases. The first phase, which started in medieval times and lasted up until the nineteenth century, saw the establishment and proliferation of pre-industrial, bustling city harbors. The second phase, one of rapid industrial and commercial growth, started in the nineteenth century and lasted into the early twentieth century. Industrial growth brought with it larger ships, with more cargo that needed to be stored, and therefore an expansion of ports and port facilities. These developments were further deepened and upgraded in the third phase, which roughly corresponded to the period between the two World Wars, during which "Fordist industrial production and its guiding themes of precision, efficiency, economy, reliability, and speed" ruled the day.[11] As ships became much larger and heavier and ports had to adapt accordingly, beginning in the 1960s large and technologically modern ports began moving away from traditional harbor areas near the city center and into designated areas designed to accommodate changes in transport technology. It was within this fourth phase that containerization revolutionized not only sea-bound transportation of goods but also dock labor and port facilities.[12]

But the prominence of these ports, marvels of modernity in their own right, was not to last long. The fifth phase, beginning in the 1980s, saw a steady deterioration of many port cities as even larger and technologically more advanced ships began calling on fewer, larger ports that could accommodate them. As Schubert maintains, "the post-Fordist city disintegrated into a polycentric fragmented structure with aggravated social conflict."[13] Deeper

---

[9] Lars Amenda, "China-Towns and Container Terminals: Shipping Networks and Urban Patterns in Port Cities in Global and Local Perspective, 1880–1980," in Carola Hein, ed., *Port Cities: Dynamic Landscapes and Global Networks* (London: Routledge, 2011), p. 53.

[10] Hein, et al., "Port cityscapes," p. 805.

[11] Dirk Schubert, "Seaport Cities: Phases of Spatial Restructuring and Types and Dimensions of Redevelopment," in Carola Hein, ed., *Port Cities: Dynamic Landscapes and Global Networks* (London: Routledge, 2011), p. 56.

[12] Ibid., pp. 58–9.

[13] Ibid., p. 59.

seaports and better highways and railway systems, which facilitated greater transportation ease and speed, gave a marked advantage to some ports over others, resulting in the accrual of advantage to a few ports at the expense of many others.

Schubert has identified a sixth phase in the evolution of seaports, one in which he maintains a process of redevelopment has taken place. Often on a step-by-step basis and without much attention to devising a larger sustainable urban or regional development strategy, a process of (re)development has been taking place in many of these formerly vibrant port cities. Usually starting with their most attractive sites, this urban redevelopment often takes the shape of building new business and shopping districts, entertainment areas, and residences. Throughout the 1990s, waterfront revitalization projects became the norm in a number of port cities, a process which in many parts of Asia was accompanied by, and accomplished through, land reclamation projects (especially in cities such as Osaka, Kobe, Tokyo, and Yokohama).[14]

As Chapters 3 and 4 of this volume demonstrate, it was around this time, in the 1980s and the 1990s, we see the development of a growing dichotomy between two types of port cities in the Persian Gulf: those that embarked on massive infrastructural development, upgraded their facilities, sought to become crucial nodes in steadily expanding global networks of trade, commerce, and information, and therefore become more appealing to corporations and other actors in the global economy; and those that remained comparatively underdeveloped, failed to upgrade their facilities and infrastructures, did not receive the sustained attention of their respective central governments, and therefore did not integrate into global networks of commerce, finance, and information to the same extent as the first group. To this first group belong the port cities of Kuwait, Manama, Doha, Abu Dhabi, and Dubai; the second group includes Basra, Bandar Abbas, and Bushehr.

The 1980s and 1990s also marked a time when a number of Persian Gulf port cities began aspiring to become "global cities." Saskia Sassen, one of the pioneers in the study of global cities, argues that changes to the global economy since the 1980s resulted in the increased importance of major cities as "sites for producing strategic global inputs." Because of the continued concentration of economic ownership and control, at a time when the actual location of factories and services is being globally dispersed, some cities have assumed a special strategic role and have become what may be called "global cities."

---

[14] Ibid., pp. 64, 67.

Sassen maintains that these global cities have three main characteristics: they are "command points in the organization of the world economy"; they are key locations and marketplaces for industries that are currently key to the global economy, namely finance and specialized services; and they are "major sites of *production*, including the production of innovations, for these industries as their products are not simply a function of talent but are made."[15]

In today's global economy, the role of the city is determined by its position within the cross-currents of international transactions. Sassen calls attention to the spatial correlation between cities and the global economy. Global cities, in fact, are offshore banking centers.[16] In today's global economy, a vast number of these global circuits have emerged in which complex international organizational and financial transactions are framed. According to Sassen, "these emergent intercity geographies begin to function as an infrastructure for globalization," and rely on certain cities as critical nodes in complex global networks.[17] Global cities are therefore "strategic sites for the management of the global economy and the production of the most advanced services and financial operations that have become key inputs for that work of managing global economic operations."[18]

Size and economic connections are not necessarily indicators of whether or not a city is "global." Instead, what matters is a city's contribution to the growth of contemporary global connections.[19] As Manuel Castells puts it, "the global city is not a place but a process. A process by which centers of production and consumption of advanced services and their ancillary local societies, are connected in a global network while simultaneously downplaying the linkages with their hinterlands on the basis of information flows."[20] Global cities therefore act as "regional motors of the world economy" by providing locations for the headquarter functions of globally operating industrial corporations, and acting as "major locations for new 'knowledge-based' production chains and for highly innovative production clusters" in fields such as information technology, medical engineering, and biotechnology.[21]

---

[15] Saskia Sassen, *Cities in a World Economy*, 4th edn (London: Sage, 2012), p. 7.

[16] Ibid., p. 16.

[17] Ibid., p. 112.

[18] Ibid., p. 34.

[19] Spencer, *Globalization and Urbanization*, p. 36.

[20] Manuel Castells, *The Rise of the Networked Society*, 2nd edn (Oxford: Wiley-Blackwell, 2010), p. 417.

[21] Stefan Kratke, Kathrin Wildner, and Stephan Lanz, "The Transnationality of Cities:

These industries also foster the expansion of low-skilled and low-paid jobs, mostly in such services sectors as cleaners, food vendors, and the like.[22]

As Sassen reminds us, "there is no perfect global city."[23] The social and physical aspects of cities are characterized by fragmentation. There are "globalized" segments of the urban economy and labor force, alongside large segments of the urban economy and labor force that are not integrated into the world economy and have, at best, minimal interactions with it.[24] This distinction into globalized versus non-global aspects of cities can also be found in relation to the physical space of cities. Most parts of the city are, in general, not inhabited by globalized economic actors and activities.[25]

One way to conceptualize a global city is to examine it within the context of transnationalism. All cities are sites of the spatial dimensions of transnationalism.[26] "Cities are nodes or hubs of transnational processes; they are paradigmatic and constitutive places of transnationalism."[27] And, the more global a city, the more widespread within its fabric are what may be referred to as "transnational urban spaces." These "transnational urban spaces" are transborder social networks or ethnic communities that emerge in the context of migration, economic exchange, or political structures. Transnationality denotes "cross-border connective processes that are both social and identificational."[28] Transnationalism "draws our attention to the emergence, properties, and impacts of transnational flows, networks, and social practices."[29] As a phenomenon, transnationality needs to be distinguished from "international" or "multinational" as it "entails the emergence of a new quality of economic, social, and cultural relations both within and between the interacting organi-

Concepts, Dimensionsm and Research Fields. An Introduction," in Stefan Kratke, Kathrin Wildner, and Stephan Lanz, eds, *Transnationalism and Urbanism* (London: Routledge, 2012), p. 13.

[22] Ibid., p. 13.

[23] Sassen, *Cities in a World Economy*, p. 114.

[24] Kratke, Wildner, and Lanz, "The Transnationality of Cities," p. 6.

[25] Ibid., p. 7.

[26] Ibid., p. 2.

[27] Ibid., p. 22.

[28] Nina Glick Schiller, "Transnationality and the City," in Stefan Kratke, Kathrin Wildner, and Stephan Lanz, eds, *Transnationalism and Urbanism* (London: Routledge, 2012), p. 33.

[29] Kratke, Wildner, and Lanz, "The Transnationality of Cities," p. 1.

zations, communities, territories, and places."[30] It is important to examine the material manifestations of transnationality in cities, its consequences for the physical transformation of spaces as arenas for transnational actors and transborder activities, on the emergence of social and economic networks, and on the creation of narrative and discursive spaces that are born out of cultural production (film and literature) and the media.[31]

Much debate and disagreement exists around the question of whether or not the Middle East in general and the Persian Gulf in particular have any global cities, especially in the sense defined here. Historians and archaeologists are agreed that the Middle East region was home to some of the earliest and most advanced cities dating as far back as 4000 BCE, a number of which featured not only remarkable achievements in urban development but also in complex trade and cultural linkages with other cities elsewhere.[32] But the ancient, "global" cities of Mesopotamia did not survive into contemporary times, and neither did the civilizational glories of Baghdad, Damascus, Cairo, Isfahan, and Istanbul last beyond specific, bygone centuries. Today it is Dubai, Abu Dhabi, and Doha that aspire to become global in their infrastructures, profiles, and transboundary roles. Whether or not they are having success in this endeavor, for now at least, is an open question.

Studying Port Cities in the Persian Gulf

Studies of port cities in general and those in the Persian Gulf in particular have generally focused on several interrelated areas. The first includes the interconnected nature of regional and global networks of which port cities are a part, and the commercial, demographic, and cultural orientations that result from and which in turn reinforce these networks. Ports thrive on trade, and with trade comes multiple levels of interconnectedness with other trading centers and trading routes, and, eventually, with other metropolises that serve as nodes of commerce, information, logistics, and services.[33] The profile and role of a port city depends on dynamics resulting from the political contexts

---

[30] Ibid., p. 1.

[31] Ibid., p. 3.

[32] Colbert C. Held and John Thomas Cummings, *Middle East Patterns: Places, Peoples, and Politics*, 6th edn (Boulder, CO: Westview, 2014), pp. 62–3.

[33] See, for example, Willem Floor, *The Persian Gulf: A Political and Economic History of Five Port Cities 1500–1730* (Washington, DC: Mage, 2006); and Lawrence Potter, ed., *The Persian Gulf in History* (New York: Palgrave Macmillan, 2009).

within which port cities operate. This revolves around both the domestic political environment that affects policy-making and resource allocation to the port city, as well as the context of the larger international political economy within which ports find themselves and in which they operate.

In the Persian Gulf, these political considerations have been shaped by the region's strategic importance because of its petrochemical resources, leading to the emergence of what may be called "oil urbanization."[34] In the resource-richer countries of the Persian Gulf, oil permeates life beyond macroeconomic and political dynamics; it also shapes patterns of urbanization. These urbanization patterns, as it happens, are often uneven and at times even contradictory. Parts of the city benefit from sustained state attention and resources, and therefore infrastructural development and growth, while other parts retain much of their traditional fabric, or undergo change and transformation that is more endogenous and unplanned and uncoordinated by central authorities. The resulting urban form has been disjointed and incongruent, often making parts of the city look nothing like other parts, creating discontinuities not only in form but also in infrastructure, profile, function, and overall orientation.

These discontinuities mark the urban landscapes of the broader Middle East and also the Persian Gulf sub-region. The Middle East is one of the most rapidly urbanizing regions of the world, and, within the Middle East, the Persian Gulf features some of the highest rates of urbanization. By 2025, four countries in the Middle East and North Africa are expected to be around 90 per cent urban, three of them in the Persian Gulf region. They include Lebanon (90 per cent), Bahrain (90 per cent), Qatar (97 per cent), and Kuwait (98 per cent).[35] Historically, specific Islamic influences—legal, cultural, and symbolic—have helped shaped the urban environment throughout Muslim-majority countries.[36] But in more contemporary times the driving forces behind urban growth and planning have been those of modernity as defined by states and their leaders and planners. Not surprisingly, today's Middle Eastern cities, not unlike cities elsewhere, feature discontinuities and disjunctures, and at times even glaring contradictions, in built areas and urban forms: modern centers filled with high-rises and towers versus migrant settle-

---

[34] Nelida Fuccaro, "Visions of the City: Urban Studies in the Gulf," *Middle East Studies Association Bulletin*, Vol. 35, No. 2 (Winter 2001), pp. 177–8.

[35] Sona Nambiar, "Urban sustainability behind megacity projects," www.zawya.com, last accessed 3 March 2013.

[36] Amirahmadi and Razavi, "Urban Development in the Muslim World," p. 2.

ments on the urban periphery; formal versus informal sector activities; the *medina*, traditional core city, versus newly-built, planned areas; and the consolidation of state structures versus the erosion of the institutions of civil society.[37] As Yasser Mahgoub correctly observes, "while some architects attempt to integrate the local architecture into global cultural trends, others try to revive the traditional architectural style to protect the local identity and heritage. The resulting built environment is chaotic and lacks identity and sense of place." Mahgoub's contention that in Kuwait "processes of globalization and localization are inseparable and ... coexist" can be applied to most other aspiring global cities of the Persian Gulf, and indeed elsewhere.[38]

These contradictions may be less obvious in the aspiring global cities of Doha, Abu Dhabi, and Dubai, which seem addicted to tearing up their old neighborhoods and replacing them with new ones.[39] But they are evident elsewhere across the Persian Gulf and almost universally throughout the Middle East. These encounters with modernity and the resulting contradictions, one of the principal constitutive elements of Persian Gulf cities, are explored in the chapters to come.

Another defining characteristic of port cities everywhere is their connectivity with other cities and ports. Across the Middle East and especially in the Persian Gulf, some cities tend to be globally less connected while others are much more integrated into broader, global networks in terms of commercial and economic orientations, demographic composition and cultural disposition, and industrial, transit, and other forms of interconnectedness. By virtue of their geographic location as gateways to points near and far, their natural resources, their commercial orientation, and their demographic make-up, "Gulfi" societies have long had multiple, in-depth interconnections with communities and markets elsewhere in their vicinity and beyond.[40] By and large, this global connectedness is concentrated mostly in a few of the larger, more ambitious port cities of the Persian Gulf, having generally bypassed most of the other cities of the Middle East and North Africa. As Bruce Stanley

---

[37] Ibid., pp. 5–6.

[38] Yasser Mahgoub, "Globalization and the built environment in Kuwait," *Habitat International*, Vol. 28 (2004), p. 505.

[39] Mehran Kamrava, *Qatar: Small State, Big Politics* (Ithaca, NY: Cornell University Press, 2013), p. 6.

[40] For a collection of discussions on these historical interconnections, see Lawrence Potter, ed., *The Persian Gulf in Modern Times* (New York: Palgrave Macmillan, 2014).

INTRODUCTION

observes, "across a range of sectors, the MENA city-system plays little role in the urban world. There are many black holes and deadends, too little broker- age, not enough global cities, few weak ties, low density, poor reachability, limited isomorphism, strong primacy, and hierarchy."[41] Stanley calls for employing a network analysis to the study of cities in the Middle East, which, he maintains, draws attention to the importance of studying how power is distributed between and is applied among the cities in a network; of examin- ing the bases for the organization of a network, or a community, which may be loosely knit and spatially dispersed; and of looking at how city-systems and city hierarchies evolve over time.[42] Many of the contributions to this volume, including my own, employ network analysis as conceptualized by Stanley without necessarily using the label.

The volume's contributions also present comparative analyses of the Persian Gulf's port cities in terms of their domestic infrastructural and demographic composition, and their resource allocation domestically and in relation to global supply chains. Due largely to a belief in the "unique" nature of Persian Gulf cities, much of the literature on urbanization in the region has eschewed com- parative analysis. Instead, most studies of urbanization in the Persian Gulf treat the phenomenon as a state enterprise that is based on "modernist" visions of rulers and the bevy of consultants and architects they hire. But few examine the socio-cultural, political, and ideological structure of oil-driven urbanization, especially at the micro-level. As Nelida Fuccaro puts it, "the predominance of studies on oil urbanization precludes an understanding of oil urbanism as a way of life and as a mode of political and socio-economic organization."[43] Therefore, what is needed is a better understanding of "the political and human texture" of contemporary Persian Gulf cities.[44] As episodes of urban unrest in Kuwait and Manama have demonstrated, especially since the 2011 Arab uprisings, informal, urban-based networks can in certain instances present avenues of empowerment for various social actors such as the youth, members of a religious sect (the Shi'a in Bahrain), or specific ideological groups (Islamist activists in Kuwait). Fuccaro suggests the study of the definition of public versus private space in oil cities as a venue for social and political interaction. In particular, the distribution pattern of residential areas based on ethnicity, class, and religious affiliation needs to be

41 Stanley, "Middle East city networks and the 'new urbanism,'" p. 197.
42 Ibid., pp. 195–6.
43 Fuccaro, "Visions of the City," p. 179.
44 Ibid., p. 185.

11

more thoroughly studied.[45] These themes figure prominently in all of the contributions in this volume.

Perhaps one of the most visibly striking features of Persian Gulf port cities is their stunning architectural transformation over the last decade or so. Not surprisingly, many studies of the topic concentrate on these transformations. Ahmed Kanna takes issue with studies that see the architectural transformations of Persian Gulf cities as devoid of the larger economic and political contexts within which they take place. He writes complainingly that "rather than exhibiting a critical awareness that visual icons of so-called Gulf Arab national identity are traditions invented as part of the cultural politics of the ruling Gulf dynasties, urban experts usually take these icons at face value."[46] The international architectural firms and the star architects so frequently employed by the Persian Gulf's ruling families, he argues, see themselves as important and strong "service providers" in helping their employers reconstruct an imaginary, politically-motivated cultural landscape.[47] The critical awareness of emerging architectural forms that Kanna sees as lacking in other works informs the contributions here, including Kanna's own.

It should come as no surprise that much of these mega-development projects, as well as larger processes of urban planning and development, are carried forward with one eye firmly on political considerations. As an example, Kuwait's 2010–14 development plan encompassed an ambitious construction program in which Kuwaiti citizens would be the direct beneficiaries of the revenues thus generated. According to the plan itself, it accounts for "several development projects to be implemented by establishing public shareholding companies through the mechanism of public subscription of at least 50% of the shares, thus maximizing high return on these mega projects."[48]

---

[45] Ibid., pp. 179–80.

[46] Ahmed Kanna, "Speaking of the City: Establishing Urban Expertise in the Arab Gulf," *International Journal of Middle East Studies*, Vol. 46 (2014), p. 171.

[47] Ibid., p. 170.

[48] Adel A. Al-Wugayan, "Kuwait Development Plans," Special Program—Germany-GCC Investment and Business Forum, available at http://www.ghorfa.de/fileadmin/inhalte/GCC-Germany_Forum/Praesentationen/Session1/Dr._Adel_AlWugayan.pdf. At the time, Al-Wugayan was the Secretary General of the Supreme Council for Planning and Development of the State of Kuwait. An assessment of the development plan, along with some of the estimated costs in billions of dollars for each of the projects it includes, can be found in "Kuwait Development Plan (KDP): Progress or Retreat," *Capital Standards* (June 2013), pp. 1–8.

INTRODUCTION

Ben-Hamouche observes a similar phenomenon in Bahrain, where, he argues, most of Manama's urban development projects are driven primarily by political considerations involving the highest levels of political leadership and often bypass existing planning processes. Architectural decisions are therefore often made without due consideration of their consequences for the built environment, national heritage, and the broader patterns and processes of urban planning.[49] In addition to their functional purposes as landmarks of modernity and global ambitions, massive real estate development projects, and the land reclamations that they frequently necessitate, are also driven by the political imperative to recycle wealth to local elites with commercial resources and influence and to maintain the rentier bargain between the state and its local clients.[50]

Related to domestic political considerations is the global profile of cities like Dubai, Abu Dhabi, Doha, Manama, and Kuwait. These emerging profiles and the domestic and global ambitions behind them are explored at length in this volume. All contributions here take as their starting point links between emerging forms of urbanism in the aspiring global cities of the Persian Gulf and their efforts to carve out a position and role for themselves domestically and internationally. Architecture and urbanism are seldom devoid of political significance. But in the Persian Gulf the links between the two are particularly salient and are some of the primary drivers, if not the only drivers, of efforts at carving an emerging global profile. The message to audiences at home and abroad is one of power, wealth, and the interconnection between tradition and modernity. The result is an ever-changing, modern skyline in the cities and city states of the Persian Gulf, which, as one seasoned observer writes, "has a sort of menacing quality—by using the symbols of Arabic/Islamic architecture these new cities are projecting themselves as the new centers of the region. They are not 'tribes with flags' anymore."[51]

---

[49] Mustapha Ben-Hamouche, "Manama: The Metamorphosis of an Arab Gulf City," in Yasser Elsheshtawy, ed., *The Evolving Arab City: Tradition, Modernity, and Urban Development* (London: Routledge, 2008), p. 212.

[50] For more state efforts to recycle wealth to local elites, see Kamrava, *Qatar*, pp. 131–3. For the imperative to maintain ruling bargains, see Mehran Kamrava, "The Rise and Fall of Ruling Bargains in the Middle East," in Mehran Kamrava, ed., *Beyond the Arab Spring: The Evolving Ruling Bargain in the Middle East* (New York: Oxford University Press, 2014), pp. 17–45.

[51] Yasser Elsheshtawy, "The Great Divide: Struggling and Emerging Cities in the Arab World," in Yasser Elsheshtawy, ed., *The Evolving Arab City: Tradition, Modernity, and Urban Development* (London: Routledge, 2008), p. 21.

This Volume

The contributions to this volume explore the causes, processes, and consequences of different forms of urbanism throughout the Persian Gulf's port cities from Basra to Muscat. The volume begins with Arang Keshavarzian's contribution, which focuses on the historical interconnectedness of Persian Gulf port cities and the relationships that drew them together as part of a larger social geography. But this "glocal" orientation has fallen victim to divergent historical paths, in the process resulting also in the morphological separation of ports from cities, and creating urban spaces of privilege for some based on identity, class, and citizenship status. Ultimately, Keshavarzian argues, inter-coastal and interurban dynamics have widened the gulf within the Persian Gulf.

My own contribution in turn builds on Keshavarzian's by elaborating on the nature of the divisions and differences that have emerged in urban forms in the Persian Gulf over the last several decades, with some cities and ports slowly decaying and atrophying while others have grown and have developed not just regional but global aspirations. I take Keshavarzian's argument about divergent historical paths by Persian Gulf port cities as my starting point. Some port cities were established as company towns by Western oil enterprises, with Abadan and Dammam as primary examples, designed specifically for purposes of segregating Western employees from local ones and housing each according to hierarchy and rank. Dammam has received government attention and resources, but Abadan has mostly been left on its own, still bearing the scars of Iran's war with Iraq from 1980 to 1988. Also largely ignored are secondary port cities such as Basra, Bushehr, and Bandar Abbas, especially in comparison to the aspiring global cities of Kuwait, Manama, Doha, Abu Dhabi, and Dubai. I question whether this latter group of port cities have reached the status of "global cities" despite their expanding roles as nodes in global networks of transportation, logistics, and services. Impressive buildings and modern landmarks they have in abundance, but whether form can attract or foster substance is yet to be seen.

Stephen Ramos focuses on historical processes of state formation in what later came to be the United Arab Emirates (UAE). Through his examination of the Trucial States, or more accurately Trucial cities, Ramos traces the critical role of city states, and more specifically infrastructures, in territorial fixity, demarcation, and eventually state formation. Following a model proposed by the historian Antoine Picon, Ramos explores the role of the civil engineer and infrastructure in the construction of territory and larger spatial processes of nation-building. Ramos's contribution is key in setting the historical stage. It reminds us that the Trucial city-states, and not just today's UAE but also Qatar and Bahrain, are exceedingly young national entities, still proactively involved in processes of nation-building and identity formation, an integral part of which, at least in their eyes, is hyper-growth, outlandish architecture, mega projects, and the creation of instant cities.

This distinction between form and substance is the central focus of Ahmed Kanna's chapter. Kanna questions some of the basic assumptions regarding "the city" and, under the rubric of the anthropocene, calls attention to the relationship between the urban and the human-environmental. He argues against the "naïve realism" that praises Persian Gulf cities at face value, instead calling for sustained attention to connecting the study of the Gulf to its larger impact on human and environmental geographies.

The hyper-urbanism whose consequences Kanna points to is the focus of the contributions by Ashraf Salama and Florian Wiedmann. Salama examines the impact of global flows on regional urbanism and architecture in the region's emerging cities. Contemporary urbanism in the southern Persian Gulf includes "bespoke" infrastructure meant to accommodate global flows, as well as a decentralization of urban governance designed to encourage investments in the urban environment. Concerted efforts to build a deliberate cultural–architectural identity have been reinforced by "multiple modernities," thereby resulting in what Salama sees as a "chaotic but emotionally detached urbanism." If these aspiring cities are to succeed in their efforts at becoming global, they need to have sustainable identities of their own and to become "competitive stakeholders and game players" in both local and regional growth while developing sustainable urban structures.

Weidmann takes this line of analysis one step further, zeroing in on the role and potential impact of real estate on Persian Gulf urbanism. Weidmann focuses on the decentralization of urban governance in Dubai and the liberalization of the real estate market in Bahrain as vehicles for the two cities' global aspirations. These two examples highlight the need for two necessary ingredients by such cities if they are to give substance to their ambitions: on the one hand they need liberalization strategies in conjunction with extensive public investments, while on the other hand they need diverse, efficient, and attractive urban environments to draw in international investors and corporations that would help them become global producers and relay stations. For now, real estate is a "rather conflicted catalyst" for the region's urban growth, Weidmann argues, resulting in instant cities created out of and for speculative incentives. Developments related to, or even attempts at fostering, the post-oil economy have little or nothing to do with these lucrative and impressive-looking real estate projects.

Are these aspiring global cities sustainable? Clearly not, at least not environmentally. As they have grown upward into the sky and northward into the sea, they have changed not just lifestyles and lived environments but also the physical geography of the Persian Gulf and its landscape. The dredging of the sea and the seemingly endless land reclamations, the construction of entire cities where previously little human habitation existed, all in the harsh conditions of the desert, often appear to matter little to policy-makers in their race to construct ever more impressive and expansive urban landscapes.

Enter Masdar City, Abu Dhabi's oversized effort at environmental sustainability. In their contribution to the volume, Remah Gharib, M. Evren Tok, and Mohammad Zebian examine the idea of the construction of Masdar as part of Abu Dhabi's move to implement a neoliberal project of industry-led, but state-financed, environmentally sustainable city. Masdar is meant to be a "smart city" in which the person and the surrounding physical environment live complementary lives. Walkability, energy efficiency, and sustainable practices are meant to be the hallmarks of the experiment, complemented by a graduate institute providing the necessary scientific guidance and framework.

Given that Masdar is a work in progress, a project as yet incomplete, the chapter's authors do not critically evaluate the city's successes and failures. But future research, building on what has been presented here, does need to analyze the very sustainability of Masdar, an astoundingly expensive endeavor, in a post-oil era. Is Masdar a largely empty showcase project in a region preoccupied with its image? Does the construction of a sustainable city in the harsh environment of the desert make sense to begin with? And what kind of knowledge transfers to local actors, to what extent and at what expense? These are questions that can best be answered only after the project is fully operational.

The book's last two chapters turn our attention to two port cities that do not have global pretensions. Pooya Alaedini and Mehrdad Javaheripour focus on urban dynamics in Iran's Bandar Abbas. Despite its strategic and commercial significance, Bandar Abbas has seen a proliferation of decaying and under-serviced neighborhoods and rising levels of poverty, all products of the city's rapid but informal growth over the last four decades on the one hand, and insufficient attention and resource allocation by the central government on the other. Bandar Abbas' location as a main cargo port and home to several manufacturing industries has not enabled the city to bridge the gap between its traditional, and largely informal, economy and more modern economic enterprises and practices. The city therefore remains inadequately equipped to undergo meaningful economic and infrastructural development, or even to pull its burgeoning population out of what seems like chronic poverty.

Cities like Bandar Abbas have retained much of their traditional fabric and contain several neighborhoods within them that have yet to undergo sustained state-sponsored and state-directed change. Marike Bontenbal's chapter zeros in on one such neighborhood in Muscat, named Mutrah. Bontenbal's fieldwork has yielded interesting results. In older, more traditional neighborhoods, she concludes, residents exhibit a strong sense of identification with their lived environment and what appears to be a more positive residential experience. Although in a place like Mutrah municipal services may be lacking in quality or may even be altogether absent, and buildings and residential units tend to be older and less appealing, residents tend to have a stronger sense of "place identity," as evident in their emotional ties to their neighborhood. At least in their responses to interview questions, most express strong satisfaction in living in their neighborhood and a sense of belonging and commitment to the place. But identities and attachments are not always consistent over time, and Bontenbal finds that changing residential patterns resulting from migration of expatriate residents in and out of Mutrah have begun to affect sentiments among even long-term residents. Some of the place identities and neighborhood attachments which residents have long held are beginning to loosen in those parts of Mutrah where expatriate populations, mostly shopkeepers and petty traders from the South Asian subcontinent, are moving in.

Bontenbal's observations support those of the other contributors here. Muscat in general and Mutrah in particular may not be experiencing the "chaotic but emotionally detached urbanism" and "multiple modernities" that Salama describes in the Persian Gulf's aspiring global cities. Nonetheless, those strong sentiments of place identity and attachment anchored in traditional fabrics of older neighborhoods are experiencing stress and strain due to demographic and migration patterns. Even a traditional neighborhood like Mutra cannot escape the effects of change.

Together the chapters in this volume paint a picture of a region in the midst of profound, multidimensional and multilayered changes. The primary drivers of these changes are, first and foremost, the regional states and their policies and the resources they allocate to carry forward their aspirations and their national, regional, and international agendas. These state policies attract, and are in turn reinforced by, the emergence of transnational networks that link territories and establishments within each national entity to wider and increasingly more complex networks elsewhere. These two reinforcing phenomena—state initiatives and global networks—have given Persian Gulf urbanisms their current defining features. Some port cities (Abadan) linger on as if time has passed them by and their best days are behind them. Others, like Bandar Abbas and Basra, struggle to catch up with the times and to capitalize on their locations and their potential for importance. But they are starved of resources or suffer from inefficient administration, both in their own municipal governance and insofar as their relations with their central governments are concerned. And still others race, with themselves and with regional competitors, towards politically-defined futures that would make them integral to emerging global networks and trends. Urbanization is being employed as one of the most central elements in the race toward modernity, progress, and development, all the while with an eye toward devising a political economy at home and a supportive one abroad that would sustain and nurture domestic ruling mechanisms.

As the contributions here show, just as the urban profiles and inner dynamics of Bandar Abbas, Basra, and Mutrah cannot be adequately understood without careful attention to the causes and consequences of the political contexts within which each city finds itself, neither can we properly understand the motives and significances of hyper-urbanism in places like Doha, Abu Dhabi, and Dubai, or projects like Masdar, without paying attention to the political forces that underwrite them. State leaders do not build buildings simply for the sake of aesthetics or their love of architecture. They do so with a careful eye toward the political messages and consequences that their building efforts project, how iconic endeavors support what may even be a contrived political tradition built more on myths than facts, and how the built environment interfaces with and nurtures their own political goals and agendas. The recent construction boom in the Persian Gulf has resulted in, among other things, the proliferation of glib and excited literature taking the architectural changes of the region at face value.[52] If not necessarily a corrective, my hope is that this volume will serve as a starting point for future avenues of research on a topic of increasing importance in a region whose global position and strategic significance—for its own inhabitants more so than for anyone else—is not about to fade any time soon.

---

[52] For a critical discussion of this genre of literature on Persian Gulf urbanism, see Kanna, "Speaking of the City," pp. 169–71.

2

FROM PORT CITIES TO CITIES WITH PORTS

TOWARD A MULTISCALAR HISTORY OF
PERSIAN GULF URBANISM IN THE TWENTIETH CENTURY

Arang Keshavarzian

It is uncontroversial to say that at the beginning of the twentieth century the port cities of the Persian Gulf had a pluralistic, "hybrid," "transnational," or "anational" quality; some would even describe them as "cosmopolitan."[1] Straddling multiple empires—Ottoman, Qajar, Omani, Saudi, and British— and trafficking in various language groups, religions, genealogies, and more, this was a world for which it seems the term "frontier" was made. What is possibly more striking from the vantage point of the early twenty-first century,

---

[1] James Onley, "Transnational Merchants in the Nineteenth-Century Gulf," in Madawi al-Rasheed, ed., *Transnational Connections and the Arab Gulf* (London: Routledge, 2005), pp. 59–89; Frederick Anscombe, "An Anational Society: Eastern Arabia in the Ottoman Period," in Madawi al-Rasheed, ed., *Transnational Connections and the Arab Gulf*, pp. 21–38; Nelida Fuccaro, *Histories of City and State in the Persian Gulf: Manama since 1800* (Cambridge: Cambridge University Press, 2009).

however, is that contemporary discussions of some of these very same cities claim that they are similarly "outward looking" and interconnected to places and forces beyond their immediate environs—and in today's parlance are "global."[2] In fact, in recent years, this very characteristic has been cited as the factor differentiating these societies from the rest of the Arab world and the Middle East.[3]

Considerable research and scholarship has been generated to make sense of these recent urban forms (i.e. Dubai, Doha, Abu Dhabi) or their less "spectacular," but equally petroleum revenue-engineered cousins (e.g. Manama or Kuwait City). Some of the literature is unflinchingly triumphalist and composed of hagiographies of rulers represented as captains steering these remarkable projects.[4] Other treatments that foreground the exceptionalism of these transporta-

---

[2] This chapter does not discuss the literature and marketing industry that have developed around the notion of "global cities" since the 1990s. For an academic appraisal of some aspects of this approach, see David Bassens, Ben Derudder, and Frank Witlox, "Searching for the Mecca of Finance: Islamic Financial Services and the World City Network," *Area*, Vol. 42, No. 1 (2010), pp. 35–46. For critiques of the use of architecture and urban planning as an instrument for making claims to modernity and globalism, see Khaled Adham, "Rediscovering the Island: Doha's Urbanity from Pearls to Urbanity," in Yasser Elsheshtawy, ed., *The Evolving Arab City: Tradition, Modernity, and Urban Development* (London: Routledge, 2008), pp. 218–57; and Farah al-Nakib, "Kuwait's Modern Spectacle: Oil Wealth and the Making of a New Capital City, 1950–90," *Comparative Studies of South Asia, Africa and the Middle East*, Vol. 33, No. 1 (2013), pp. 7–25.

[3] Abdulkhaleq Abdulla, "The Arab Gulf Moment," in David Held and Kristian Ulrichsen, eds, *The Transformation of the Gulf: Politics, Economics, and the Global Order* (London: Routledge, 2012), pp. 106–24; Yasser Elsheshtawy, "Tribes with Cities," *Dubaization Blog*, 2013, http://dubaization.com/post/66097171299/tribes-with-cities, last accessed 26 May 2016; Abbas Al-Lawati, "Gulf Cities Have Long Way to Go Before Leading Arab World," *Al-Monitor*, 14 October 2013, http://www.al-monitor.com/pulse/originals/2013/10/gulf-dubai-abu-dhabi-doha-arab.html?utm_source=&utm_medium=email&utm_campaign=8369; Sultan Sooud al-Qassemi, "Thriving Gulf Cities Emerge as New Centers of Arab World," *Al-Monitor*, 8 October 2013, http://www.al-monitor.com/pulse/originals/2013/10/abu-dhabi-dubai-doha-arab-centers.html, last accessed 26 May 2016.

[4] Frank Broeze, "Dubai: Creek to Global Port City," in Lewis R. Fischer and Adrian Jarvis eds, *Harbours and Havens: Essays in Port History in Honour of Gordon Jackson* (St. John's, Newfoundland: International Maritime Economic History Association, 1999); Jeffrey Sampler and Saeb Eigner, *Sand to Silicon: Achieving Rapid Growth Lessons from Dubai* (London: Profile Books, 2003).

tion hubs, financial nodes, and speculation bubbles are more even-keeled. In these discussions, the darker moments along the path from British tutelage to monarchical absolutism are exposed;[5] yet, these works continue to speak in terms of an exceptional "Dubai model."[6] Still other scholars have marshaled rich empirical research with against-the-grain reading of sources and critical analytical insights to demonstrate how the workings of power, discourses of development, and confidence in planning both marks contemporary capitalism and binds these societies to international modes and processes.[7]

Concurrently, the last decade has also witnessed a new interest in these histories of the wider Persian Gulf and its hinterlands during the late nineteenth and early twentieth century period in which new rounds of imperial rivalry, center–periphery struggle, and technological innovation disrupted the older order and introduced new alliances and forms of governance. We have studies that have focused on individual cities,[8] surveys of the northern coast and the expansion of the Qajar's authority to the Persian Gulf and Gulf of

[5] Christopher M. Davidson, "Arab Nationalism and British opposition in Dubai, 1920–66," *Middle Eastern Studies*, Vol. 43, No. 6 (November 2007), pp. 879–92.

[6] Martin Hvidt, "The Dubai Model: An Outline of Key Development-Process Elements in Dubai," *International Journal of Middle East Studies*, Vol. 41 (2009), pp. 397–418.

[7] Reem Alissa, "The Oil Town of Ahmadi since 1946: From Colonial Town to Nostalgic City," *Comparative Studies of South Asia, Africa and the Middle East*, Vol. 33, No. 1 (2013), pp. 41–58; Kaveh Ehsani, "Social Engineering and the Contradictions of Modernization in Khuzestan's Company Towns: A Look at Abadan and Masjed-Soleyman," *International Review of Social History*, Vol. 48, No. 3 (2003), pp. 361–99; Ahmed Kanna, *Dubai: The City as Corporation* (Minneapolis, MN: Minnesota University Press, 2011); Pascal Menoret, *Joyriding in Riyadh: Oil, Urbanism, and Road Revolt* (Cambridge: Cambridge University Press, 2014); Stephen Ramos, *Dubai Amplified: The Engineering of a Port Geography* (Burlington, VT: Ashgate, 2010); Robert Vitalis, *America's Kingdom* (Stanford, CA: Stanford University Press, 2006).

[8] Willem Floor, *The Persian Gulf: The Rise and Fall of Bandar-e Lengeh: The Distribution Center for the Arabian Coast, 1750–1930* (Washington, DC: Mage, 2010); Willem Floor, *Bandar Abbas: The Natural Trade Gateway of Southeast Iran* (Washington, DC: Mage, 2011); Fuccaro, *Histories of City and State in the Persian Gulf*; Vanessa Martin, *The Qajar Pact: Bargaining, Protest and the State in Nineteenth-Century Persia* (London: I. B. Tauris, 2005), pp. 29–47; Reidar Visser, *Basra, the Failed Gulf State: Separatism and Nationalism in Southern Iraq* (New Brunswick, NJ: Transaction, 2005).

Oman,[9] and examinations of the interactions across and between the two coasts.[10] Taken together they demonstrate that this maritime world was not an isolated "sub-region" and backwater of modern history, nor can the era be reduced to notions of stasis and decline or be merely viewed as a prelude to the pre-oil era. The Persian Gulf, like other bodies of water, was more a bridge and conveyor-belt than a border or a chasm.

What are strikingly absent, however, are analyses that study the entire twentieth century or compare these urban forms across the temporal divide that is marked by major economic and geopolitical transformations, including the emergence of the petroleum political economy, the retreat of British Empire and ascendance of US hegemony, and the shift from a world of imperial frontiers to nation-state borders. This chapter consciously seeks to disrupt the standard markers of periodization that have narrowed the temporal scope of analysis of the Persian Gulf and Arabian Peninsula. Thus, I offer a broad comparative perspective on the nature of urban forms and relationships at the beginning and end of the long twentieth century. While ultimately we will need analyses and debates about the processes and causes of this shift, my arguments will be limited to sketching a rubric for distilling this shift, rather than fully describing or explaining it.

A second conceptual approach is to focus on these urban centers as "port cities" by considering how this form of urbanism has been *reworked by and for* new technologies, modes of accumulation, and forms of political control.[11] Port cities offer a vivid example of how local conditions interact along and with multiple scales. This relational process is captured by Carola Hein, who contends that

> [M]aritime and associated networks create dynamic, multi-scaled, and interconnected cityscapes. I call them *port cityscapes*, and they exist around the world. Port cities are literally connected through shipping, trade, or traders, but also other

---

[9] Lawrence G. Potter, "The Consolidation of Iran's Frontier on the Persian Gulf in the Nineteenth Century," in Roxane Farmanfarmaian, ed., *War and Peace in Qajar Persia: Implications past and Present* (London: Routledge, 2008), pp. 125–48.

[10] Floor, *The Persian Gulf*; Sultan Muhammad al-Qassemi, *The Myth of Arab Piracy in the Gulf* (London: Routledge, 1986).

[11] By this I do not mean that these cities are only port cities and that non-maritime factors have little influence on the urban fabric of these societies. As the chapter illustrates, "the hinterland," government policies, and caravan routes and translocal political economies are all critical in understanding the ports and shifts in the urban form.

networks—of diasporas, trade groups, religious congregations, ethnic groups, elites, family, migration, artisans, slaves, shipworkers, etc.—that relate people symbolically through kinship and other social ties.[12]

Historically, port cities are where networks of exchange operated, goods were traded, credit was dispersed, connections to other port cities were sustained, and political, religious and social practices, as well as ideas and non-human organisms, circulated. These coastal cities owe their origin and the ebbs and flows of their development to the functioning of ports and the trade they enabled. To balance and keep working all of these multi-directional processes, port cities had to adapt to survive. Both the ports and these cities have developed according to the demands of "the hinterland," long-distance trade, and transformations in technologies associated with shipping, logistics, and warehousing. These physical ports are thus in a dialectical relationship with urban space as well as trade patterns and state policies.

Finally, this chapter seeks to move beyond discussions of the Persian Gulf in the twentieth century wherein this body of water is treated as a boundary that renders the northern and southern shores as distinct places and incomparable cases.[13] The focus on port cities and the maritime dimension of these sub-national polities forces us to consider the Persian Gulf as a readily traversed frontier and interconnected set of relationships mapping a shifting social geography with multiple centers and peripheries.[14] The culturally plural, fluid, and highly networked nature of these societies has been illustrated by a substantial body of literature on the nineteenth and early twentieth century (see Map 2.1). While this does not mean that national or even translocal politics (e.g. Pan-Arabism) are irrelevant or that variations do not exist along the littoral or over time, the goal here is to provide a more expansive analytical lens and to encourage less nationalistic historiographies that valorize "security" and regional "stability" in realist and geopolitical terms. Thus, I con-

---

[12] Carola Hein, ed., *Port Cities: Dynamic Landscapes and Global Networks* (London: Routledge, 2011), p. 5.

[13] This tendency is almost universal in international relations and policy writing. However, in the last two decades it has become the norm in more academic works and projects to define "the Gulf" in exceedingly nationalist terms. Consequently, the geographies and littorals are decoupled, and ultimately the peoples and societies are reified.

[14] Sugata Bose, *A Hundred Horizons: The Indian Ocean in the Age of Global Empire* (Cambridge, MA: Harvard University Press, 2006); Charles King, *The Black Sea: A History* (Oxford: Oxford University Press, 2004).

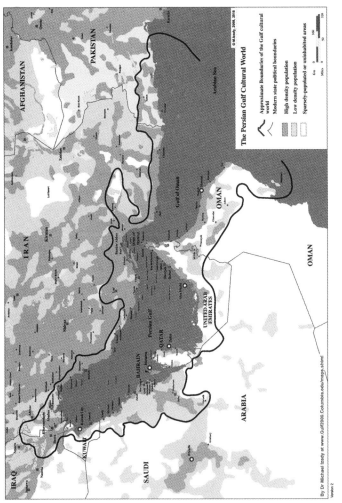

2.1: The Persian Gulf cultural world

Map by Michael Izady

Source: http://gulf2000.columbia.edu/images/maps/GulfCultralWorld0804_lg.png

sciously incorporate examples from, and think through differences between, cities and ports such as Basra, Bushehr and, Bandar Abbas, and locales on the southern coast that have tended to receive greater attention in "Gulf Studies" circles that have become increasingly institutionalized in North Atlantic academic and policy worlds.[15] The aim is not to suggest that all ports or cities on the Gulf were or are the same or follow a single historical path, but to explore how these diverse locales experienced similar yet dramatic changes in the political economy.

Based on these three observations, this chapter poses the following questions: how do the Persian Gulf's two different forms of transnational urbanism separated by a century compare, and what does this tell us about the urban process as well as transnationalism? My argument is that the Persian Gulf has always been transnational or "glocal";[16] but the processes and mechanisms have changed in a way that has resulted in (a) a morphological separation of ports from cities, (b) a less integrated regional network of ports, and (c) cities where homogeneity and unity, in terms of identity, class, and citizenship status, are privileged, and differences are rendered as threats that must be neutralized and controlled. These transformations operate at multiple geographic scales and are products of both technical changes and state policies under evolving capitalist conditions. Hence, social boundaries and territories have not been strictly articulated on national or urban scales, nor can they adequately be studied as such.

Port Cities and Gulf Regionalism in an Era of Empires

"Port cities" can be thought of as urban places and societies that develop in a close and multidimensional relationship to maritime activities of a port. Thus, there is an intimate spatial and functional association between the city and the port. In the context of the available maritime and logistical technologies of the nineteenth century and early twentieth century, we can also speak of a system of port cities in which steamships and other vessels, such as dhows, made frequent calls at multiple ports along a maritime routes or circuits. The urban

---

[15] An important recent exception is David Commins, *The Gulf States: A Modern History* (London: I. B. Tauris, 2012).

[16] Erik Swyngedouw, "Neither Global nor Local: 'Glocalization' and the Politics of Scale," in Kevin R. Cox, ed., *Spaces of Globalization: Reasserting the Power of the Local* (New York: Guilford Press, 1997), pp. 137–66.

form that prevailed on the shores of the Persian Gulf until the collapse of the pearling economy and global depression of the 1930s was the port city.

Within the confines of the Persian Gulf and during the *fin de siècle*, there were a whole host of locales that could be described as port cities. These were towns and cities that combined access to the sea and ample drinking water.[17] Some cities, for instance Manama and Bushehr, enjoyed greater levels of trade and a more enduring status as commercial hubs. Other port cities declined or grew in stature during this era—Bandar Lengeh's waning and the ascent of Dubai captures this dual dynamic. Part of the variation was because not all of these harbors were created equal, and at this juncture the quality and safety of these "natural harbors" and anchorage facilities were a critical matter that benefited ports such as Bandar Lengeh, but hindered the growth of Doha, Abu Dhabi, and Basra. Critical port cities were located at either end of the Gulf. Basra, despite enjoying less than ideal shipping facilities (discussed below), marked the northerly terminus of not only Gulf traffic, but routes extending to the subcontinent and East Africa. Muscat, situated beyond the Straits of Hormuz and located just over 700 nautical miles from Basra, bookended the Gulf and its string of port cities.

What was traded between and shipped to and from these port cities? The main goods exported from the region were pearls, shells, horses, salt fish, tobacco, opium, and dates that were marketed for Bombay and Zanzibar, but from there were distributed to other destinations on the Indian Ocean littoral, in Western Europe, and in the United States. Meanwhile, other commodities were imported to or circulated across the Gulf—examples of such goods are wheat, barley, textiles, timber, rice, tea, coffee, lamp oil, and slaves.

It was the pearl fishing industry, however, that was the cornerstone of the political economy of these societies, with the cash economy and demand for labor fostering capital accumulation and urban growth. Driven by growing global demand, the 1880s to 1920s marked a boom period for the pearl industry. Based in coastal towns and villages with small populations, the sector drew on and exploited a labor force that was necessarily translocal. Ship hands, divers, and other laborers included slaves and recently emancipated migrants from Africa and Baluchestan.[18] Also, Bedouin populations from the Arabian hinterland were attracted to the seasonal employment in the coastal centers, as were Persians and Arabs who migrated from various

---

[17] Peter Lienhardt, *Sheikhdoms of Eastern Arabia* (New York: Palgrave, 2001), p. 114.
[18] Fuccaro, *Histories of City and State in the Persian Gulf*, p. 26.

regions of the Gulf sphere.[19] At the height of the boom, "according to some estimates, one-quarter of the male population along the Arabian shore worked in the pearl industry in one capacity or another."[20] These cities and ports were dominated by the pearling and its attendant activities; for instance, the city of Kuwait in 1904 had a population of 35,000, possessed 461 pearl boats, and employed 9,200 men in this sector.[21] The importance of pearling is reflected by the fact that in 1910 the British vice consul felt it necessary to provide two population figures for Bandar Lengeh, one for the summer (8,000) and one for the winter (12,000) when the pearling fleet returned.[22] Translocal labor currents and seasonal ebbs and flow were paralleled by geographically mobile capital that financed boats and expeditions by merchants drawn from various tribal families based in desert oases and port cities across the Gulf and Indian Ocean as well as from different ethno-linguistic and religious backgrounds.

While in some cases pearl divers were able to finance their own boats or create cooperatives, the typical practice was debt peonage, whereby captains, themselves often indebted to merchants, would extend advances to divers, pullers, and seamen at the start of the pearling season, which had to be repaid via the catch and sale of pearls.[23] These debts, understood by merchants and captains as profit-sharing rather than wages, frequently transferred across season and could be inherited. This system generated a series of dependencies and forms of bondage across seasons and between pearl divers and their families, and between them and a host of ship captains, financiers, and merchants that zigzagged across the Gulf. Ultimately this economy was vulnerable to vagrancies of global markets for pearls.

---

[19] Robert Carter, "The History and Prehistory of Pearling in the Persian Gulf," *Journal of the Economic and Social History of the Orient*, Vol. 48, No. 2 (2005), pp. 157 and 179.

[20] Commins, *The Gulf States: A Modern History*, p. 120; see also Rosemarie Said Zahlan, *The Making of the Modern Gulf States* (London: Unwin Hyman, 1989), p. 22.

[21] Carter, "The History and Prehistory of Pearling in the Persian Gulf," p. 154; Jill Crystal, *Oil and Politics in the Gulf: Rulers and Merchants in Kuwait and Qatar* (Cambridge: Cambridge University Press, 1990), p. 24; Richard Lawless and Ian J. Seccombe, "Impact of the Oil Industry on Urbanization in the Persian Gulf Region," in Hooshang Amirahmadi and Salah S. el-Shakhs, eds, *Urban Development in the Muslim World* (New Brunswick, NJ: Rutgers University Press, 1993), p. 184.

[22] Floor, *The Persian Gulf*, p. 9.

[23] Lienhardt, *Sheikhdoms of Eastern Arabia*, p. 29.

When commerce was booming a significant portion of capital fed back into the urban economies and accounts of shopkeepers and landowners.[24] Pearl fishing required a substantially larger work force than the coastal towns could provide, and these port cities profited in many ways from labor migration, the influx of capital, and burgeoning consumerism. Talking to Peter Lienhardt in the 1950s, one Kuwait merchant based in Dubai reflected on the boom years of the first quarter of the twentieth century, "Those were times when the poor had money; prosperity comes from the poor, not from the rich."[25] Meanwhile, Carter associates the pearl economy's boom era with changes in urbanism; specifically, with "an overall increase in population beyond that allowed by the food-production capacity of the region, as cash was available to bring in foodstuffs from external sources. The increasing population became concentrated into coastal centres, which maximized benefits from the pearling industry."[26] This socioeconomic world was enmeshed with various transregional forces, and in certain instances (e.g. Basra and Bushehr) merchants were disadvantaged by integration into an international capitalist economy and displaced by European trade.[27] Yet, these port cities enjoyed benefits too; Fuccaro concludes that:

> local shipping maintained a solid profile sustained by pearl trade with India and by the exchange of goods for local consumption with Iran, Iraq, and the Arabian Peninsula. The continuation of intercoastal trade was also assisted by the size of British ships, which could only approach large harbours. Native shipping was also able to support the bulk of regional trade in the late 1920s and early 1930s, when the collapse of pearling and the depression in the world markets restrained the circulation of international commodities.[28]

As implied in the above description, these port cities and the larger arena in which they operated were socially multicultural. People spoke many languages and dialects, practiced various religions or branches of the same religion, and identified themselves in multiple ways—kinship and tribal affiliation, social status and profession, or loyalty to and protection from various and competing authorities. This was colorfully captured by the future Viceroy

---

[24] Fuccaro, *Histories of City and State in the Persian Gulf*; and Lienhardt, *Sheikhdoms of Eastern Arabia*, pp. 150–64.

[25] Lienhardt, *Sheikhdoms of Eastern Arabia*, p. 152.

[26] Carter, "The History and Prehistory of Pearling in the Persian Gulf," p. 169.

[27] Hala Fattah, *The Politics of Regional Trade in Iraq, Arabia, and the Gulf 1745–1900* (Albany, NY: State University of the New York Press, 1997); Martin, *The Qajar Pact*.

[28] Fuccaro, *Histories of City and State in the Persian Gulf*, p. 59.

of India, George Curzon, in his travelogue where he described the steamship that he took through the Persian Gulf: "surely a more curious study in polyglot or polychrome could not well be conceived."[29] For Curzon, the multilingual and translocal nature of this social world made the Persian Gulf, or what he formulated as "The Persian Question," critical for British India and, ultimately, the resilience of the British Empire.

The pearl economy and its attendant mercantile activities also undergirded the political system by forging governing coalitions of rulers and merchant families. The merchants provided the financial resources required by the ruling tribal families and local governors representing the Qajars and Ottomans. As Crystal related,

> Merchants extracted revenues from pearl divers rather than peasants, and gave a portion of these extracted revenues to the ruler through customs duties, pearl boat taxes, and personal loans. Their political power grew from their economic strength. Their ordinary input into decision-making came from the social institutions of marriage ... and *majlis* ... which gave them informal but daily access to the rulers.[30]

This relative balance between merchants and rulers, whether independent monarchies or representatives of central authorities in Tehran or Baghdad, suggests that these places are best characterized as "city-societies" rather than "city-states."[31] At this time centralized states did not exist and instead distant sovereigns worked through intermediaries, who both had their own interests and enjoyed varying degrees of local authority and efficacy. Fuccaro concludes that these port cities developed as "'voluntary' associations with their immigrant populations of non-tribal stock and mobile workforce" relying on kin and patronage hierarchies within and beyond the cities.[32] Hence, prior to the Great Depression and advent of oil exploration and revenue generation, effective control over these port cities and the balance of power between rulers (or their representatives) and merchants favored the latter.

A System of Port Cities: Integrated, Yet Differentiated

If the political economy of these port cities produced functionally integrated urban spaces that bound social groups together through a system of debt- and

---

[29] George N. Curzon, *Persia and the Persian Question*, 2 vols. (London: Frank Cass, [1892] 1966), Vol. 2, p. 468.
[30] Crystal, *Oil and Politics in the Gulf*, p. 4.
[31] Fuccaro, *Histories of City and State in the Persian Gulf*, p. 14.
[32] Ibid., p. 71.

profit-sharing, these port cities themselves were woven together into an inter-coastal network. Because social relations extended beyond the immediate shoreline and into the mainlands via caravan routes, Anscombe describes these societies before World War I as a "networked region."[33] These networks were vehicles for capital accumulation, exchange, labor movements, and consumption as well as embodiments of the "polyglot and polychrome" world that bred imperial attraction and anxiety during the long nineteenth century.[34] Most notably, a number of merchant families established trading houses in multiple locations in the Gulf as well as along the Indian Ocean and Red Sea coasts. As such, the merchant families of the Gulf enjoyed multiple branches based in myriad port cities and trades. James Onley describes one such family, the Safars, who operated in Basra, Bushehr, Shiraz, Manama, Muscat, Mokka, and Bombay, to name just a few of the places where the extended family owned homes and trading houses during the nineteenth and early twentieth century.[35] Establishing multiple commercial centers was good business because it enabled the family to establish trade, credit, and kinship ties with various locations and communities in order to guard against risk associated with vola-tile markets and politics. Finally, this pre-oil mercantile economy was fused together via colonial banking institutions based in Iran, Iraq, and India.[36]

Although these merchants invested in land and property, their capital and social acumen were highly mobile and responsive to shifts in duties and cus-toms regimes. Therefore, these ports competed to attract long-distance trade, with customs offices enticing this mercantile capital by reducing their rates or even establishing "free ports."[37] In turn, merchants who already had region-wide footholds moved, or threatened to do so, in response to changing cus-toms duties and rivalries. Two famous episodes were the 1905 relocation of merchants from Bandar-Lengeh to Dubai and the 1909 relocation of mer-chants and pearl boats from Kuwaiti to Bahrain.[38] Unlike in the earlier

---

[33] Anscombe, "An Anational Society: Eastern Arabia in the Ottoman Period," p. 31.
[34] Engseng Ho, "Empire through Diasporic Eyes: A View from the Other Boat," *Comparative Studies in Society and History*, Vol. 46 (April 2004), pp. 210–46.
[35] Onley, "Transnational Merchants in the Nineteenth-Century Gulf."
[36] Adam Hanieh, *Capitalism and Class in the Gulf Arab States* (New York: Palgrave Macmillan, 2011), pp. 78–82.
[37] Fattah, *The Politics of Regional Trade in Iraq, Arabia, and the Gulf.*
[38] Floor, *The Persian Gulf*, 101; Fatma al-Sayegh, "Merchants' Role in a Changing Society: The Case of Dubai, 1900–90," *Middle Eastern Studies*, Vol. 34, No. 1 (January 1998), pp. 87–102.

episode, the merchants returned to Kuwait, but only when the Sabah ruling family acquiesced to their demands to reduce duties two years later.[39] While this option to exit empowered merchants vis-à-vis administrative officials, it also reflected and inscribed the regional dimensions of port cities.

Additionally, empires and diasporas sewed the Gulf together and related it to the wider Indian Ocean world. First, many economic, religious, and kinship relations were built on centuries-long relationships across the Indian Ocean Basin and caravan routes extending from the port cities.[40] Until the mid-1800s the Omani oceanic empire, with outposts in southern Iran, generated connections across and beyond the Gulf. Meanwhile, the Qassemi dynasty based in Sharjah and Ras al-Khaimah also controlled, leased, and claimed rights to various ports and islands in the straits of Hormuz region.[41] With the steady development of Britain's treaty and protectorate system, and hegemonic control over the Gulf, a new dimension to these forms of transregionalism emerged at the turn of the last century. The British Raj generated an additional form of cosmopolitanism in a region that was already plural. These cosmopolitans were not citizens of the world, but protected persons of the British Empire. Some of the most prominent merchant families benefited from this access, while they also functioned as British agents and became important intermediates for British officials in the region and India. British security facilitated trade by the East India Company and locals, or at least by those that Britain deemed not to be "pirates." Britain incorporated the merchant families as part of their imperial apparatus of "protected persons subjects" and employed them as brokers in their relations with recognized sheikhs.[42] Meanwhile, in the 1860s, the British India Steam Navigation Company established a bi-weekly service connecting Karachi to Basrah via Muscat, Bandar Abbas, Lingah, Bushire, and Manamah.[43] Dubai was added in 1904, an indication of its rising status as a port city and mercantile node.[44]

---

[39] Crystal, *Oil and Politics in the Gulf*, pp. 24–35.

[40] Bose, *A Hundred Horizons*; Engseng Ho, *The Graves of Tarim: Genealogy and Mobility across the Indian Ocean* (Oakland, CA: University of California Press, 2006).

[41] Potter, "The Consolidation of Iran's Frontier on the Persian Gulf in the Nineteenth Century."

[42] James Onley, "Transnational Merchants in the Nineteenth-Century Gulf."

[43] Broeze, "Dubai: Creek to Global Port City," p. 165.

[44] The British, however, limited innovations by limiting access to technologies, e.g. they denied Iran from acquiring navy ships; delayed the building of railroads in the

The British political resident used his powers vis-à-vis the sheikhs to ensure that the debts owed by Arab merchants to Indian merchants were paid.[45] In sum, a web of maritime, economic, and social connections bound the unequal peoples and myriad ports into a "civilizational unit" whose parts had more in common with each other than with the historic and emergent inland centers of Baghdad, Riyadh, or Tehran.[46]

Being integrated into a commercial circuit or social arena did not mean that these port cities were indistinguishable from one another. A critical factor differentiating the port cities and coastal regions at the beginning of the twentieth century was their relationships with hinterlands. To varying degrees, the hinterlands provided labor, finances, commodities for export, and markets for imports. At the same time, the hinterland represented a threat to coastal societies and port cities. There were two basic modalities. For cases in which the port cities were relatively free from emergent central governments with significant revenues and bureaucracies (e.g. Manama, Dubai, Kuwait, Doha), the mercantile communities were protected from institutional attacks from state-builders, but remained vulnerable to Bedouin raids that could be organized by ruling families and tribal federations against traders and sailors. In the second case, the ports were nominally part of larger political units or land-based empires with central governments based in Riyadh, Istanbul/Baghdad, and Tehran. Hence, these coastal towns were vulnerable to these emerging authorities' desires to penetrate the largely autonomous cities in order to extract taxes and project their sovereignty.

This captures the experience of places such as Qatif, Basra, Bushehr, Lengeh, and Bandar Abbas. In these cases where the port cities were located in the incipient nation-states of Iran, Iraq, and Saudi Arabia, merchants and maritime workers had to contend with factors such as expanding customs apparatuses and increasing levels of duties that tended to repel mercantile

---

region; and withheld newer pearling ships. See Christopher Davidson, *The United Arab Emirates: A Study in Survival* (Boulder, CO: Lynne Rienner, 2005), pp. 32–4. Moreover, British "protection" isolated these societies from non-British worlds (Said Zahlan, *The Making of the Modern Gulf States*, pp. 13–4). Finally, recognizing and patronizing specific rulers and families managed to limit contestation in these societies and "froze" politics in many of these cases.
[45] al-Sayegh, "Merchants' Role in a Changing Society," pp. 95–6.
[46] Potter, "The Consolidation of Iran's Frontier on the Persian Gulf in the Nineteenth Century," p. 128.

activities to port cities free of such restrictions. In these cases, commercial traffic and capital tended to be directed to capital cities and trade routes independent of the Persian Gulf. For instance, in the late nineteenth century, Iran's Gulf trade was downgraded as routes and networks directed commerce from Russia and Europe via Baghdad and northern Iran.[47] With the development of the oil industry in Abadan after the First World War, the center of economic gravity shifted further North. Saudi Arabia offers a different set of factors that weakened the mercantile activities of its Gulf towns (e.g. Qatif). On the one hand, much of its trade routes and population centers were connected to the Red Sea and north. Even after the 1970s oil boom, Saudi's mercantile class was drawn disproportionately from the western province of Hijaz.[48] Meanwhile, the Saudi rulers consolidated their position on the peninsula by extracting resources in the form of feudal tribute from nomadic tribes, rather than borrowing or taxing commercial activities and port cities. Finally, in Iraq, Basra's activities were shaped by the gravitational pull of Baghdad's economy and Britain's colonial policies at the turn of the century.[49] Despite Basrawi merchants being supportive of the separatist movement calling for autonomy for Basra, the combination of economic investments in Baghdad and Iran and poor port facilities hindered the development of Basra's economy and political autonomy.[50] This was in part due to British policies aimed at keeping Iraqi oil off the market,[51] and consequences of the drawing of the Kuwaiti–Iraqi border.[52] In short, Basra became a provincial capital in the Iraqi state, rather than the capital of a Persian Gulf city-state.

[47] Martin, *The Qajar Pact*, pp. 29–47.
[48] Hanieh, *Capitalism and Class in the Gulf Arab States*, p. 75.
[49] Visser, *Basra, the Failed Gulf State*.
[50] Priya Satia, "Developing Iraq: Britain, India and the Redemption of Empire and Technology in the First World War," *Past and Present*, Vol. 197, No. 1 (2007), p. 221.
[51] In order to obstruct the export of petroleum from Iraq, oil company and imperial interests collaborated to block the building of railroads and pipelines through present-day Iraq and limited the development of Basra's port facilities; see Timothy Mitchell, *Carbon Democracy: Political Power in the Age of Oil* (London: Verso, 2012), pp. 43–54.
[52] Ultimately, post-World War I, British High Commissioner Percy Cox restricted Iraq's access to the Persian Gulf when he drew Iraq's boundaries in a way that benefited Kuwait, which itself was claimed by the Iraqi government. Iraq sought to gain access to the strategically important islands of Bubiyan and Warba and with that direct access to the Gulf. The two islands directly blocked the approaches to Iraq's only deep-water port at Umm Qasr via the shipping lanes running through the

In spite of, and because of, these variations, trade networks stitched together these port cities, the peoples who inhabited them, and further afield the caravan routes operating across diverse physical and political geographies. This process was spatially and socioeconomically uneven and resulted in its own forms of competition and exploitation. These relationships, dependencies, movements, and rivalries engineered qualities that can be termed regionalism. This Persian Gulf region, moreover, was manifest at the level of the urban too.

Cities with Ports: the Production of Gulfs on Multiple Scales[53]

By the beginning of the twenty-first century, it is unlikely that a visitor to Dubai, Bandar Abbas, Doha, or Kuwait City will witness commercial ships or spend time in these ports. This does not mean that these cities lack maritime facilities or that there is a shortage of "foreigners" residing and visiting these locales. In fact, Dubai enjoys one of the ten busiest ports in the world and has the greatest maritime traffic among all the ports in West Asia and the Mediterranean in terms of capacity and handling of twenty-foot equivalent units (TEUs). Instead, the point I am making is that the majority of visitors to these cities arrive via highly regulated airplanes and airports, which interface with the "outside" world in ways that are more regulated and spatially stratified than the earlier order. Ports, in both sea and air versions, exist. However, they are spatially and socially apart from the urban fabric,[54] and often legally detached from the "mainland."[55] While there are specific regional

---

narrow Khor Abdullah waterway. The islands were the focus of the 1973 Iraqi–Kuwait border skirmish, and after 1991 Kuwait transformed Bubiyan into a military base. See Kristian Coates Ulrichsen, "Basra, Southern Iraq and the Gulf: Challenges and Connections," Kuwait Programme on Development, Governance and Globalisation in the Gulf States, London School of Economics, Research Paper No. 21, February 2012. Iraq officially recognized Kuwait's ownership of the two islands in 1994.

[53] Note that I do not want to imply that the transformations I describe were linear, incremental, and uncontested. I am employing the notion of "port cities" and "cities with ports" as a heuristic, and it is imperfect and incomplete like any other.

[54] Ramos, *Dubai Amplified*.

[55] Arang Keshavarzian, "Geopolitics and the Genealogy of Free Trade Zones in the Persian Gulf," *Geopolitics*, Vol. 15, No. 2 (May 2010), pp. 263–89.

factors that have generated this outcome, there are also more general forces engineering this "retreat of the waterfront."[56]

Ports, Containerization, and the Urban Form

What has led to this "retreat of the waterfront," and what have been the consequences for the Gulf's cities and the port system? Two structural factors reconstituted the relationship between ports and societies during the course of the twentieth century. First, the emergence of a political economy of oil displaced not only the pearling economy, but the host of relationships that sociologically assembled port cities. Oil wealth brought with it possibilities for major infrastructural projects and fueled consumerist societies by overvaluing local currencies and directing productive assets into the service sector. While the pearling economy was decimated by global economic depression and competition with East Asian cultured pearls in the 1920s–1930s, those merchants who were able to survive and curry the favor of the new rentier states were able to profit as importers and agents for foreign companies. In the smaller Gulf states, this process was lubricated by their peculiar status as British "protectorates," which cemented the "sheikhly" political system, engineered the petroleum industry, and designed various aspects of urban planning and construction.[57] In the larger Gulf littoral states of Iran, Iraq, and Saudi Arabia, the political economic processes of state formation were also deeply intertwined with the extraction and export of petroleum and international struggles over accumulation and petrodollar recycling.[58]

Thus, these former "city societies" either became more precisely "city-states with ports" (e.g. Kuwait, Qatar, Dubai, etc.), or provincial cities with ports (e.g. Bandar Abbas, Dammam, Basra). In the former cases, the cities with ports are the seats of governments of rentier states that are less dependent on

[56] Brian Stewart Hoyle, "The Port–City Interface: Trends, Problems, and Examples," *Geoforum*, Vol. 20, No. 4 (1989), pp. 429–35.

[57] Davidson, *The United Arab Emirates*; Kanna, *Dubai: The City As Corporation*; al-Nakib, "Kuwait's Modern Spectacle"; Ramos, *Dubai Amplified*.

[58] Kaveh Ehsani, "The Social History of Labor in the Iranian Oil Industry: The Built Environment and the Making of the Industrial Working Class (1908–1941)," PhD dissertation, Leiden University, 2014; Keshavarzian, "Geopolitics and the Genealogy of Free Trade Zones in the Persian Gulf," pp. 263–89; Menoret, *Joyriding in Riyadh*; Charles Tripp, *A History of Iraq*, 3rd edn (Cambridge: Cambridge University Press, 2007); Visser, *Basra, the Failed Gulf State*; Vitalis, *America's Kingdom*.

merchants and the domestic economy for revenue. In the latter cases, these provincial ports are frequently distant from major population centers, industrial regions, and capital cities that host national decision-making bodies. In all of these cases, during the course of the century, the balance of power and the relationship between institutions of rule and residents (both citizens and non-citizens) have been reconfigured in ways that favor rulers.

If the political economy generated greater autonomy for political decision-makers from the mercantile community, the "containerization revolution" in the mid-twentieth century was a second significant structural shift that directly dislodged ports from the urban core by the century's end.[59] Containerization refers to the adoption in the 1960s of the International Standards Organization container measuring 20 feet long, 8 feet wide, and 8 feet tall, or a twenty-foot equivalent unit (TEU).[60] These standardized units, which could be transported, loaded, and unloaded across different modes of transport radically drove down costs of international shipping, and ratcheted up the speed of commerce. By facilitating transoceanic trade, containerization ultimately transformed the global redistribution and management of manufacturing, commercial patterns, and attendant maritime and logistics technologies (i.e. sizes of ships, cranes, and berths). It made possible "integrated distribution management." Containerization introduced new opportunities and demands on port facilities. It also mechanized the process and dislocated significant segments of the labor force—and with it their political power as represented in unions. "Because economies of scale are the essence of container transport, and as a result of vastly improved productivity at the quayside and on board ship, current demand is for fewer berths." Hilling and Hoyle continue, "Likewise, the high costs of constructing and equipping a full con-

---

[59] It should be noted that oil export generated its own maritime demands. By 1970, oil accounted for 60 per cent of international seaborne cargo measures in terms of tonnage (Mitchell, *Carbon Democracy*, p. 37). The percentage has declined to 31 per cent in 2012, but has doubled in absolute terms (see *Review of Maritime Transport Report* in 2013, http://unctad.org/en/pages/newsdetails.aspx?Original VersionID=668, last accessed 26 May 2016).

[60] D. Hilling and B. S. Hoyle, "Spatial Approaches to Port Development," in B. S. Hoyle and D Hilling, eds, *Seaport Systems and Spatial Change: Technology, Industry, and Development Strategies* (Chichester: John Wiley & Sons, 1984), pp. 10–11; Marc Levinson, *The Box: How the Shipping Container made the World Smaller and the World Economy Bigger* (Princeton, NJ: Princeton University Press, 2008).

tainer terminal together with the ship-owner's desire to minimise his ports of call has led to marked concentrations of traffic at fewer ports."[61]

While the capital-rich economies of the post-1970s Gulf region could cover many of these costs, they still had to take on the engineering and spatial demands of building these container terminals that place a premium on space. To facilitate economies of scale associated with containerization, terminals were built outside cities (e.g. Shahid Rajaei Port in Bandar Abbas and Shuaiba Port in Kuwait). In the particular case of Jebel Ali Port in Dubai, the entire port was a man-made operation. "Green field sites" were chosen to build capacity and to generate demand via a massive, capital-intensive, and ever expanding logistics zone for the handling of ever larger ships and supertankers and volumes of cargo; more recently in Jebel Ali such a site was used for a new massive airport for passengers and cargo. "Interestingly, the political interplay [between] these competing urban claims have ... encouraged port expansion beyond boundaries in favor of cheaper and, more abundant land for expansion, and fewer interests groups to mobilize politically and prevent port development 'in their (urban) backyard.'"[62] Thus, these port and mega-projects functioned as means *and* ends to territorial control.[63]

Before turning to the issue of how these various cities relate to one another, and what became of the port system of the early twentieth century, I must mention another factor that contributed to keeping peoples of the cities simultaneously connected, but apart. During the century, a variety of regional urban forms were employed as spatial and legal methods to separate and control people based on race and class. First in Iran and then subsequently in Bahrain, Kuwait, and Saudi Arabia, the various company towns established in and around oil facilities institutionalized spatial segregation to reduce labor costs, discipline minds and bodies, and manage potential mobilizations.[64]

[61] Hilling and Hoyle, "Spatial Approaches to Port Development," p. 10.
[62] Ramos, *Dubai Amplified*, p. 36.
[63] For example, on Jebel Ali Port and Free Trade Zone in Dubai, see Keshavarzian, "Geopolitics and the Genealogy of Free Trade Zones in the Persian Gulf" and Ramos, *Dubai Amplified*; on Kish in Iran, see Keshavarzian, "Geopolitics and the Genealogy of Free Trade Zones in the Persian Gulf"; on Salalah in Oman see Matthew Greene, "Evolution of an Omani Port: Interpreting the development of the Port of Salalah," MA thesis, Near Eastern Studies, New York University, May 2014.
[64] Alissa, "The Oil Town of Ahmadi since 1946"; Mona Damluji, "The Oil City in Focus: The Cinematic Spaces of Abandan in the Anglo-Iranian Oil Company's

Additionally, land and housing policies were devised to distribute welfare paternalistically to citizens and to demarcate the spatial boundary between them and non-citizens.[65] These urban forms have displaced the old urban quarters of the port city that are now populated by the urban poor and non-citizens. This separation has been "policed" by both new and tried technologies of state and markets. In the hyper-rich contexts of UAE or Kuwait, where the ratio of citizen to non-citizen has plummeted, forms of security are aimed at monitoring the "threat" from non-citizens, and to discipline citizens.[66] Conceptions of "family" and "tribe" have been mobilized alongside discourses and spatializations of "authenticity" to naturalize differences and define citizenship in what Ahmed Kanna calls "neoorthdoxy."[67] Meanwhile, in the economies of the Gulf where laborers are neither "imported" nor "guests," such as in Bandar Abbas, unemployment, fear of unemployment, and migration to economic centers away from the coast functions to discipline labor.[68]

The Withering away of the Port City System

Beyond manufacturing new ports and new relationships between cities and ports, containerization rearticulated relationships among ports. Economic interests of the shipping industry since the 1960s have led to a more vertically integrated port-system. Because of the requirement that ports provide dedicated terminals and infrastructure for loading and unloading containers and the high costs of ever larger container ships, companies want to limits port calls on their "mainline service." Thus, there has emerged the possibility for a single port to become the entrepôt for the entire region. Due to a number of local and international interests and contingencies, such as wars and sanctions,

Persian Story," *Comparative Studies of South Asia, Africa and the Middle East*, Vol. 33, No. 1 (2013), pp. 75–88; Ehsani, "Social Engineering and the Contradictions of Modernization in Khuzestan's Company Towns"; Vitalis, *America's Kingdom*.

65 Paul Dresch, "Foreign Matter: The Place of Strangers in Gulf Society," in John W. Fox, Nada Mourtada-Sabbah, and Mohammed al-Mutawa, eds, *Globalization and the Gulf* (London: Routledge, 2006), pp. 200–22; al-Nakib, "Kuwait's Modern Spectacle."

66 Noora Lori, "National Security and the Management of Migrant Labor: A Case Study of the United Arab Emirates," *Asian & Pacific Migration Journal*, Vol. 20, Nos. 3/4 (2011), pp. 315–37.

67 Kanna, *Dubai: The City as Corporation*, p. 109.

68 See Alaedini in this volume, Ch. 10.

Dubai's Jebel Ali port and logistical hub was able to take advantage of this possibility.[69] Ultimately, Jebel Ali, the "first-mover" in adopting technologies for this new maritime era and a port that has been willing and able to accommodate US naval demands, figures prominently in the new hierarchy of Gulf ports. For instance, while in 1982 Dammam outpaced Dubai, by 1986 Jebel Ali overtook its Saudi rival and has not relinquished its status as the leading maritime facility in the Gulf in terms of TEUs handled. Notably, Dubai's dominant position is in spite of attempts by the GCC countries to limit the rise of a single regional hub.[70] Jebel Ali's logistics capacities have allowed it to play as critical a role for the US Navy as does the United States Fifth Fleet's base in Manama.[71]

Consequently, over the course of the twentieth century, connections across and between cities with ports have not diminished, but have become more centrally regulated and more vertical than in the era when merchants, diasporas, empires, and small wind- and coal-powered ships wove the port cities together. This is reflected in supertankers and mammoth container ships existing in the Persian Gulf alongside a steady trafficking of goods via *dhows*. This grey economy, and even illicit trade, that has encompassed commercial activities to and from Iran and Iraq typically must remain small-scale to avoid detection and is not suitable or profitable for container ships and large terminal operators.[72] Thus, it is externalized by this shipping system and placed behind a veil of illegality and informality, in much the same way as the *lumpenproletariat* is rendered invisible spatially, yet visible legally. This is yet another instance of how internationalization tears down certain boundaries and obstacles to exchange, but must also create new boundaries to maintain hierarchies and generate surplus. The cities upon the Persian Gulf, like other urban spaces, are manifestations of patterns of power and the reproduction of social relations of capitalism.

[69] Keshavarzian, "Geopolitics and the Genealogy of Free Trade Zones in the Persian Gulf."
[70] Broeze, "Dubai: Creek to Global Port City," p. 184.
[71] This statement is based on data provided via personal communication with the US Naval Forces Central Command, Department of the Navy, 2 June 2009.
[72] Narges Erami and Arang Keshavarzian, "When ties don't bind: smuggling effects, bazaars, and regulatory regimes in post-revolutionary Iran," *Economy and Society* (2015); Ahmed Kanna, "Dubai in a Jagged World," *Middle East Report* 243 (Summer 2007), pp. 22–9; Pete Moore, "Making Big Money on Iraq," *Middle East Report* 252 (Fall 2009), pp. 22–9.

Conclusion

This chapter has offered a means for describing the variation between cities of the Persian Gulf littoral at the beginning of the twentieth century and their contemporary manifestations. It posits that a central characteristic of these urban spaces was their relationship to the sea as mediated by the technologies of shipping and capital accumulation associated with pearling, petroleum, and petrodollar recycling. It was in these urban spaces that multiple processes came together with all their friction, exclusions, and conflicts.

I argue that at the cusp of the last century, in functional and political economic terms, these were "port cities" that wedded physical places and social relations to maritime mercantilism. After a series of secular changes, including the breakdown of the pearling economy and emergence of the oil economy as well as the shift from the era of empires to nation-states, the containerization revolution facilitated the development of spatial and functional separations between ports and cities. This is a physical, legal, and social divide that is both policed by these new states and results in more divergent urban experiences across the Persian Gulf. Hence my reference to these urban forms as "cities with ports." Accompanying this transformation has been a shift at the regional scale too. While the port cities were knitted together via dense shipping and economic structures bridging and transcending the Gulf littoral, these "cities with ports" have developed into a functional hierarchy for the purposes of shipping, compression of time-space, and accumulation. The "regional" scale has morphed from the Persian Gulf to the transoceanic. In its wake, the Gulf is riddled with rivalries, inequalities, and forms of distinction. In other words, intercoastal and inter-urban dynamics have deepened the gulf.[73] Rather than accepting the states' nationalist projects and attempts to secure state and national boundaries via homogenizing and differentiating populations, the aim here is to focus our attention on the multiple scales through which socioeconomic forces transform the region at once, but along paths that are distinct, yet interrelated.

The transformation in these cities sheds light on how "cosmopolitanism" in the early twentieth century differs from "globalism" in the early twenty-first

---

[73] For some discussion on inter-city competition, see Adham, "Rediscovering the Island: Doha's Urbanity from Pearls to Urbanity"; and Yasser Elsheshtawy, "Cities of Sand and Fog: Abu Dhabi's Global Ambitions," in Yasser Elsheshtawy, ed., *The Evolving Arab City: Tradition, Modernity, and Urban Development* (London: Routledge, 2008), pp. 258–304.

century. First, it is important not to assume that the social pluralism of these port cities and port systems reflected equality in terms of rights and responsibilities, or to assume that it necessarily produced non-exclusionary and tolerant worldviews and political projects. Differences in occupation and religion did matter.[74] Transnationalism also produced anti-imperialism and notions of nationalism, political movements, and identifications focusing on differences. For instance, it was the British India Steam Navigation Company ships that distributed Arab nationalist newspapers.[75] Moreover, as the frontier nature of the region gave way to hardening notions of nationhood, struggles over who was "foreign" became prominent. Thus, cosmopolitanism was a form of "tolerance" mediated by various forms of social and economic relations, rather than explicit and institutionalized forms of protection of difference. Pluralism in the "global city" is a far cry from both the diversity and interconnected world of the port cities at the beginning of the twentieth century or the ideal-type ethical notions of "cosmopolitanism" grounded in laws and protected by a public sphere. Metaphorically speaking, these have become "airport cities" in which social diversity is part of and essential for the city, but this pluralism is simultaneously confronted with a host of laws, security apparatuses, and forms of spatial segregation.

---

[74] Inter alia, Laurence Louër, *Transnational Shia Politics: Religious and Political Networks in the Gulf* (New York: Columbia University Press, 2012).
[75] Broeze, "Dubai: Creek to Global Port City," p. 167.

3

CONTEMPORARY PORT CITIES IN THE PERSIAN GULF

LOCAL GATEWAYS AND GLOBAL NETWORKS

Mehran Kamrava

Over the last two decades or so, a subtle but steady shift has been taking place in the Middle East, with the region's centers of economic, commercial, diplomatic, and political gravity shifting increasingly away from the Levant and North Africa and toward the Persian Gulf region. An integral cause and consequence of this shift has been the apparent emergence of a number of "global cities" across the southern shores of the Persian Gulf, stretching from Kuwait down to Abu Dhabi and Dubai. A region-wide urban chasm has developed in the process, in which Arab and Middle Eastern cities can be divided into the two general categories of "struggling" and "emerging," a division drawn mostly between the ways in which large clusters of cities are coping with ongoing processes of globalization.

According to Yasser Elsheshtawy, the Middle East's "great divide" is being driven primarily by real estate conglomerates, fueled by global capital and oil wealth. The Arab cities of the Persian Gulf—most notably Doha, Manama, Kuwait, Abu Dhabi, and Dubai, as well as Riyadh—have emerged as models to which the other cities of Middle East and Arab regions are aspiring.[1] "The Gulf model," itself a product of what Elsheshtawy calls "moments of change", has brought with it the massive migration of laborers in search of employment, and of skilled professionals and semi-skilled workers, replicating the astounding imbalances that mark the Middle East's economy at a smaller scale within each of the emerging cities.[2] Active engagement with and participation in globalization may have propelled the Middle East's "emerging global cities" into a higher plain of infrastructural development and modern urbanism, but it has also brought them armies of foreign workers and unsettling levels of demographic imbalance.

This chapter examines port cities along the Persian Gulf, going beyond Elshehtawy's dichotomy of "struggling" and "emerging" cities, although agreeing with his basic thesis that some have become the beneficiaries of sustained attention and resources while others suffer from seeming policy neglect and are starved of resources. Building on Arang Keshavarzian's historical account of Persian Gulf urbanism in this volume (Chapter 2), this chapter traces the evolution and current profiles of three types of port cities along the Gulf. They are, in ideal types, company towns, many of which have seen better days; secondary port cities, which, by virtue of being "secondary" receive nowhere near the attention and resources that their "primary" counterparts receive; and what I call "aspiring global cities," which have ambitions of being global cities but do not seem to be quite there yet.

There is a correlation between being a primary city and aspiring to become a central node in multiple global networks in trade and commerce as well as finance, transportation, and logistics. Besides Dubai, all of the other aspiring global cities of the region are capital cities, and all, including Dubai, are primary cities. As such, they are the chief locations for the country's concentrated economic and political power, national symbols and heritage sites (such as museums, national libraries, and sports stadiums), trade and commercial activities, cultural life, and religious centers (national mosques). These cities predominate in the life of the entire country and overshadow all other urban formations; in fact, Kuwait, Qatar, and to a lesser extent Bahrain are all essen-

---

[1] Yasser Elsheshtawy, "The Great Divide: Struggling and Emerging Cities in the Arab World," in Yasser Elsheshtawy, ed., *The Evolving Arab City: Tradition, Modernity, and Urban Development* (London: Routledge, 2008), pp. 8–9.

[2] Ibid., pp. 9–10.

tially city states, the primary city is essentially the whole state. Not surprisingly, they are the chief beneficiaries and recipients of both public and private attention and resources, the primary sites for investments and infrastructural growth, and, invariably, the biggest urban centers in terms of population and geographic size.[3]

The three-tier division of Persian Gulf port cities into company towns, secondary port cities, and aspiring global metropolises has come about as a result of the confluence of three separate yet interlocking and reinforcing developments. The first dynamic revolves around geostrategic factors involving the larger region, most notable of which have been the 1980–88 Iran–Iraq war; Iraq's invasion, occupation, and ejection from Kuwait in 1990–91; sanctions and restrictions on Iraq throughout the 1990s and the 2000s; the US invasion and occupation of Iraq beginning in 2003; and international tensions involving Iran and its nuclear program and steadily comprehensive trade sanctions imposed on the country since the mid-2000s. Related directly to these geostrategic factors have been differential state policies and the capabilities of the region's various states to allocate resources toward projects of urban and infrastructural development. Iran and Iraq have hardly been in a position to embark on meaningful urban development projects hundreds of miles away from their capital cities, and even if they had the political will to do so, they have neither the infrastructural mechanisms nor the opportunities and chances to engage with regional and international trading partners. Iran and Iraq's economic woes and policy handicaps have unfolded at a time of inverse riches for their smaller, agile, and ambitious neighbors to the south.

This reversal of fortune, the third development, has not been limited to the Persian Gulf and actually involves the larger Middle East. Sometime in the 1980s, as Iran and Iraq were busy exhausting themselves in what came to be the longest war of the twentieth century, the states of the Gulf Cooperation Council (GCC) decided proactively to engage the global economy, to invest their expansive oil revenues in domestic infrastructures and financial institutions, and to present themselves as attractive, stable alternatives to international investors scared off from the rest of the Middle East. Unlike their larger, politically more troubled, and economically clunky counterparts elsewhere in the region, GCC countries welcomed rather than shied away from globalization, seeking—sometimes with greater success than others—to make them-

---

[3] For more on primary cities, see Mehran Kamrava, *Politics and Society in the Developing World*, 2nd edn (London: Routledge, 2000), pp. 81–5; and Saskia Sassen, *Cities in a World Economy*, 4th edn (London: Sage, 2012), pp. 62–5.

selves critical nodes in emerging networks of global transportation and logistics, banking and finance, and corporate headquarters and decision-making.[4] Their rhetoric of cooperation and unity notwithstanding, the states of the GCC have often competed over political and strategic goals and objectives. But where that competition is most intense, and at times even bitter, is in positioning themselves as attractive destinations for multinational corporations and international investors, and ultimately as global cities.

For the time being, it would require a leap of faith to consider the capital port cities of the GCC—Kuwait City, Manama, Doha, Abu Dhabi, and Dubai—as global cities in the sense defined by Chapter 1 of this volume. By itself, consumption ought not to be confused with development. A global city needs to be also a hub of production of advanced services as part of a broader global network.[5] For now, the cities of the GCC are at best only consumers of infrastructural and knowledge products from elsewhere. Whether their deep pockets and their voracious appetite for imports of all kinds will pave the way for them to give substance to their aspirations of becoming global cities is yet to be seen. Clearly, they have both the ambition and, steadily, the imported infrastructure to also become proactive nodes of production of services and information in expansive global networks. But they still have some way to go from being primarily consumers to also becoming producers. Only Dubai has become somewhat of an exporter of architectural services, selling the "Dubai model" of glass and steel towers to other cities in the region. But even that niche is far too small and its production outlet far too much of a trickle to signal the emirate's arrival as a "global city."

Thus while global networks may be increasing and expanding across the GCC's gleaming port cities, for now the flow of services and products within them remains overwhelmingly one-way, keeping these cities as aspiring rather than actual global cities. They remain mostly local gateways, not unlike the company port towns of Abadan in Iran and Dammam in Saudi Arabia in the early decades of the twentieth century, or the port cities of Basra in Iraq and Bandar Abbas and Bushehr in Iran in the 1960s, 1970s, and 1980s. Like the two iterations of aspiring global nodes before them, the GCC port cities of today see themselves as pioneering hubs, not just of hydrocarbon production

[4] Anoushiravan Ehteshami, *Globalization and Geopolitics in the Middle East* (London: Routledge, 2009), pp. 130–48.
[5] Manuel Castells, *The Rise of the Networked Society*, 2nd edn (Oxford: Wiley-Blackwell, 2010), p. 417. See also the discussion of global cities in Chapter 1 of this volume.

but also of logistics and transportation. However, both the inability of the region's company towns and secondary port cities to become actual nodes of information and service production, and the ravages of the geostrategic developments over which they themselves had little control, have today relegated them to cities with, at best, marginal importance within their respective national economies and, even less, within the broader region. They can serve as models to avoid for the aspiring port cities within their neighborhood.

Company Towns

Oil profoundly impacted urbanization patterns across the Persian Gulf, but it did so differently throughout the region. In Iran, the company town of Abadan grew from a small, dusty town in the early years of the 1900s to a city of around 250,000 people in the 1950s. New towns of Dhahran, Al Khobar, and Damman also grew rapidly in Saudi Arabia. In the city-states of Kuwait, Bahrain, and Qatar, however, it was the old traditional urban centers that grew in domination and significance as a result of the oil industry.[6] In these smaller countries, separate oil company towns developed only sparsely—as in Ahmadi in Kuwait and Awali in Bahrain. This was because most oil installations were located relatively close to existing population settlements, and because the activities of the oil companies were on a somewhat smaller scale compared to those in Iran and Saudi Arabia. Nevertheless, oil wealth completely transformed traditional patterns of urban development in the sheikhdoms, destroying traditional special structures of cities and introducing Western planning models and policies.[7] In the process, the dominant role of these capital cities—Kuwait City, Manama, and Doha—were reinforced as they grew in size, and in economic and commercial significance.

A company town refers to a settlement or city designed, built, owned, maintained, and managed by a private company or a state-owned enterprise.[8] In company towns, the "urban fabric centers around features implanted by the

---

[6] Richard I. Lawless and Ian Seccombe, "Impact of the Oil Industry on Urbanization in the Persian Gulf Region," in Hooshang Amirahmadi and Salah S. El-Shakhs, eds, *Urban Development in the Muslim World* (New Brunswick, NJ: Transaction, 1993), p. 185.

[7] Lawless and Seccombe, "Impact of the Oil Industry on Urbanization in the Persian Gulf Region," p. 207.

[8] John Garner, *The Model Company Town* (Amherst, MA: University of Massachusetts Press, 1984), pp. 6–7.

company," and the economic enterprise around which the city was designed and built dominates the political, social, and cultural lives of the city.[9] They are "essentially a temporary pioneering device, especially suited to conditions obtaining in nations undergoing rapid economic development."[10] Company towns tend to fall into one of the two categories of extractive or manufacturing towns, and are designed to provide basic infrastructure and housing to the full spectrum of employees needed to run complex industrial operations such as mining and petroleum. As such, they pay detailed attention to urban form and planning, and are often based on the deliberate company policy of segregation by employee class, level of skill, or national origin. A hierarchy of dwelling types is especially noticeable in the larger company towns.[11] By the early twentieth century, the assumption behind the design of company towns was to ensure a "scientific" urban design in which "through continuous intervention in all aspects of the quotidian life of the labor force and their families, to mold them into skilled and efficient, but also docile, 'happy', and modern 'human capital.'"[12] These assumptions often translate into the provision of villas with modern amenities, open spaces and green lawns, and parks and recreational facilities.

As part of its expansive efforts in Iran after the discovery of oil in 1908, the Anglo Persian Oil Company (APOC) designed and built nine industrial company towns in Khuzestan province in the first quarter of the twentieth century.[13] These towns were built to accommodate the increasing numbers of engineers and technicians being imported into the country, mainly from Britain and the United States, to manage and run the booming petroleum sector. The expansion of the oil industry in south-western Iran beginning in the early 1900s and in the southern states of the Persian Gulf in the 1930s resulted in the employment of considerable numbers of non-locals, especially Westerners, in the local oil sectors. By 1950, some 40 per cent of the employees of Aramco, Qatar Development Company (QDC), and Bahrain Petroleum Company (BAPCO) were classified as "non-indigenous," and a

[9] J. D. Porteous, "The Nature of the Company Town," *Transactions of the Institute of British Geographers*, Vol. 51 (November 1970), p. 133.

[10] Ibid., p. 127.

[11] Ibid., p. 135.

[12] Kaveh Ehsani, "Social Engineering and the Contradictions of Modernization in Khuzestan's Company Towns: A Look at Abadan and Masjed–Soleyman," *International Review of Social History*, Vol. 48, No. 3 (December 2003), p. 375.

[13] Ibid., p. 361.

significant number of those considered "indigenous" were from elsewhere in the region, most notably Bahrain, the Trucial States, Oman, and Baluchestan. Altogether, by 1950 some 22,000 foreign workers were employed by the oil companies operating in the Persian Gulf region.[14]

In Khuzestan as elsewhere, the location of the company towns had little to do with environmental conditions or existing settlements and communities, but were instead decided upon by requirements of the oil industry.[15] This meant that the choice of the location of the town was dictated by considerations of extraction, storage, transportation, and distribution.[16] According to Ehsani, in addition to providing housing and facilities for the oil company's labor force, company towns serve the additional purpose of using "the carefully designed urban space for training, monitoring, controlling, and, in short, socializing this labor force according to the demands of the company."[17] In Abadan, there was "an obsession to use urban space as an instrument of controlling the population" through building neighborhoods far apart from one another and separating them with large swathes of barren land or wide roads, placing police stations in such a way as to make surveillance of workers' quarters easier, and ending most roads in bottlenecks rather than linking them through traffic exchanges in order to make intermingling and pedestrian interaction more difficult.[18]

One of the consequences of the construction and population of company towns was the introduction of "a new model of social engineering and hierarchical modernization" into Iranian social life by such powerful actors as transnational capital, the central state, and professional elites.[19] Senior European staff, for example, received the largest villas with green lawns in park-like settings, and lower-rank employees received progressively smaller dwellings depending on their descending rank and levels of skills.[20] These same patterns

---

[14] Lawless and Seccombe, "Impact of the Oil Industry on Urbanization in the Persian Gulf Region," pp. 189–90.

[15] Ehsani, "Social Engineering and the Contradictions of Modernization in Khuzestan's Company Towns," p. 376. Neglect of environmental conditions is an endemic feature of almost all company towns, especially older ones. See, for example, Porteous, "The Nature of the Company Town," p. 134.

[16] Ehsani, "Social Engineering and the Contradictions of Modernization in Khuzestan's Company Towns," p. 383.

[17] Ibid., p. 362.

[18] Ibid., pp. 389–90.

[19] Ibid., p. 361.

[20] Ibid., p. 384.

of interaction were replicated elsewhere across the Persian Gulf and Middle
East regions among pretty much similar sets of actors, thus influencing the
social structure of the oil cities, emerging political dynamics and ideological
threads, and broader patterns in state–society relations.[21] As Lawless and
Seccombe explain:

> In Abadan, as in all 'oil company towns' in the Persian Gulf, urban planning
> expressed Western rather than Islamic values. Probably the most striking feature
> was the strict segregation of the inhabitants by ethnicity and occupational status, a
> policy that gave rise to sharp breaks between adjacent areas containing population
> groups of markedly different status. In this way, the strictly hierarchical occupa-
> tional structure of the company was faithfully reflected in the spatial patterning of
> the city's residential areas. Significantly, the influence of the company's policies on
> the spatial patterning of the city's population remained after the company was
> nationalized and the number of foreign employees declined dramatically.[22]

Urban planning and urban forms influenced family practices and interactions as well. Company towns had their concepts, urban forms, and housing
plans imported from Europe and the United States en masse, and with literally
no modification to fit local conditions. These new designs soon forced changes
to local family structures. Smaller living spaces forced the breakdown of
extended families into nuclear ones. The replacement of the traditional central
courtyard with tiny garden plots eliminated or significantly reduced natural
air circulation and necessitated the use of fans and other electrical appliances.
Separate kitchens with running water and an operative sewage system
improved hygiene and reduced mortality rates.[23]

Though initially an almost entirely APOC-created space, with its street
layouts and urban plans drawn up in the company headquarters in London,
Abadan steadily attracted migrant workers from around the country, and,
gradually, a new sense of social identity of its own, with its inhabitants considering themselves Abadani.[24] Over time, Abadan and other Iranian company
towns developed a dualistic feature, whereby a dichotomy appeared between

---

[21] For an examination of similar developments in Iraq, for example, see Arbella Bet-
Shlimon, "The Politics and Ideology of Urban Development in Iraq's Oil City:
Kirkuk, 1946–58," *Comparative Studies of South Asia, Africa and the Middle East*,
Vol. 33, No. 1 (2013), pp. 26–40.

[22] Lawless and Seccombe, "Impact of the Oil Industry on Urbanization in the Persian
Gulf Region," p. 200.

[23] Ehsani, "Social Engineering and the Contradictions of Modernization in Khuzestan's
Company Towns," pp. 387–8.

[24] Ibid., pp. 377–8.

the "formal" town, which, as planned and maintained by the company, was hierarchical and segregated, and the "informal" town, which was an amalgam of styles, cultures, and social groups. Ehsani describes the formal parts of Abadan as follows:

> The formal space of Abadan ... consisted of several segregated neighborhoods, the residents of which were carefully assigned housing according to their job, rank in the company roster, and even race, nationality, and ethnicity. A rigid and inflexible hierarchy defined the neighborhood, street, alley, and specific house of each individual employee according to his rank, work record, skill, and even ethnicity, and assigned a house to his family (all employees being male).[25]

To showcase its urban planning accomplishments and to attract more of its European employees to the oil city, in 1949 the Anglo Iranian Oil Company (AIOC) started making a film about Abadan called *Persian Story*.[26] Ironically, the company finished the film in 1951, just as Iranian nationalist sentiments were reaching a peak and the AIOC's Iranian operations were becoming nationalized by PM Mussadiq's government. Hailing its efforts at bringing about the city's growth and urban planning as a major engine of modernity in Iran, the following passage appeared underneath the *Persian Story*'s recorded script:

> Abadan, means more than oil; it means people—men and women, Persians and Europeans, to whom Abadan is not just industry but home. So side by side with the giant Refinery grow all the other amenities of a modern city where the races meet—schools and colleges, hospitals and clubs and clinics; and the two peoples share the work, so do they share the leisure. In the heart of the oil city stands the reason for it all, the enormous purpose of all the rest: the great Refinery, the biggest in the world.[27]

Needless to say, the film's portrayal of Abadan and its amenities as mixed and multi-ethnic was a gross misrepresentation of the reality on the ground.

As with most other company towns, however, Abadan soon witnessed the growth of a "spontaneous" city with its own "native" architecture, bazaars, informal and unplanned residential areas, and even places of illicit and illegal

---

[25] Ibid., p. 384.

[26] In 1953, in light of the Iranian government's move to nationalize the oil industry, APOC was renamed the Anglo Iranian Oil Company (AIOC), and in 1954 it renamed itself once more, this time to British Petroleum Company (BP).

[27] Quoted in Mona Damluji, "The Oil City in Focus: The Cinematic Spaces of Abadan in the Anglo-Iranian Oil Company's Persian Story," *Comparative Studies of South Asia, Africa and the Middle East*, Vol. 33, No. 1 (2013), p. 84.

activity such as goods smuggling, prostitution, and drug trafficking.[28] Together, in contrast to the formal parts of the city whose life and rhythm were dictated by the oil company, and later the Oil Ministry, the informal parts of the city "presented a lively, adventurous, exciting, untamed, and unsupervised public arena to all citizens, whether employed by the company or not."[29] In his examination of the early history of Iranian company towns, Kaveh Ehsani argues that they had a vibrant cultural landscape "thanks to the heterogeneity and energy of their population, as well as the forbidding scales the cities had reached despite the company's wishes."[30]

A few decades after Abadan's growth under the auspices of APOC, a similar pattern of urbanization took place in relation to the company town of Dammam in Saudi Arabia. Dammam was formed in 1923 when the Al-Dawaser tribe moved from Bahrain to the mainland and settled there, and then, along with the nearby city of Dhahran, expanded considerably after Aramco started establishing "camps" there for expanding numbers of oil workers.[31] Beginning in the 1950s, Aramco began building single-family unit "villas" for its employees, and by the 1970s these types of seemingly "modern" homes had also gained increasing popularity among local, middle-class Saudis.[32] Similar to APOC's initiatives in Abadan, Aramco's urban planning was designed deliberately to segregate its employees from the local population. The account of one American visitor to Dammam in 1956 is illustrative of the manifestations of proliferating, segregated, Western-style grid-iron subdivisions:

> Not one westerner would have difficulty in identifying the senior staff "camp" as a settlement built by Americans in our southwestern tradition of town planning. It is an area of single-story dwellings for employees and their families. Each house is surrounded by a small grassed yard usually enclosed by a hedge.[33]

Company towns may have been planned and built by the oil companies, but over time the company becomes just another presence in the city rather than its defining centerpiece and benefactor, and the cities assume their own

28 Ehsani, "Social Engineering and the Contradictions of Modernization in Khuzestan's Company Towns," p. 392.
29 Ibid., p. 393.
30 Ibid., p. 361.
31 Mashary Al-Naim, "Dammam, Saudi Arabia," in Murray Fraser and Nasser Golzari, eds, *Architecture and Globalization in the Persian Gulf Region* (Burlington, VT: Ashgate, 2013), p. 57.
32 Ibid., pp. 64–5.
33 Quoted in ibid., p. 60.

internal rhythm and dynamics, their own identities, and their own forms. Its genesis as a company town all but forgotten, Dammam has today expanded beyond recognition, home to ever-increasing numbers of migrant workers, more from the South Asian subcontinent today than from the United States. As one observer notes:

> plenty of new neighbourhoods were constructed in the last two decades to meet the population growth. Compared to the surrounding older cities, especially Qatif, urban and social identity has undergone incredible transition in Dammam. The different cultural backgrounds of newcomers to the area, along with the presence of huge numbers of expatriate labourers, have heightened this crisis of identity.[34]

Although not nearly to the same extent as Doha, Abu Dhabi, and Dubai, Dammam has also sought to commercialize its skyline by encouraging the construction of high-rise towers along major thoroughfares and expressways.[35] At the very least, the city has successfully transformed itself from a sterile company town not too long ago into a thriving secondary port city today.

Abadan has been far less fortunate in more recent times, its trajectory one of decline rather than growth. Nasser Golzari maintains that Abadan's modern origins as a British company town, its overwhelming reliance on the oil industry for many decades, and its devastation and depletion during the course of the Iran–Iraq war have all today resulted in a fair amount of "confusion" over the city's current and future identity.[36] During Iran's eight-year war with Iraq, the city suffered devastating infrastructural damage, much of which is yet to be repaired. Although the war ended in 1988, and the country underwent what the government labeled a "construction crusade" in the 1990s, Abadan and its sister city of Khorramshahr have remained largely neglected by the central government in Tehran, becoming at best service cities and at worst "non-place[s] within the national and global market places."[37] The scars of war still linger on the city's infrastructure and its sense of self. The government in Tehran seems ill-equipped to do much for now to repair and heal the city's wounds. Clearly, Abadan's days as a consequential metropolis in Iran and beyond are behind it.

[34] Ibid., p. 69.
[35] Ibid., p. 70.
[36] Nasser Golzari, "Abadan and Khorramshahr, Iran," in Fraser and Golzari, eds, *Architecture and Globalization in the Persian Gulf Region*, p. 227.
[37] Ibid., p. 220.

Secondary Port Cities

A second category of urban formation found along the Persian Gulf is the secondary port city, of which Basra, Bandar Abbas, Bushehr, and today's Dammam are prime examples. As their designation implies, secondary cities lack the power and significance of primary cities, are smaller in size and population, and do not have the economic diversity and infrastructural depth and resources of their bigger counterparts. Frequently, the economy of secondary cities is dominated not by the specialized services and the financial sectors, nor even by large-scale manufacturing industries, but instead by the informal tertiary sector requiring lower levels of skill and technical specialization. Although in recent decades many of these cities have seen major improvements in service delivery, urban planning, infrastructural growth and development, and sustained administrative, economic, and political attention by the central government, secondary cities still lag considerably behind the capital city or other primary cities in overall levels of political and economic significance, the allocation of resources, and levels and forms of engagement with other centers of importance and influence within the country and abroad.[38]

With the exception of Dammam, the story of the Persian Gulf's secondary port cities—whether of Basra in Iraq, or Bushehr and Bandar Abbas in Iran—is one of untapped and underdeveloped potential, caused by willful or inadvertent neglect by the capital city, wars and international tensions, and inhospitable climates for domestic and international investments. Not surprisingly, secondary port cities have for the most part maintained their urban fabric, seen as an archival record of all building activities undertaken in a city, whether spontaneously or planned, from its foundation to the present. Urban fabric may be defined as "an accumulation of many successive activities that reflect the age and maturity of the city."[39] On the one hand, these activities reflect the work and preferences of the private sector, which has been historically guided by considerations of Islamic law, or *fiqh*, regarding such matters as personal privacy, donations, inheritance, ownership, the placing of easement, and the like. This, Ben-Hamouche argues, resulted in a certain natural level of "architectural diversity and urban dynamism." On the other hand, the

---

[38] For more on secondary cities, see Kamrava, *Politics and Society in the Developing World*, pp. 85–7.

[39] Mustapha Ben-Hamouche, "Complexity of urban fabric in traditional Muslim cities: Importing old wisdom to present cities," *Urban Design International*, Vol. 14, No. 1 (2009), p. 33.

urban fabric reflected the efforts of the public sector aimed at structuring the city based on the policies and preferences of the state and its affiliated urban planners. "The older the city, the more complex its urban fabric."[40]

But an old urban fabric does not necessarily translate into a city's adaptability to changing circumstances, and its accommodative capacity to cope with the stresses and strains of demographic growth and technological change. This inability to cope with and accommodate changing demographic, technological, and urban currents can be readily seen in both Bandar Abbas and Basra. In Bandar Abbas, for example, various new communities growing in the city have not been well integrated into the urban mainstream, giving the city a look of incongruity and neglect.[41] The general decline of the agricultural sector and comparatively easy and lucrative trade in smuggled goods has made Bandar Abbas a receiving and transit city for migrants from nearby towns and rural areas, resulting in the growth of various slum areas in the city's periphery.[42] Water pollution and improper sanitation in Bandar Abbas have resulted in repeated occurrences of "red tide"—resulting from accumulation of polluted algae—off the city's coastal waters in the Persian Gulf. Outbreaks of illness due to contaminated water supplies are also not uncommon in the city.[43]

In an effort to address some of these problems, beginning in 1985 the Iranian government launched an ambitious program of urban development. Aimed at providing much needed urban plans and facilities to the inner cities of major metropolitan areas, the plan gave the public greater say and participation in developmental issues while reducing government and municipal expenditures.[44] According to a study conducted ten years after the program was first launched, the effort has been largely successful and has, to varying degrees, prevented the emergence of new squatter settlements while providing basic infrastructural services and amenities (roads, water, drainage, sewerage, and electricity) to existing urban areas.[45]

But a number of major structural problems continue to persist. Inadequate economic opportunities in the formal sector have turned Bandar Abbas into

---

[40] Ibid., p. 22.
[41] Widari Bahrin, "Bandar Abbas, Iran," in Fraser and Golzari, eds, *Architecture and Globalization in the Persian Gulf Region*, p. 314.
[42] Ibid., p. 317.
[43] Ibid.
[44] Mohammad Mehdi Azizi, "The Provision of Urban Infrastructure in Iran: An Empirical Evaluation," *Urban Studies*, Vol. 32, No. 3 (1995), p. 507.
[45] Ibid., p. 521.

GATEWAYS TO THE WORLD

a major smuggling hub. The city's location serves as an ideal transit route for smuggled goods into the country, and illegal transit by speedboat into Oman and the UAE—only a two-hour journey—is not uncommon.[46] The city's port facilities, meanwhile, remain underdeveloped and nowhere near competitive given the size and current demands of marine transport, with Tehran turning its attention to Bushehr and even further west to the small and still developing port of Chabahar near the Pakistani border.

Further up the Persian Gulf coast and closer to Iran's oil facilities is the port city of Bushehr, whose urban profile is not that different from Bandar Abbas. Although Bushehr has long been one of the country's more cosmopolitan urban centers, thanks to its strategic importance and its geographic location as a main entrepôt, it experienced relative economic decline in the 1960s and 1970s. As one of the country's main port cities, Bushehr has in recent years benefited from the central government's largesse and attention as part of the Islamic Republic's efforts to jumpstart its economy and to engage the world through trade and commerce. In 2008, a master plan for urban growth and planning was devised for the city, along with plans to expand existing road networks to other major cities inland.[47] But these economic and infrastructural development efforts fall short of enabling the city to live up to its economic and strategic potential. Bushehr still lags in urban service delivery, suffers from poor overall economic performance (having chronically high rates of unemployment), and has failed to develop its potential in areas such as industrial manufacturing, transportation, and tourism.[48]

Neglect, untapped potential, and decay are not limited to Iran's port cities along the Persian Gulf. Basra, Iraq's only port on the Gulf and its sole outlet to the open sea, has suffered a similar fate. Despite its strategic location and its abundant natural resources in oil, gas, agriculture, and water, the city of Basra continues to suffer from neglect and infrastructural decay. According to a joint study conducted in 2009 by the Basra Business Associations and the Center for International Private Enterprises (CIPE):

> Basra lags behind in all walks of economic life and suffers due to its weak, poor economy. Its economy is characterized by clear infrastructure inefficiency, and poor or nonexistent electric, water and municipal services. The productive sectors such

---

[46] Bahrin, "Bandar Abbas, Iran," p. 314.
[47] Semra Aydinli and Avsar Karababa, "Bushehr, Iran," in Fraser and Golzari, eds, *Architecture and Globalization in the Persian Gulf Region*, p. 246.
[48] Ibid., p. 248.

as agriculture and industry are still using outdated production methods and machinery which has made them incapable of coping with the citizen's needs and competing with foreign imports. Job opportunities for citizens are also insufficient, hindering efforts to curb the continued unemployment problem in Basra. All these factors have yielded further macroeconomic imbalances and deteriorating living standards for the people of Basra.[49]

In the later 2000s, the central government launched a number of initiatives aimed at Basra's urban renewal, most of which appear to have been derailed due to the country's larger problems. The Basra governorate has been awarding a number of contracts to architectural firms, mostly based in Kuwait, Dubai, and Abu Dhabi, to develop the city's waterfront with areas made up of multi-use residential, commercial, and entertainment districts. In 2010–11, moreover, the Basra Provincial Council devised an ambitious development strategy, in which it hoped "to make Basra a developed city with integrated infrastructure where the best delivery of services are available" and to make the city "the economic capital of Iraq and a distinguished economic center in the region."[50] The development strategy outlined goals to improve the city's sewerage and potable water delivery systems, to construct additional water desalination plants to ensure adequate supplies of drinking water, to adopt a master plan for the city's business districts and residential and green areas, to renovate existing roads and bridges and increase existing road capacity, and to facilitate commercial and industrial investment opportunities for potential investors.

Problems persist, however. In addition to Iraq's unstable security situation, an "absence of state of the art technologies and materials that can handle emerging developments worldwide," corruption, poor infrastructure, and multiple "administrative and bureaucratic impediments" continue to plague Basra's economy and infrastructure.[51] Problems with the city's four main marine ports—Umm Qasr, Khor Azzubeir, Abu Flous, and Al Maʿaqal—are emblematic of the city's predicament. They all operate at a level consistently far below capacity because of a history of neglect by the central government in Baghdad. Most have access to inadequate and unreliable transport vehicles and are incapable of coping with new developments in the international shipping and trans-

---

[49] Center for International Private Enterprises, "Agenda of Basra Province" (Washington, DC: CIPE, 2009), p. 8.

[50] Basra Provincial Council, "Basra Provincial Development Strategy, 2011–2015," Basra, Iraq, 2010–2011.

[51] Center for International Private Enterprises, "Agenda of Basra Province," pp. 10–11.

port industries.[52] Compounding their difficulties are frequent administrative and budgetary turf battles that often paralyze their operations.

Similarly, Basra's agricultural, industrial, and trade sectors all suffer from major structural deficiencies and difficulties that result from their own operations and the larger political and economic environments within which they operate. The transportation sector faces inadequate port facilities, decayed roads and bridges, poor air transport, poor service delivery to carriers at border points, and continued reductions in small and medium support enterprises such as car rental companies and trucking firms. Similarly, the banking sector, as with the rest of the country, remains underdeveloped and is largely unable to operate, never mind compete, in the global arena.[53]

Iran and Iraq, being gripped by their own domestic political and economic problems for the last several decades, belligerents in bloody and devastating wars, and subject to comprehensive and punishing international sanctions regimes for the last decade or so, have been unable, or unwilling, to develop their port cities in the Persian Gulf despite their strategic, economic, and commercial needs. Basra, Bushehr, and Bandar Abbas have maintained their traditional urban fabrics, as if largely left behind in time by a good few decades. Targeted for urban renewal projects and infrastructural upgrades at one point or another, such initiatives either failed to take off altogether or at best have had incomplete and marginal consequences. The cities' port facilities are outdated, operate at far below capacity, cannot accommodate larger ships with heavier loads, and can hardly address the trade and commercial needs of the country. These secondary port cities may have fared better than Abadan in the long term, but only slightly. They remain, however, far behind in terms of infrastructural development and global engagement compared to the nearby aspiring global cities that have capitalized on their misfortunes.

Aspiring Global Cities

In the aspiring global cities of the Persian Gulf, the forces of globalization are reshaping the very structure and form of the city. Global investments dominate the local real estate market. "Traditional cityscapes, propagated by advances in transportation and telecommunication, are being drastically transformed to make room for new places of global consumption and material culture; that is,

---

[52] Ibid., pp. 79–80.
[53] Ibid., pp. 12–13.

suburban office complexes, business and technology parks, shopping malls, and, even whole 'edge cities.'"[54] Elsheshtawy divides these emerging global cities into those early modernizers—"cities which have a more developed encounter with modernity"—in which Kuwait, Manama, and Riyadh can be categorized, and the more dormant cities, such as Doha and Abu Dhabi, that are only now beginning to assert themselves proactively as emergent global cities.[55] Doha and Abu Dhabi, and no doubt Dubai as well, are deliberately and proactively seeking to transform themselves overnight from once-poor fishing villages into contemporary metropolises with global profiles.[56]

The era of meaningful change in the Gulf's aspiring cities can be traced back to the late 1980s, when the GCC states began investing their expansive revenues in infrastructural, commercial, and financial endeavors that were domestically oriented. Existing roads were expanded and new ones were built; specialized hospitals were established; port facilities were upgraded and new ones were created; national airlines began competing regionally and airports began aspiring to become regional and global hubs; new universities and technical colleges were established; and international hotel chains inaugurated more and more opulent hotels near the coastal areas and along the corniche.[57]

It was not always like this, and snapshots of each of the cities a mere few decades ago illustrate the amazing scale and dizzying speed of change along the southern shores of the Persian Gulf. Until well into the early 1960s, for example, Abu Dhabi, as the locals depicted it, was left behind in the eighteenth century. Even the signing of an oil concession in 1953 had failed to result in tangible changes to the dusty town, as the ruler at the time, Sheikh Shakhbout, was a "stubborn conservative" who "refused to part with any of his money."[58] In fact, it was not until the late 1960s that Sheikh Zayed, by then well-established in his rule, embarked on an ambitious plan to build the city anew almost overnight. Throughout the 1970s the city raced to rebuild and rediscover itself, aided in the process by higher oil prices, seeing an increasing number of official govern-

[54] Fuad K. Malkawi, "The New Arab Metropolis," in Elsheshtawy, ed., *The Evolving Arab City*, p. 35.

[55] Elsheshtawy, "The Great Divide," p. 12.

[56] Ibid., p. 13.

[57] Sulayman Khalaf, "The evolution of the Gulf city type, oil, and globalization," in John W. Fox, Nada Mourtada-Sabbah, and Mohammed al-Mutawa, eds, *Globalization and the Gulf* (London: Routledge, 2006), p. 249.

[58] Quoted in Yasser Elsheshtawy, "Cities of Sand and Fog: Abu Dhabi's Global Ambitions," in Elsheshtawy, ed., *The Evolving Arab City*, p. 264.

ment buildings, hospitals, schools, and mosques, and, beginning in the late 1970s and the early 1980s, even high-rise towers and luxury hotels.[59] By one count, in the late 1960s and the early 1970s, around 40 per cent of Abu Dhabi's workforce was devoted to the construction sector as the city was being built.[60] According to a 1988 master plan, Abu Dhabi's size was to grow through land reclamation in order to accommodate its rapid growth in population, and, additionally, through the extension of wide, grid-pattern roads. At the same time, the plots of land handed out by the ruler's office in the central parts of the city were not that large, resulting in the construction of densely packed towers throughout the city center. These urban patterns, of wide grid-pattern roads in the outlying areas and densely-packed towers in central areas, continue to mark Abu Dhabi's urban landscape until today.[61]

Doha also remained a sleepy pearling town well into the early decades of the twentieth century, one in which tribal affiliations directly influenced patterns of demographic distribution. Each tribe was clustered into a district (*fereej*), with eight main districts (*fereejan*) making up the small area that comprised the city. The harbor remained the city's main focal point, where the open markets, the shipyards, and a number of meeting places (*majalis*) were located.[62] Khaled Adham paints a vivid picture of Doha's urban layout around this time:

> The housing stock was composed of a few hundred simple one floor dwellings huddled closely together along narrow winding alleys. Other structures that dotted the cityscape included the *barasti* and the Bedouin tents. Members of the tribe were given land by the sheikh upon their request, usually to accommodate a large increase in the family or for newlyweds to start a new one.[63]

In the mid-1950s, as the discovery of oil began having what were at first modest financial rewards, Doha's urban face started to change with the construction of asphalt roads, an electric power plant, schools and hospitals, and various construction projects. This coincided with the increasing flow of both low-skilled and professional migrant workers into the country, and the pre-

[59] Ibid., p. 270.
[60] Jane Bristol-Rhys, "Socio-Spatial Boundaries in Abu Dhabi," in Mehran Kamrava and Zahra Babar, eds, *Migrant Labor in the Persian Gulf* (New York: Columbia University Press, 2011), p. 65.
[61] Elsheshtawy, "Cities of Sand and Fog," pp. 272–3.
[62] Khaled Adham, "Rediscovering the Island: Doha's Urbanity from Pearls to Spectacles," in Elsheshtawy, ed., *The Evolving Arab City*, pp. 223–4.
[63] Ibid., p. 224.

cipitous, though mostly unplanned and spontaneous, growth of the city to accommodate its expanding size. Within two decades of the discovery of oil in Qatar, from the 1950s to the 1970s, Doha's geographic size grew tenfold, the population increasing by nearly 600 per cent, and the number of foreigners residing in the city by nearly 1,000 per cent.[64]

Throughout the 1960s and the early 1970s, urban growth took place in Doha with little attention to spatial planning or architectural form. It was only after the country's formal independence in 1971 and the establishment of various government agencies and an expanding bureaucracy that many of the city's older streets, residential areas, and entire neighborhoods were bulldozed and replaced by newer variants designed to accommodate evolving tastes and in size and population.[65] Equally important was the redistribution of land by the state, and more specifically by the Emir, for purposes of political legitimacy and consolidation, along with an aggressive land reclamation project to expand the city's size and prime real estate along the coastline. Adham argues that this growth was driven primarily by massive increases in population and the influx of migrant workers by the tens of thousands, resulting in what he labels as "urbanity of necessity."[66] This was taken over in the 1990s, when the new Emir aspired to fashion Qatar's modern identity with a distinct image in the world community by an "urbanity of the spectacle," during which world-renowned architects were commissioned to give the city a physical appearance commensurate with its expansive wealth and its global ambitions.[67] This phase, which began in the mid-1990s and continues until today, has witnessed the construction of numerous mega-projects meant to impress and inspire, signaling the city's attractiveness to its growing hordes of wealthy residents and Western and professional expatriates. The most notable of these projects include multiple skyscrapers and towers changing Doha's skyline, the Villaggio Mall, countless luxury hotels and residential towers, Lusail City, the Aspire Dome and Sports Complex, the enormous Education City campus, the Museum of Islamic Art, Katara Cultural Village, and, perhaps most importantly, the Pearl artificial island.[68]

Kuwait's pre-oil profile was slightly different from that of Abu Dhabi and Doha, featuring robust industries revolving around pearling, seafaring, and

[64] Ibid., pp. 226–7.
[65] Ibid., pp. 230–31.
[66] Ibid., p. 236.
[67] Ibid., pp. 236–40.
[68] Ibid., p. 247.

trading with other littoral cities of the Persian Gulf.[69] Before the launch of the oil industry in 1946, Kuwait was in fact a thriving port city. The passage from a port economy to an oil economy profoundly affected the process of city formation in Kuwait, creating new economic realities with new spatial consequences and planning requirements.[70] As Farah al-Nakib puts it in relation to Kuwait, for the country's leaders and planners, "their capital city had to satisfy the global gaze."[71] An ambitious development plan was launched in 1950 by the new ruler Abdullah al-Salem, as a result of which many of the historic parts of the city were torn down and underwent what the government touted as "wholesale reconstruction."[72] Before long, newly planned spaces began appearing in many parts of the city.

Manama has pretty much followed a similar trajectory, though Bahrain's limited oil resources compared to its neighbors has had consequences for the speed of urban infrastructural development in the country and the scale of the capital city's global ambitions. Mustapha Ben-Hamouche divides the development of Manama into three phases. The first phase was one of "autonomous urbanism," in which the city evolved naturally and as a result of natural demographic changes, water supply, and the location preferences and choices of the various tribal groupings. The second phase ushered in an era of "bureaucratic urbanism," in which first the British imperial administration and after 1971 the independent Bahraini government began projects of land registration, urban planning, service provision, road works, land reclamation, and devising housing policies. These processes and projects continued into the third phase, one of "global urbanism," which began in the 1990s and has brought with it mega-projects such as the Bahrain Financial Harbor, the Bahrain World Trade Center, the Al-Zamal Tower office complex, and the Abraj al-Lulu towers of luxury residential units.[73]

Although not quite seeking to compete with Dubai, which has successfully positioned itself as the main entrepôt to the rest of the Persian Gulf and indeed the rest of the Middle East, Bahrain's efforts at engaging with globali-

---

[69] Farah al-Nakib, "Kuwait's Modern Spectacle: Oil Wealth and the Making of a New Capital City, 1950–90," *Comparative Studies of South Asia, Africa and the Middle East*, Vol. 33, No. 1 (2013), p. 7.

[70] Ibid., p. 8.

[71] Ibid., p. 18.

[72] Ibid., p. 10.

[73] Mustapha Ben-Hamouche, "Manama: The Metamorphosis of an Arab Gulf City," in Elsheshtawy, ed., *The Evolving Arab City*, pp. 184–211.

zation have been driven by its attempts to emerge as the region's financial and business hub. The "post-oil era" has led to the emergence of what Ali Alraouf has called Manama's "hybrid urbanism." No longer conditioned by hydrocarbon revenues, Alraouf maintains that Bahrain is engaged in a process of "self-stylization" in which "any proposed structure is ultimately measured by its ability to thrive in new and unpredictable conditions."[74]

These and other similar projects all demonstrate attempts at global ambitions and aspirations through real estate and infrastructural development. National, economic, and cultural differences notwithstanding, processes of urban development, and the current urban profiles and aspirations of the port cities of the southern Persian Gulf, feature remarkable parallels and similarities. Doha, Dubai, Abu Dhabi, and Kuwait City have all sought to position themselves as global cities through real estate, in the process employing the built urban environment and architectural form as places of fantasy and entertainment.[75] Dubai has played a particularly pioneering role in this regard, having in the process forged a special, symbiotic relationship with Abu Dhabi. Dubai's boom would not have been possible without the wealth of Abu Dhabi, and, especially since the mid-2000s, Abu Dhabi is in many ways seeking to emulate the Dubai model while trying to avoid some of the pitfalls which have befallen Dubai. One of these pitfalls includes the construction of a number of costly white elephant projects that have lain dormant and remain unoccupied and unused.[76]

Given the opulence and hype surrounding Dubai, it is easy to accuse other regional cities of wanting to replicate the model it represents in real estate and urbanism-led development. And, undoubtedly, both competition with and emulation of Dubai play big roles in guiding aspects of urban growth patterns elsewhere in the Persian Gulf. Dubai's Palm Islands and the World archipelago, for example, no doubt served as inspirations for the development of the Saadiyat island off Abu Dhabi and the Pearl island in Qatar, to name only two examples.[77] Interestingly, as an indication that Dubai may indeed be emerging

---

[74] Ali A. Alraouf, "Manama, Bahrain," in Fraser and Golzari, eds, *Architecture and Globalization in the Persian Gulf Region*, p. 98.

[75] Adham, "Rediscovering the Island," p. 252.

[76] Elsheshtawy, "Cities of Sand and Fog," p. 262.

[77] The first such artificial island built in the Persian Gulf was the Green Island in Kuwait, built in 1988. It was not until the Palm, however, that artificial islands began to be constructed on a massive scale to house numerous business and entertainment facilities and residential areas.

as a central node in a global—or at least regional—network of information and service provision, a number of Dubai-based architectural firms and development companies are now busily providing services and advice for urban development projects elsewhere in the region.[78] But the urban forms of each of these aspiring global cities, and the dynamics driving their ambitions, need to be analyzed on their own, specific merits. As Khaled Adham puts it in relation to Doha, "while it is true that Dubai may have instigated, or speeded up, Doha's recent development and construction boom, these developments have lives and dynamics of their own. To put it differently, once the ball of development started rolling in Doha in the mid-1990s, it acquired its own dynamic energy, which is affected by both internal and external logics."[79]

Few examples illustrate this uniqueness better than the construction of the Jebel Ali port, industrial area and free zone off Dubai, which, according to one observer, "marks a definitive historical moment when Dubai's global aspirations were first realized through port engineering and construction."[80] Originally built between 1976 and 1979, the Jebel Ali port underwent a major expansion beginning in 2001 and is today the world's largest man-made harbor and the biggest port in the Middle East.[81] This coincided with a rise in chronic levels of political instability elsewhere in the region, thus resulting in the growing importance and increased trade volume in Jebel Ali port. The port in particular and Dubai in general have been the beneficiaries of the fallouts of the Iranian revolution of 1978–9; the Iran–Iraq war of 1980–88 and the so-called "tanker war" it entailed; military conflict between Iraq and Arab allies in the early 1990s and US–Iraqi tensions throughout the 1990s; the US invasion of Iraq in 2003; and the increasingly comprehensive trade and economic sanctions imposed on Iran by the US and the European Union in the 2000s. As Stephen Ramos has correctly observed, "regional conflict, in its own way, provided a degree of economic stability for Dubai by spurring increased regional trade through its ports. Dubai was able to take advantage of events within the region, identify them as opportunities for its own benefit, and provide both facilities and policies to capitalise on these trade-related opportunities."[82]

---

[78] Alraouf, "Manama, Bahrain," p. 95.

[79] Adham, "Rediscovering the Island," p. 248.

[80] Stephen J. Ramos, "Dubai's Jebel Ali Port: Trade, Territory and Infrastructure," in Carola Hein, ed., *Port Cities: Dynamic Landscapes and Global Networks* (London: Routledge, 2011), p. 233.

[81] For a full discussion of Jebel Ali, see ibid., pp. 230–43.

[82] Ibid., p. 242.

With one of the few deep water harbors in the Persian Gulf, expansive and updated storage facilities, and accessible land and sea transit routes, the Jebel Ali port has helped propel Dubai into becoming an unparalleled center of regional commerce and transit. A significant portion of the world's trade with Iran, as well as many of the goods entering and leaving Oman, Qatar, and Saudi Arabia, go through Jebel Ali. The port marks one of the defining points of advantage that Dubai appears to have over its regional competitor cities, and even when Doha's deep water port comes on line in 2014–15, Jebel Ali is still likely to benefit from "early starter" advantage. In its global aspirations, Dubai has a headstart over the competition.

The real estate developments around the Jebel Ali port and elsewhere in Dubai and in the rest of the region have been guided by certain assumptions about ideal architectural forms. Much of these ideal forms, especially in the early years, have been associated with Western imports. In their rush to modernize, in many countries of the GCC "western regulations and administrative systems have been integrally adapted and sometimes copied regardless of local practices and the rooted legal heritage."[83] Contemporary architecture in Saudi Arabia actually originated in the first half of the twentieth century, with the building of housing projects by Aramco between 1938 and 1944.[84] Similarly, next door in Kuwait, the capital city's master plan was devised by a London-based architectural firm.[85] The plan called for the demolition of old houses and neighborhoods in order to make way for modern villas, wider roads for increased car traffic, and new infrastructure and facilities such as schools and hospitals.[86]

Importation and reliance on foreign, mainly Western, architects continue to this day, and most Gulf cities employ the services of European and American planners and consulting firms to design their cities and the built environment. In fact, as just one example, much of the planned city for the area surrounding Jebel Ali was designed to resemble US company towns and

---

[83] Mustapha Ben-Hamouche, "Complexity of urban fabric in traditional Muslim cities," p. 32.

[84] Mashary A. Al-Naim, "Riyadh: A City of 'Institutional' Architecture," in Elsheshtawy, ed., *The Evolving Arab City*, p. 118.

[85] This was also the case with Riyadh, where the urban master plan was devised in the late-1960s by a Greek consultant, Constantinos Doxiadis, and subsequently revised in the mid-1970s by a French consultancy.

[86] Yasser Mahgoub, "Kuwait: Learning from a Globalized City," in Elsheshtawy, ed. *The Evolving Arab City*, pp. 154–6.

the British garden city, made up of self-contained residential communities surrounded by green belts and park-like areas.[87]

The importation of Western urban forms has not been without its critics, both in the academic and the policy worlds, and especially in local society. Elsheshtawy laments the waning of distinct urban identities in the Persian Gulf's aspiring global cities: "officials in the Gulf are turning towards Western architects and planners to plan, design, form and shape their cities. The 'new Middle East' is based on Western conceptions of what our cities should look like. Arabs have disappeared from contributing to the design of their built environment."[88] In Kuwait, the resulting urban environment was seen as "unfriendly, hostile and lacking a sense of belonging."[89] Yasser Mahgoub, a veteran architect, described the city's architectural style as "comparable to visiting a Disneyland of residential manifestation."[90] According to Mahgoub, "as the case of Kuwait illustrates, the absence of local architects and planners, especially during the early stages of development, contributes to the creation of an alienated place."[91] Other Gulf intellectuals have decried the demise of the pluralistic civic tradition and cosmopolitan cultures of their cities, due largely to the intrusion of Western transnational corporations and their commercial interests at the expense of local culture and tradition. This is compellingly portrayed in the Saudi writer Abdelrahman Munif's 1984 novel, *Cities of Salt* (*Mudun al-Milh*).[92]

Beginning in the 1980s and the 1990s, two interrelated architectural trends emerged in the Gulf: on the one hand encouraging the intrusion of Western design concepts into the region, while on the other hand seeking to remedy and reverse it. The first trend was the spread of what might be called "institutional architecture," with states sponsoring the construction of architectural landmarks for various institutions such as government ministry buildings, hospitals, universities, and the like. A second, related trend that emerged

---

87 Ramos, "Dubai's Jebel Ali Port," p. 238. For more on "garden cities," see Robert A. M. Stern, David Fisherman, and Jacob Tilove, *Paradise Planned: The Garden Suburb and the Modern City* (New York: Monacelli Press, 2013).

88 Elsheshtawy, "The Great Divide," pp. 22–3.

89 Mahgoub, "Kuwait," p. 156.

90 Ibid., p. 162.

91 Ibid., p. 181.

92 Fuccaro, *Histories of City and the State in the Persian Gulf*, pp. 3–4. *Cities of Salt* is available in English: Abdelrahman Munif, *Cities of Salt*, Peter Theroux trans. (New York: Random House, 1988).

about a decade later was the spread of "neo-traditional architecture," again under the auspices of state patronage, as a direct reaction to the perceived and actual "de-Arabization" of cities such as Doha, Abu Dhabi, and Dubai.[93] The neo-traditionalist movement represented a "strong regionalist movement calling for a rethinking of the western models of urban planning and architecture implanted into … Gulf countries."[94] It continues to mark the contemporary era, which has also seen a fixation with constructing mega-projects costing billions of dollars.

As far as institutional architecture is concerned, it was actually Riyadh that set the regional trend. This was reflected both in process and product. The process was one of deliberate planning, in Riyadh's case by the Arriyadh Development Authority (ADA), while the product represented buildings and institutions meant, in addition to their functional utility, to project power and authority.[95] This relationship appears to have been reversed in the 1990s in the case of Dubai, which then served as a model that Riyadh, as well as other aspiring global cities in the region, sought to emulate both in form and in economic power.[96]

In Saudi Arabia, ADA was established in 1983 as perhaps the country's most important urban management institution; it embarked on a number of massive construction projects, all with the aim of developing and projecting a distinct cultural identity through architecture. Led mainly by American and European architectural firms throughout the 1980s and the early 1990s, this led to the emerging trend of "new traditionalism."[97] The assumption behind this new traditionalism is to design urban landscapes and spaces in ways that reflect local cultural significance, both real and imagined, despite and through the perceptual language of Western architecture. In Al-Naim's words, "these projects reveal an ability to generate design principles from traditional archi-

---

[93] Andrzej Kapiszewski, "De-Arabization in the Gulf: Foreign Labor and the Struggle for Local Culture," *Georgetown Journal of International Affairs*, Vol. 8, No. 2 (Summer 2007), p. 81.

[94] Alraouf, "Manama, Bahrain," p. 86.

[95] Al-Naim, "Riyadh," pp. 136–7.

[96] Ibid., pp. 145–6.

[97] Ibid., p. 134. Some of the more notable urban landscapes built in Riyadh during this period include the Ministry of Foreign Affairs (1983); the King Khaled International Airport (1983); the first, second, and third phases of the massive Qasr Al-Hokm park and shopping district in Riyadh (1984, 1992, and 1994 respectively); the campus of the King Saud University (1984); and the Diplomatic Quarter (1987).

tecture and recycle them in contemporary practice."⁹⁸ The aspiring global cities of the Persian Gulf are dotted with such projects. Doha's neo-traditional architectural landmarks include the Emiri Diwan, the Al Fanar religious complex, Souq Wakif, the National Museum, and the Museum of Islamic Art. In Dubai and Abu Dhabi, in addition to official buildings such as the Masdar complex on the outskirts of the capital city, many of the more recent hotels and tourist attractions are constructed using traditional designs that are either reminiscent of an imaginary Arabian past—the Emirates Palace Hotel in Abu Dhabi—or are somehow meant to represent a continuation of local culture and heritage.

Similar developments were occurring in Kuwait, where in the 1980s the government commissioned a number of world-renowned architects to design famous monuments throughout the city: the national airport, the parliament building, the Ministry of Foreign Affairs, the Central Bank, and the Kuwait Water Towers. In addition to designing monuments meant to signify wealth and power, the architects were mandated to incorporate elements of traditional Islamic architecture into their designs in ways that reflected Kuwait's heritage and culture.⁹⁹ Perhaps no landmark better symbolizes the move toward new traditionalism than the Kuwait Water Towers, imitating traditional Arabian perfume containers, which were inaugurated in 1977.¹⁰⁰ In the aftermath of the Iraqi invasion of Kuwait in August 1990 to February 1991, the 1990s saw a concerted effort by Kuwaiti architects to reassert local identity through the design of public buildings and private villas. Although the results were often mixed, there was nevertheless an effort to incorporate traditional-looking elements like towers and trees into the design of most buildings.¹⁰¹

As far as residential architectural design is concerned, most cities of the Persian Gulf appear to have passed through three parallel, distinct, but overlapping phases. Yasser Mahgoub outlines these three phases in the architectural evolution of Kuwait city. In the first phase, traditional courtyard houses, which often reflected local needs and circumstances, especially in terms of the environment, dominated the urban landscape. In the second phase, many of these houses were demolished and replaced by Western-style villas, most of which reflected Mediterranean architecture found in Egypt, Lebanon, and

⁹⁸ Ibid., p. 137
⁹⁹ Mahgoub, "Kuwait," pp. 165–6.
¹⁰⁰ Ibid., p. 167.
¹⁰¹ Ibid., pp. 172–4.

Syria, from where their architects came. Many of these villas were designed "using strange shapes and forms" that had little to do with the life inside them. The third phase, beginning in the 1980s and the 1990s, has witnessed a rediscovery of the virtues of traditional architecture, reflecting the broader regional style known as new traditionalism.[102]

It is important to note that much of the contemporary neo-traditional architecture is inspired by an imaginary "Arabia." By their own admission, many of the star architects commissioned to design signature pieces that hark back to an imaginary past know little or nothing about the Middle East or Arab heritage and culture. Many of their designs are inspired by exotic stories about and images from classical Cairo, Damascus, or Baghdad rather than the actual cultures and heritage of the cities for which they are designing buildings.[103] As Elsheshtawy observes, "Architects are creating their own context."[104]

The Persian Gulf states, of course, have themselves been implicit in their creation of imaginary pasts that suit their contemporary political purposes. In fact, as part of their efforts to project a global image, and also to forge imagined continuities between present political realities and the distant past, literally all Arab states of the Persian Gulf have embarked on very expensive, highly ambitious campaigns to design and build world-class museums. Many of these museums have become architectural showpieces in the burgeoning urban landscapes of the southern coast of the Persian Gulf. The trend began with the construction of the Kuwait National Museum in 1983, followed by the National Museum of Bahrain, which opened in Manama in 1988. Not to be left behind, as part of a determined effort to carve out a place for itself as a capital of Arab arts and culture, the emirate of Sharjah has opened some twenty museums since 1988.[105] In 2008, Doha opened the Museum of Islamic Art, built on an island of its own; and a new National Museum, shaped in the form of a desert rose and touted as an "unparalleled new institution" of art in the country and the region, is scheduled for inauguration sometime around 2016–17.[106] The emirate of Abu Dhabi, for its part, has commissioned high-profile architects to design three large museums: the Guggenheim, the

---

[102] Ibid., p. 158.

[103] Elsheshtawy, "Cities of Sand and Fog," pp. 290–92.

[104] Ibid., p. 292.

[105] Mounir Bouchenaki, "The Extraordinary Development of Museums in the Gulf States," *Museum International*, Vol. 63, Nos. 3–4 (2011), pp. 96–7.

[106] http://www.dezeen.com/2010/03/24/national-museum-of-qatar-by-jean-nouvel/, last accessed 26 May 2016.

Louvre–Abu Dhabi, and the Zayed National Museum. The Guggenheim in Abu Dhabi, scheduled for completion by 2017, is intended to be twelve times bigger than the original in New York.[107] Each of these building is more spectacular than the one built before it, and all are designed by world-renowned architects for whom the only limitation appears to be imagination. The museums each have "budgets beyond anything to be seen anywhere else in the world."[108] As Mounir Bouchenaki has commented, the "observable new trend of commissioning great names of international contemporary architecture to design museums for a region hitherto little known for buildings of this kind probably reflects a political drive to construct a new identity for these countries and to develop new cultural attractions as part of the modernization of their societies."[109]

The construction of these museums is part of a broader effort to build ever larger, ever more impressive edifices. Across the Persian Gulf, wealthy sheikhs and businessmen try to outdo each other by commissioning famous Western architectural firms to design and construct ever more outlandish landmarks to make an indelible impression on their city's skyline. Dubai and Abu Dhabi have been especially keen to outdo each other in building extremely tall towers (see Table 3.1).

A few examples from Abu Dhabi illustrate the point. In describing Abu Dhabi's urban profile since the mid-2000s, Elsheshtawy calls it the "age of mega-projects and star architects."[110] With the passing of Sheikh Zayed in 2004 and the ascension to power of Sheikh Khalifa bin Zayed Al Nahyan, Abu Dhabi entered a new period of hyper-growth, when many of the city's older neighborhoods and even landmarks were torn down and replaced by high-rise towers, showpiece projects, and a brand new Souq built in traditional Arabic design.[111] One of these showcase projects is the Saadiyat Island, which is meant to be the cultural hub of not just Abu Dhabi and the UAE but indeed of the larger Persian Gulf region and the entire Middle East. The renowned architect Frank Gehry was commissioned to design a version of the Guggenheim museum for the emirate, the Guggenheim Abu Dhabi; and Jean Nouvel, another star architect, was given the task of designing a version of the

---

[107] Bouchenaki, "The Extraordinary Development of Museums in the Gulf States," p. 96.

[108] Ibid., p. 101.

[109] Ibid., p. 95.

[110] Elsheshtawy, "Cities of Sand and Fog," p. 274.

[111] Ibid., pp. 281–5.

Table 3.1: Tallest towers in the Persian Gulf

Gulf Ranking	Int. Ranking	Tower Name	Country	City	Height (m)	Pinnacle (m)	Floors	Built
1	–	Kingdom Tower	K.S.A.	Jeddah	1000	–	167	2019
2	1	Burj Khalifa	U.A.E	Dubai	828	829.8	163	2010
3	3	Abraj Al-Bait Towers	K.S.A	Mecca	601	601	120	2012
4	–	Qatar National Bank Tower	Qatar	Doha	510	–	101	2014
5	–	Diamond Tower	K.S.A	Jeddah	432	–	93	2017
6	–	Marina 101	U.A.E	Dubai	426.5	–	101	2015
7	17	Princess Tower	U.A.E	Dubai	414	414	101	2012
8	18	Al Hamra Tower	Kuwait	Kuwait City	412.6	413	80	2011
9	20	23 Marina	U.A.E	Dubai	395	395	89	2012
10	–	Capital Market Authority Headquarters	K.S.A	Riyadh	385	–	77	2014
11	–	The Domain	U.A.E	Abu Dhabi	381	–	88	2014
12	23	Central Market Project	U.A.E	Abu Dhabi	381	–	88	2012
13	25	Elite Residence	U.A.E	Dubai	380.5	–	87	2012
14	30	Almas Tower	U.A.E	Dubai	363	363	68	2009
15	33	JW Marriott Marquis Dubai Tower 1	U.A.E	Duabi	355	–	82	2012
16	33	JW Marriott Marquis Dubai Tower 1	U.A.E	Dubai	355	–	82	2013
17	35	Emirates Office Tower	U.A.E	Duabi	355	356.4	54	2000
18	–	Lamar Tower 1	K.S.A	Jeddah	350	–	72	2014
19	40	Ahmed Abdel Rahim Al Attar Tower	U.A.E	Dubai	342	342	76	2010
20	43	The Marina Torch	U.A.E	Dubai	337	–	79	2011
21	–	ADNOC Headquarters	U.A.E	Abu Dhabi	335.3	–	65	2014
22	–	DAMAC Heights	U.A.E	Duabi	335	–	85	2016
23	46	Rose Tower	U.A.E	Dubai	333	333	72	2007
24	51	The Index	U.A.E	Duabi	328	328	80	2010
25	51	Al Yaqoub Tower	U.A.E	Dubai	328	328	69	2013
26	54	The Landmark	U.A.E	Abu Dhabi	324	324	72	2012
27	58	Burj Al Arab	U.A.E	Dubai	321	321	60	1999
28	62	HHHR Tower	U.A.E	Dubai	317	317.8	72	2010
29	66	Ocean Heights	U.A.E	Dubai	310	310	72	2010

Louvre Museum on the island. Other cultural showcase projects include a maritime museum, a performing arts center, nineteen art pavilions, and a branch campus of New York University.[112] In 2007, the emirate's government modified the city's master plan to account for a rapid increase in population and to guide the city's global aspirations while vowing to become a "contemporary expression of an Arab city."[113]

Kuwait, eager not to be left behind, developed in the first decade of the 2000s an obsession with mega-projects and especially with ever taller high-rise buildings. A case in point is the Burj Mubarak Al Kabir, also referred to as "the Tower of a Thousand and One Nights," at 1,001 meters standing proudly taller than the 800-meter Burj Dubai.[114] In 2006, the Kuwaiti government also announced the building of a new city of 250 square kilometers, Madinat Al-Hareer or City of Silk, north of the Kuwait bay area. With its master plan approved in June 2014, the city is meant to be "founded on the rich heritage of Arab gardens, towns, palaces, and markets. It balances Centers of Fair with Centers of Commerce as a rich garden city" and will comprise four new city centers, namely Finance City, Leisure City, Culture City, and Ecological City.[115] The city's centerpiece will be the Burj Mubarak Al Kabir, the Tower of a Thousand and One Nights, which is meant to complement each of the four cities. According to the architectural firm designing the city, Eric R. Kuhne and Associates:

> Every City has a symbol that stands as an icon for the world to know. For Madinat Al Hareer, we have many: a grand waterway on the Bayside of Kuwait, a new resort & leisure community on the Riverside, a new centre of culture on the Gulfside, and a new wildlife sanctuary and science academy on the Desertside. But on the skyline, we will have a new icon as the skyline pinnacle of Madinat Al Hareer: the Burj Mubarak Al Kabir, the Tower of A Thousand and One Arabian Nights. Standing 1001 metres tall, it will house 7 vertical villages combining offices, hotels, leisure, and residential into a vertical city centre that reaches for the heavens. This "sky city" will combine the ceremonial grandeur of a great city, the heroic routine of everyday life, and all the support services and facilities that are accustomed to the finest hospitality offers for any community in the world. It seeks to be one of the taller

[112] Ibid., p. 291.
[113] Quoted in ibid., p. 276.
[114] Mahgoub, "Kuwait," p. 177. In 2009 Burj Dubai was renamed Burj Khalifa in a gesture laden with symbolism, given the bail-out of Dubai by Abu Dhabi following the global financial crash and the Dubai debt crisis.
[115] Quoted in ibid., p. 177.

72

CONTEMPORARY PORT CITIES IN THE PERSIAN GULF

towers in the world. The design is inspired by the defiant flora of the desert as much as the rich folklore of Arabic heritage described in Kitāb 'Alf Layla wa-Layla. These stories of life become a metaphor for the complexity of lives that will emerge from Madinat Al Hareer, the City of Silk.[116]

By some accounts, the cost of City of Silk is estimated at around $77 billion.[117] In introducing the concept of the City of Silk, the architectural firm designing it was explicit in drawing the city's connections with the rest of the region:

> Today, we announce a new Golden Age for the Middle East with Madinat Al Hareer, the City of Silk. Far more than just a property development, Madinat Al Hareer builds upon the momentum and courage begun 20 years ago by our sister cities of Dubai, Abu Dhabi and Doha that have created a new sense of excitement and prosperity for the Arabian Gulf.[118]

Although not a port city, it is worth mentioning that the obsession with modernity and image has not left even the ancient city of Mecca unscathed. Successive Saudi kings, calling themselves Custodians of the Two Holy Mosques, have overseen the wholesale destruction of historic buildings and entire neighborhoods—lest they turn into places of worship and replace devotion to God—and have replaced them with shapeless, supposedly modern structures such as government offices, shopping strips, and malls. Today, the city's centerpiece is no longer the Grand Mosque housing the Kaaba but instead the Mekka Royal Clock Tower Hotel, inaugurated in 2012, which at 1,972 feet stands as one of the world's tallest buildings.[119]

All of this hyper-growth and development, crucially, has occurred within the context of highly segregated urban spaces throughout the Persian Gulf's aspiring global cities. Oil wealth, and the activities of the oil companies, changed the demographic make-up of many Gulf cities as the oil industry imported hordes of foreign workers and attracted others from peripheral areas.[120] Under the terms of the concession agreements, oil companies often

---

[116] http://www.civicarts.com/madinat-al-hareer.php

[117] "Kuwait Development Plan (KDP): Progress or Retreat," *Capital Standards* (June 2013), p. 1.

[118] http://www.civicarts.com/#!madinat-al-hareer/bf6oo

[119] See Ziauddin Sardar, "The destruction of Mecca," *International New York Times* (2 October 2014), p. 6. Sardar writes that "the rulers of Saudi Arabia and the clerics have a deep hatred of history. They want everything to look brand new."

[120] Lawless and Seccombe, "Impact of the Oil Industry on Urbanization in the Persian Gulf Region," p. 210.

undertook to employ local nationals, but at the same time reserved the right to import foreign labor in order to guarantee "efficient" operations.[121] Today, in contrast to the glass and steel buildings, on the fringes of each city and in neighborhoods seemingly far from the reaches of modernity, overcrowded neighborhoods feature small houses in which rooms are rented to multiple tenants. While these older, rental houses are often extremely profitable for their owners, most migrants working in the booming construction sector can barely afford the rooms on offer; most, therefore, live in the accommodation provided by their employers.[122]

The overall pattern of distribution of populations throughout the city is based on class, ethnicity, and nationality, and is highly segregated, with members of the so-called "diasporic elite" living in luxury high-rise buildings or gated communities and walled accommodations, commonly referred to as "compounds."[123] Gated communities were originally an import of Aramco and meant to insulate and protect its American employees from native Saudis; they have now proliferated across the aspiring global cities of the Persian Gulf, as well as Riyadh and fashionable parts of Beirut.[124]

Jane Bristol-Rhys' study of socio-spatial boundaries in Abu Dhabi maps out the city's segregation into "insurmountable spatial boundaries" in areas of residence, leisure, shopping, and most other social activities. The spatial segregation is often expressed through a grammar of its own, distinguishing "laborers from workers; workers from expats; and all migrants from Emiratis."[125] In Qatar, similarly, on Fridays public shopping malls and the *souq* are designated as family spaces and are not open to bachelors, "bachelor" being a codeword for male migrants from South Asia, married or not. Even on weekdays, the more expensive and exclusive section of the city's swanky Villaggio mall is protected by security guards who prevent migrant workers from entering the section. A number of Abu Dhabi's parks and public beaches are also desig-

---

[121] Ibid., p. 190.

[122] Mahgoub, "Kuwait," pp. 159–60.

[123] Andrew M. Gardner, "Gulf Migration and the Family," *Journal of Arabian Studies*, Vol. 1, No. 1 (June 2011), p. 11.

[124] Georg Glasze, "Segregation and seclusion: the case of compounds for western expatriates in Saudi Arabia," *GeoJournal*, Vol. 66 (2006), pp. 83–6. See also Georg Glasze and Abdallah Alkhayyal, "Gated housing estates in the Arab world: case studies in Lebanon and Riyadh, Saudi Arabia," *Environment and Planning B: Planning and Design*, Vol. 29 (2002), pp. 321–36.

[125] Bristol-Rhys, "Socio-Spatial Boundaries in Abu Dhabi," p. 67.

nated as "family areas," many protected by fences and charging entry fees to ensure access by only approved groups.[126]

Tensions and anxieties often arise in Manama's residential areas where populations of both locals and migrants are found. The anxiety is often justified by locals on grounds of the moral threat that bachelor migrants pose toward their family life and women and children.[127] Andrew Gardner argues that these anxieties "are not the product of empirical experience, but rather are best understood as the articulation of a collective anxiety concerning the security of these states' social and cultural integrity."[128] In fact, as one Kuwaiti citizen told another anthropologist, these anxieties can often be traced back to "seeing strangers around you everywhere."[129]

Sulayman Khalaf distinguishes migrant worker housing into five general types: residential camps and ad hoc shanty towns mostly occupied by recent and temporary arrivees; old traditional houses of nationals that were deserted by their owners and lack modern amenities and conveniences; high-rise residential buildings and suburban villas rented by foreign middle-class professionals; villas and residential townhouse compounds purpose-built for professional expatriates and their families; and residential buildings of much lower quality, built mostly in the 1970s in rows and in what are now older and more congested parts of town, housing lower-middle-class families from the Arab world and the Indian subcontinent.[130]

The segregation of migrant workers and other foreigners permeates the life of the Persian Gulf's aspiring global cities. In the cities of the Arab world, the spatial segregation of social groups is not a new historical phenomenon, with the different quarters of the city serving as an extension of private space.[131] But segregation within the Dohas and Dubais of the region has taken on new dimensions. Most semi-skilled and unskilled migrants in these cities live in "labor camps" located on the periphery of the city and away from the city's commercial center. Dubai and Qatar have gone so far as to draw up plans for separate planned cities for laborers, while Kuwait has opted for the construction of a number of dormitory satellites in the suburbs of Kuwait Bay. Oman,

---

[126] Ibid., p. 78.

[127] Gardner, "Gulf Migration and the Family," pp. 20–21.

[128] Andrew Gardner, "Labor Camps in the Gulf States," *Viewpoints: The Middle East Institute* (February 2010), p. 57.

[129] Gardner, "Gulf Migration and the Family," p. 21.

[130] Khalaf, "The evolution of the Gulf city type, oil, and globalization," pp. 251–3.

[131] Glasze and Alkhayyal, "Gated housing estates in the Arab world," p. 321.

on the other hand, saw no need for the planning of new cities or a major expansion of its existing urban centers.[132]

Housing patterns for nationals also reflect economic disparities, with wealthy elites often building gigantic mansions and palaces (*qaser*) in prime locations;[133] villas belonging to the upper middle classes, whose consumerist attitudes prefer larger villas of five to seven bedrooms; and houses provided freely by the state to low-income social groups comprising mostly recently settled Bedouin tribal families, called *'sha'beyya* (people's community).[134] In Abu Dhabi, interestingly, the modified master plan both into account and accounts for spatial segregation of the city's population, providing large areas for new Emirati housing inspired by traditional family structures, along with a diverse mixture of affordable housing options for low-income foreign residents.[135]

In the 1980s, extended-family compounds began appearing, in which both ties within extended family as well as the independence of the nuclear family were maintained. In these compounds, members of an extended family occupy clusters of villas next to each other or placed within the same compound, allowing for a common entrance into the compound but private entrances into each of the villas within it.[136] As far back as the early 2000s, researchers were calling attention to the transition of Gulf families from extended ones into "nuclear families characterized by extended relations."[137] This has had consequences for patterns of housing and urban growth.

What all of this has amounted to is an ironic mixture of cosmopolitanism and global outlook and profile with deeply entrenched mechanisms to ensure segregation and minimal intermingling among the cities' different populations. There is also a fair amount of deliberate segregation, at times self-segregation, often along ethnic and nationality lines. Khalaf astutely observes that the Persian

---

[132] Alexander Melamid, "Urban Planning in Eastern Arabia," *Geographical Record*, Vol. 70, No. 4 (October 1980), pp. 473–6.

[133] Khalaf perfectly describes these palaces: "they are distinguished by their immensity, high encircling walls, arched gates with cannons or statues bespeaking grandeur and power, and lush landscaped gardens." Khalaf, "The evolution of the Gulf city type, oil, and globalization," p. 253.

[134] Ibid., pp. 253–5.

[135] Elsheshtawy, "Cities of Sand and Fog," p. 276.

[136] Glasze and Alkhayyal, "Gated housing estates in the Arab world," p. 324.

[137] Yahya El-Haddad, "Major Trends Affecting Families in the Gulf Countries," in United Nations, *Major Trends Affecting Families* (New York: United Nations, 2003), p. 222.

Gulf's aspiring global cities have become stages for "segregated multicultural lifeways and identities." "Multiculturalism has entered into the very making of the city and shaped it in its present-day particular form," he writes. "Because of its large multi-ethnic social makeup, the Gulf city lacks a dominant, integrated and homogenous cultural ethos or character that one can find in metropolises such as Cairo, Beirut, London, Bombay, or Hong Kong."[138]

Conclusion

This chapter has identified three ideal types of port cities across the Persian Gulf, namely company towns, secondary cities, and aspiring global cities. A combination of policy neglect, inadequate resources, and geostrategic developments has impeded the potential significance of secondary cities and company towns both at home and abroad. Conversely, a number of factors have coalesced to propel the aspiring global cities to the international limelight, and, more importantly, regional influence. There has been a dramatic shift in significance and influence in favor of the southern shores of the Persian Gulf, especially insofar as active engagement with global networks of trade and commerce, finance and banking, transportation, and infrastructural depth are concerned.

That this shift in significance has occurred is hardly ever questioned. What is less clear is what this shift actually means for broader regional and global dynamics and trends. In some quarters at least, there is a general sense of skepticism about the emerging global cities of the Persian Gulf, as cities of "sand and fog," somehow lacking in authenticity and merely benefitting from temporary spikes in wealth and capital speculation.[139] According to Elsheshtawy, "cities such as Abu Dhabi may adopt the forms of a global city—exclusive mixed use developments, international museums and centers of learning, world class airports etc.—but in the end one could argue that they are merely recycling ideas, or serving global capital—without adding a substantive, alternative discourse to urban development."[140]

Elsheshtawy's poignant remarks cannot be easily dismissed. Gulf cities are seen, and see themselves, as showcases, and have become centers of conspicuous consumption dotted with massive mansions, luxury office buildings, fancy hotels and residential towers, and luxury cars.[141] Some observers have gone so

---

138 Khalaf, "The evolution of the Gulf city type, oil, and globalization," p. 259.
139 Elsheshtawy, "The Great Divide," p. 11.
140 Elsheshtawy, "Cities of Sand and Fog," p. 297.
141 Khalaf, "The evolution of the Gulf city type, oil, and globalization," pp. 256–9.

far as to argue that "the UAE and Qatar have been consciously constructed as specialized geographic zones for the global elite and transnational capitalism."[142] Referring to the intent conveyed through the advertising of Qatar's Pearl development, Adham makes the following point: "Catering to a particular lifestyle, the project intends to create a hybrid place of fantasy with a permanent atmosphere of festivity."[143] This description of the Pearl in Qatar applies equally perfectly to the Palm Jumairah in Dubai, the Saadiyat Island in Abu Dhabi, and the Amwaj Islands in Bahrain.

But consumerism should not be confused with development, and neither should fantasy be mistaken as reality. The question that needs answering is the extent to which these aspiring global cities have the substance to become central nodes of production and exchange of complex information, goods, and services in today's interdependent world. For now, they are mostly on the receiving end of the global flows, overwhelmingly consumers rather than also being producers and conveyors. Dubai's comparative position as a global city appears to be on a firmer footing relative to the rest of the pack, thanks largely to the Jebel Ali port and its slow trickle of exporting its own real estate model to other cities in the region. But a busy deep water port and lucrative architectural practices do not a global city make. Until their voracious appetite for consumption is complemented by a capacity to produce, the aspiring global cities of the Persian Gulf will remain just that, aspirants.

[142] Jerry Harris, "Desert dreams in the Gulf: transnational crossroads for the global elite," *Race and Class*, Vol. 54, No. 4 (2013), p. 86.
[143] Adham, "Rediscovering the Island," p. 249.

4

AN HISTORICAL EXAMINATION OF TERRITORY AND INFRASTRUCTURE IN THE TRUCIAL STATES

Stephen J. Ramos

During the past two decades, the Gulf region has courted international atten-tion for its architecture and urbanism.[1] Fascination with the mode, pace, and scale of the region's urbanization grew, and a sub-genre of literature poured out in an attempt to understand so-called "Gulf cities."[2] Sharp observers

---

[1] There is a nomenclature debate concerning "Persian Gulf" and "Arabian Gulf," but it is not central to my argument. I will use the term "Gulf" to describe the body of water and region.

[2] Ahmed Kanna, ed., *The Superlative City: Dubai and the Urban Condition in the Early Twenty-First Century* (Cambridge, MA: Harvard University Press, 2013); AMO, Archis, Pink Tank, NAi, eds, *Volume 23: Al Manakh 2: Gulf Continued* (Abu Dhabi: Abu Dhabi Planning Council, 2010); Ole Bouman, Mitra Khoubrou, Rem Koolhaas, eds, *Volume 12: Al Manakh/Dubai Guide, Gulf Survey, Global Agenda* (Netherlands: Stichting Archis, 2007); Sulayman Khalaf, "The Evolution of the Gulf City Type, Oil, and Globalization," in John W. Fox, Nada Mourtada Sabbah, and Mohammed Al-Mutawa, eds, *Globalization and the Gulf* (New York: Routledge, 2006), pp. 244–65; Yasser Elsheshtawy, *Planning Middle Eastern Cities: An Urban Kaleidoscope in a Globalizing World* (New York: Routledge, 2004).

quickly realized, however, that the term and scale of "city" did not appropriately describe the urbanization and settlement processes.[3] Terms such as "megalopolis," "archipelago," and "urban landscape" (to name a few) were then proposed as scalar lenses through which to interpret what was happening in the Gulf, and how it seemed both to represent and to influence urban circumstances in other parts of the world.[4]

There has been a concurrent, renewed interest in territory, coupled with calls to retrieve it as the most appropriate scale at which to discuss contemporary spatial phenomena of architecture and urbanism.[5] Within the field of geography, a common critique since 1973 has been the notable under-examination of the concept of territory.[6] In sum, this critique claims that conceptualization of territory has been reductive, either because of focus on its relational nature without the deeper historical background, or the reification of bounded space without an understanding of how the space was configured.[7] John Agnew articulated the "territorial trap" to summarize the flaws of its conceptualization, but Stuart Elden points out that the warnings have not

[3] Gareth Doherty, "Bahrain's Polyvocality and Landscape as a Medium," in Jala Makhzoumi, Shelly Egoz, Gloria Pungetti, eds, *The Right to Landscape: Contesting Landscape and Human Rights* (Burlington, VT: Ashgate, 2011), pp. 185–96; Stephen Ramos, *Dubai Amplified: The Engineering of a Port Geography* (Burlington, VT: Ashgate, 2010); Pier Vittorio Aureli, "Toward the Archipelago: Defining the Political and the Formal in Architecture," *Log*, Vol. 11 (2008), pp. 91–119; Albert Pope, "We are all Bridge-and-Tunnel People," *Log*, Vol. 12 (2008), pp. 41–58.

[4] See also Allen J. Scott, *Global City-Regions: Trends, Theory, Policy* (Oxford: Oxford University Press, 2001); Roger Simmonds and Gary Hack, eds, *Global City Regions: Their Emerging Forms* (London: Spon, 2000); Edward W. Soja, *Postmetropolis: Critical Studies of Cities and Regions* (Malden, MA: Blackwell, 2000).

[5] Hashim Sarkis, "Geo-Architecture: A Prehistory for an Emerging Aesthetics," *Harvard Design Magazine*, Vol. 37 (2014 special issue, ed. Eve Blau and Rahul Mehrotra), pp. 124–9; Stuart Elden, *The Birth of Territory* (Chicago, IL: University of Chicago Press, 2013); Antoine Picon, "What Has Happened to Territory?" in David Gissen, ed., "Territory: Architecture Beyond Environment," *Architectural Design*, Vol. 80, No. 3 (2010 special issue), pp. 94–9.

[6] Elden, *The Birth of Territory*; Jean Gottmann, *The Significance of Territory* (Charlotte, VA: University Press of Virginia, 1973); John Ruggie, "Territoriality and Beyond: Problematizing Modernity in International Relations," *International Organization*, Vol. 27 (1993); Claude Raffestin, *Pour une Géographie du Pouvoir* [For a geography of power] (Paris: Libraires Techniques, 1980).

[7] Elden, *The Birth of Territory*.

invited more precise reflection, but rather seem to have stymied further exploration.[8] Elden concludes that it is "through a historical conceptual examination that moving beyond the 'territorial trap,' rather than simply skirting around it, is possible."[9] Under Roman law, territory is defined as "all land included within the limits of any city,"[10] and given the city-state nature of the Trucial States, and conflict carry-overs even after UAE federation, this simplified, working definition will serve as a framework for the chapter to illustrate the dynamic between Trucial cities and their surrounding territories.

Over the century-and-a-half preceding the federation of United Arab Emirates (UAE), the historical, socio-cultural, and political meanings of territory move from one of a tribal, nomadic, subsistence culture loosely moving among pearling, wells, and grazing lands to a stricter territorial definition for oil speculation, concession leases, and production. Shifting tribal allegiances were dialectically tied to fluid territorial powerscapes when British interests were focused on maritime trade. British strategic territorial concerns moved from open maritime trade routes to including coastal and hinterland territories for their oil potential once it was discovered in other parts of the region. James Onley's work on the region's Pax Britannica of the nineteenth and early twentieth centuries describes how social, economic, and spatial power relationships changed as the symbiotic period of pearling and animal husbandry moved to oil exploration and production.[11] British oil concession negotiations were conducted through the ruling sheikhs of each Trucial State, which at once gave them a clear power endorsement and ruling advantage over other potential pretenders to the ruling position. The results of British endorsement

---

[8] John Agnew and Stuart Corbridge, *Mastering Space: Hegemony, Territory, and International Political Economy* (London: Routledge, 1995); Elden, *The Birth of Territory*.

[9] Elden, *The Birth of Territory*, p. 3; see also Alexander B. Murphy, "The Sovereign State System as Political-Territorial Ideal: Historical and Contemporary Considerations," in Thomas Biersteker and Cynthia Weber, eds, *State Sovereignty as a Social Construct* (Cambridge: Cambridge University Press, 1996), pp. 81–120.

[10] Hugo Grotius, *Corpus Juris Civilis*, Digest, L.xvi. 239.8. The definition continues that "territory" may also inspire fear because of a magistrate's right to remove people from the territory; Joe Painter, "Territory-Networks" (paper presented at the annual meeting of Association of American Geographers, Chicago, 7–11 March 2006, pp. 6–7).

[11] James Onley, "The Politics of Protection: The Arabian Gulf Rulers and the Pax Britanica in the Nineteenth Century," *Liwa: Journal of the National Center for Documentation and Research*, Vol. 1, No. 1 (2009), pp. 25–46.

essentially codified the towns where the rulers resided as the centers of power over surrounding territories, and served as historic precedent for UAE federation in 1971 to be both a modernization and an urbanization project.[12]

Infrastructure, of course, prepares land for urbanization, and the role of infrastructure in this transformative process of territorial meaning acted as a central instrument and medium through which political dreams and desires were expressed throughout the region's quasi-colonial and post-colonial circumstances. Infrastructure served the British and Emirati leaders in their modern territorial "quest for order,"[13] and as an end unto itself, to order the very nature of the state.[14] Infrastructural elements informed the British land surveying campaigns in the region of the late 1950s, along with land boundary negotiations among leaders that followed. These hinterland efforts occurred in parallel to the maritime trade infrastructure projects on the urban coastal settlements. The precedent of infrastructure as essential claim to territorial definition and ownership helps to explain the wave of duplicated infrastructure in the region during the 1970s after British withdrawal. Antoine Picon, in an article appropriately titled "What Has Happened to Territory?",[15] underscores the importance of the civil engineer and infrastructure in the construction of territory and the larger spatial processes of nation-building.[16] The relationship between territorial signification and infrastructure deployment formed the essence of the UAE discourse on nation-building and development. I have argued elsewhere that the examination of circulatory infrastructure is essential in understanding urbanization in the Gulf,[17] and I would like to build on that argument to propose further that territory is the appropriate scale to understand Gulf urbanization, both historically and today.

---

[12] See Julian Walker, "Practical Problems of Boundary Delimitation in Arabia: The Case of the United Arab Emirates" in Richard Schofield, ed., *Territorial Foundations of the Gulf* (New York: St Mark's Press, 1994), pp. 109–16.

[13] Zygmunt Bauman, *Modernity and Ambivalence* (Cambridge: Polity Press, 1991).

[14] Timothy Mitchell, *Rule of Experts: Egypt, Techno-Politics, and Modernity* (Berkeley, LA: University of California Press, 2002); Mathew Edney, *Mapping an Empire: The Geographical Construction of British India 1765–1843* (Chicago, IL: University of Chicago, 1997).

[15] Picon, "What Has Happened to Territory?"

[16] See also Fernand Braudel, *Civilization and Capitalism: 15th–18th Century* (New York: Harper & Row, 1982), cited in Picon, "What Has Happened to Territory?"

[17] Ramos, *Dubai Amplified.*

TERRITORY AND INFRASTRUCTURE IN THE TRUCIAL STATES

This chapter incorporates historical examination of both the period when the Trucial States under the larger British Empire moved to independence, and the formation of the United Arab Emirates in 1971, to explore the changing significance of territory, and dynamic territorial configuration, in this process. I consider the role of infrastructure, and how it served as a territorial medium that also moved from designating tribal influence to serving as a signifier for territorial fixity and demarcation. Through this empirical/historical analysis, the intention is to contribute to larger theorizing of territory, urbanization, and post-colonial nation formation.

Background: The British, Trucial States, and UAE Formation

Located in the lower Gulf region, the United Arab Emirates is a group of seven emirates—Abu Dhabi, Ajman, Dubai, Fujairah, Ras al-Khaimah, Sharjah, and Umm al Quwain—that formed a federation on 2 December 1971.[18] Pirouz Mojtahed-Zadeh discusses issues of boundary within the Gulf region dating at least as far back as the pre-Islamic border pillars mentioned in the *Shahnameh*, and among states including the Abbasid Caliphate of Baghdad (AD 749–1248) and the Safavids of Persia (AD 1501–1722).[19] From 1835 through 1971, the emirates were part of a larger British protectorate system known as the Trucial States, based on the British backing of certain ruling families through "truces" or pacts, with the understanding that British interests would be supported in the region.[20] Throughout the nineteenth and early twentieth centuries, these interests were mainly focused on the peaceful passage of maritime trade routes, which ran between Britain and its colonies in India and East Asia. In 1954, the British Political Resident in Bahrain, Rupert Hay, put it thus: Before the First World War, Great Britain was concerned with little more than the protection by sea of the ports in which various Shaikhs had their capitals, and she refrained from accepting responsibility for the maintenance of peace on land.[21]

---

[18] Ras al-Khaimah officially joined two months later on 11 February 1972: Shihab M. A. Ghanem, *Industrialization in the United Arab Emirates* (Aldershot, Hants: Avebury, 1992).

[19] Pirouz Mojtahed-Zadeh, *Security and Territoriality in the Persian Gulf: A Maritime Political Geography* (Richmond, Surrey: Curzon Press, 1999).

[20] Malcom C. Peck, *The United Arab Emirates: A Venture in Unity* (Boulder, CO: Westview Press, 1986).

[21] Rupert Hay, "The Persian Gulf States and their Boundary Problems," *Geographical Journal*, Vol. 120, No. 4 (1954), p. 433.

As early as the fifteenth century, if trade routes could move uninterrupted through the Persian Gulf region, European powers were not involved in the societal affairs of settlements as a traditional colonial ruling class, nor did European merchants bother to explore trade extensively within the region, believing that it required more effort than either the climate or the local economies were worth.[22]

The opening of the Suez Canal in 1869 increased maritime trade routes and connectivity between Europe and Asia, thereby raising the Gulf/Indian Ocean region's strategic importance.[23] French, Russian, German, and Ottoman expeditions to court diplomatic relationships, either real or imagined, precipitated greater British commitment to the region, which, of course, required a similar reciprocal commitment from the Trucial States. In March 1892, exclusive agreements were signed which stated that no territorial sovereignty could be ceded to any other international power without British consent.[24] This changed the Trucial States' status from simply a commercial interest for Britain to a strategic one, and this would be particularly important for the future oil exploration concessions of the early twentieth century. Oil discovery in Persia and Saudi Arabia at the beginning of the twentieth century, and shortly thereafter in Kuwait and Bahrain, brought a more specific and intentional interest from the British to the region. Soon afterward, oil exploration was carried out in all of its Gulf protectorates.

Tumultuous political and economic events throughout the region during the 1960s culminated in the British government's announcement in early 1968 that it would withdraw all interests east of the Suez Canal by the end of 1971.[25]

22 Roger Owen, "Cities of the Persian Gulf: Past, Present and Future" (lecture delivered at the University of Nicosia, Cyprus, 14 October 2008).

23 Thomas Rammin, "The Ensemble of Port Development Factors in the Mediterranean Region: 1815–1999," PhD dissertation, Harvard University Graduate School of Design, 1999.

24 Onley, "The Politics of Protection"; David Roberts, "The Consequences of the Exclusive Treaties: A British View," in Brian R. Pridham, ed., *The Arab Gulf and the West* (London: Croom Helm, 1985); Husain M. Al-Baharna, *The Legal Status of the Arabian Gulf State: A Study of Their Treaty Relations and Their International Problems* (Manchester: Manchester University Press, 1968); J. B. Kelly, "The Legal and Historical Basis of the British Position in the Persian Gulf," St. Anthony's Papers, No. 4, *Middle Eastern Affairs*, Vol. 1 (London: Chatto & Windus, 1958), pp. 119–40.

25 Tore T. Peterson, *The Decline of the Anglo-American Middle East: A Willing Retreat* (Brighton: Sussex Academic Press, 2006); Simon Smith, *Britain's Revival and Fall*

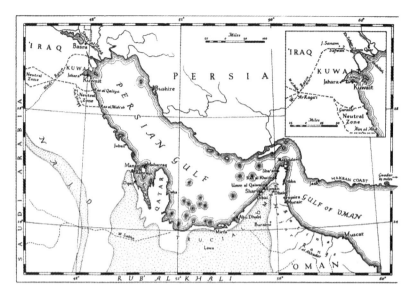

4.1: Map of the Persian Gulf in 1954

Source: Rupert Hay, "The Persian Gulf States and Their Boundary Problems,". *Geographical Journal*, Vol. 120, No. 4 (1954), p. 433.

British withdrawal essentially coincided with increased oil revenue flowing into Abu Dhabi and Dubai, the two emirates that had discovered oil within their territories in 1958 and 1966, respectively.[26] As Shihab Ghanem asserts, oil discovery and federation simultaneously and essentially mark the birth of the modern UAE.[27] But British withdrawal also meant the end of its backing of rulers, and, by extension, the territorial arrangements made under their Trucial endorsements. The oil-producing Trucial States—Dubai, Abu Dhabi, Bahrain, Qatar—all offered to pay for the £12,000,000 cost of the British

---

in the Gulf: Kuwait, Bahrain, Qatar, and the Trucial States, 1950–71 (New York: Routledge Curzon, 2004); Glen Balfour-Paul, *The End of Empire in the Middle East: Britain's Relinquishment of Power in Her Last Three Arab Dependencies* (Cambridge: Cambridge University Press, 1991).

[26] Sharjah would discover oil shortly after federation in 1972 (Ghanem, *Industrialization in the United Arab Emirates*).

[27] Ghanem, *Industrialization in the United Arab Emirates*.

military presence to continue in the region.[28] Their reluctant independence is counter-intuitive, particularly in comparison to other British experiences with the region. Below I explore some of the territorial reasoning and history that help to explain this.

Territorial Flux and Protection

The total UAE land area is 83,600 square kilometers, of which Abu Dhabi comprises approximately 80 per cent of the territory with 67,340 square kilometers, followed distantly by Dubai, with 4,114 square kilometers, or 5 per cent, and the other five emirates making up the remaining 15 per cent.[29] The land, in section, falls into four geographic categories of coast and coastal plain, interior desert, an upland plain, and interior rugged mountains.[30] The region's geographic diversity has marked two distinct cultures: coastal settlements dedicated to trade, shipbuilding, fishing and pearling, and other socio-economic activities oriented toward the sea; and interior settlements and nomadic Bedouin communities based on agriculture and animal husbandry. In her work on the geographic and economic conditions of the lower Gulf region before oil was discovered, Frauke Heard-Bey points out that tribes of the region included many subsections that were individually sea-oriented or nomadic, but intermingled with one another in tribal confederation as the basis for "the creation of a nation-state within a large and geographically very varied territory."[31] This intermingling included marriage within the different sections, and intensive trade based on seasonal pearl and date harvests. These two forms of economic cultures within the territory, among larger tribes, were often collaborative (a negotiation among tribal *dar*).[32] Taking into account the region's

---

[28] Onley, "The Politics of Protection"; Kelly, "The Legal and Historical Basis of the British Position."

[29] Khaled Kassar, *1000 Numbers and Reasons Why Dubai*, 2nd edn (Beirut: BISC Group, 2007).

[30] Erhard. F. Gabriel, *The Dubai Handbook* (Ahrensburg: Institute for Applied Economic Geography, 1987); Peck, *The United Arab Emirates*.

[31] Frauke Heard-Bey, *From Trucial States to United Arab Emirates* (New York: Longman, 1982), p. 34.

[32] *Dar* loosely translates into tribal territory. See John C. Wilkinson, *Arabian Frontiers: The Story of Britain's Boundary Drawing in the Desert* (New York: I. B. Tauris, 1991), Part V; Richard Schofield, "Borders and Territoriality in the Gulf and the Arabian Peninsula," in Richard Schofield, ed., *Territorial Foundations of the Gulf* (New York: St Mark's Press, 1994), pp. 1–77.

resource scarcity, both in terms of limited arable land and seasonal fishing possibilities, this mutual interaction and dependence was a pragmatic survival mechanism. Before oil explorations, it is widely suggested that the political unit for territorial sovereignty in the Gulf region was "people-centered," based on personal agreements rather than precise territorial definition.[33]

Fluctuating boundaries contingent on political or pastoral circumstances did not, however, always foster collaborative and peaceful tribal relationships.[34] Ali Mohammed Khalifa describes how violence was ever present among tribal states, or between the tribes within them, precisely over territorial elements essential for survival: grazing lands, water holes, fishing and pearling rights, and, eventually, stricter definitions of territorial boundaries.[35] The Bani Yas and the Qawasim were rival tribes in the late eighteenth and early nineteenth centuries. Because the British treaties focused specifically on maritime truce, the Bani Yas were benefited due to their land-based power, in contrast to the Qawasim sea prowess. Though treaties sought to end the warring factions of the region, the Qawasim and Bani Yas would continue their inter-tribal battling to the end of the nineteenth century.

Pearling coastal settlements emerge in the late eighteenth and early nineteenth centuries throughout the Gulf, as "essentially tribal outposts which prospered as centers of trade and of the pearling industry."[36] Pearling prosperity attracted some tribes to coasts, and due to scarce resources, competition among tribes was a central part of coastal settlement, management, and rule. The coastal settlements in the pearling era mark the origin of subsequent

---

[33] John C. Wilkinson, *Arabian Frontiers*; J. P. Bannerman, "The Impact of the Early Oil Concessions in the Gulf States," in Richard I. Lawless, ed., *The Gulf in the Early Twentieth Century: Foreign Institutions and Local Responses* (Durham: Centre for Middle Eastern and Islamic Studies, 1986), pp. 76–90.

[34] Richard Schofield and Gerald Blake, *Arabian Boundary Disputes on the Arabian Peninsula*, vols. 7 and 25 (Cambridge: Archive Editions, 1988); Rosemarie Said Zahlan, *The Origins of the United Arab Emirates: A Political and Social History of the Trucial States* (New York: St Martin's Press, 1978).

[35] Ali Mohammed Khalifa, "The United Arab Emirates: Unity in Fragmentation—A Study in Ministate Integration in a Complex Setting, 1968–1976," PhD dissertation, University of California, Santa Barbara, 1978; Henry Rosenfeld, "The Social Composition of the Military in the Process of State Formation in the Arabian Desert," *Journal of the Royal Anthropological Institute of Great Britain and Ireland*, Vol. 95 (1965), pp. 75–86.

[36] Nelida Fuccaro, "The Making of Gulf Ports Before Oil," *Liwa: Journal of the National Center for Documentation and Research*, Vol. 2, No. 3 (2010), p. 20.

urbanization processes of the region.[37] The region was generally organized around nomadic Bedu tribes in the interior who would charge protection taxes for passage through their territory, smaller villages where tribes engaged in the kind of complementary fishing/agricultural activities mentioned above, and the coastal towns where pearling and trade were centered.[38] Scarcity fostered a need for protection through allegiances, which could then change quickly. It is this dynamic territorial configuration that better describes the "people-centered" nature of the territory, where violence and flux were ever present.[39] Zahlan clarifies that while more fixed authority emanated from their capital village coastal settlements, "the foremost measure of a coastal ruler's strength and prestige was his ability to command tribes of the interior ... the extent of a ruler's territory was governed by the extent to which tribes roaming the area would support him in time of need."[40] John C. Wilkinson's observation is particularly instructive:

> Ownership notions in Arabian tribal societies were confined to mobile property and to nodes of intensive land use where inputs and labour and capital had created agricultural land, permanent wells, towns, etc. Such nodes of intensive settlement, gave rise to usufructuary rights in the surrounding areas, both on the coast and in the desert. In these peripheries it was the use of resources that mattered and the interests of groups could overlap and indeed complement each other. The essential right that had to be preserved in territorial organization was mobility in space. Boundary drawing lay in the social system, that is, in who was recognized as a member of the group, while reciprocal relationships were defined in terms of family, clientship, neighbourliness and military alliance. The whole was rationalized in personal terms of descent, and the accompanying code of behaviours translated into terms of 'honour and shame,' stemming from *asl* (origin). Family and clan networks, perceived or real, therefore determined the relationships of trade, society, and political power, not exclusive territorial rights.[41]

[37] Ibid.; Nelida Fuccaro, *Histories of City and State in the Persian Gulf; Manama since 1800* (Cambridge: Cambridge University Press, 2009).

[38] Julian Walker, "Social and Economic Developments in Trucial Oman in the First Half of the Twentieth Century," *Liwa: Journal of the National Center for Documentation and Research*, Vol. 2, No. 3 (2010), pp. 33–47.

[39] Onley, "The Politics of Protection"; Rosenfeld, "The Social Composition of the Military."

[40] Zahlan, *The Origins of the United Arab Emirates*, 6.

[41] John C. Wilkinson, "Britain's Role in Boundary Drawing in Arabia: A Synopsis," in Richard Schofield, ed., *Territorial Foundations of the Gulf* (New York: St Mark's Press, 1994), p. 97.

The tribal territorial field involved multiple factions and constantly shifting allegiances, wherein dependence on tribal support meant that Bedu tribes were the "preponderant force" of the Trucial hinterland region, "able to hold Rulers, merchants, and common people to ransom,"[42] up to the early 1950s.

With pearls as the largest single income source, a sheikh's pearling fleet was among his most valuable possessions. It guaranteed him the resources and influence necessary to buy and/or coerce tribal allegiances, and meant security not only for his rule, but also for the hinterland trade routes that were known to be under the influential sphere of the Bedu.[43] As Onley points out, "That no sheikh could rule his people without a command of economic power explains why all rulerships were town-based, at the heart of economic activity in the Gulf."[44] Thus, the sheikh's town location was the center and seat of power, but this power was negotiated, and required a strategic relationship with surrounding hinterland territory, and the associate tribal groups, in order to maintain and manage it. The intricacies of the protection system have been amply cited and researched among Arabian tribes.[45] British presence essentially "upped the ante," wherein British protection meant the military backing of the then strongest military force in the world, the Royal Navy, and elevated the sheikh's political status in the eyes of other tribes, and within his own.[46] British support upset the territorial power negotiation, tipping the balance in favor of the coastal town centers, and empowered sheikhs over the tribal leaders of the interior. As Olney points out, "In the 1950s and 60s, the British helped the coastal rulers to achieve complete control over these dependencies,

---

[42] J. P. Tripp, "Political Agency, Trucial States, February 15, 1957, No. 6 Dispatch to Sir Bernard Burrows," in Richard Schofield, ed., *Arabian Boundary Disputes on the Arabian Peninsula*, Vol. 22 (Cambridge: Archive Editions, 1991), p. 77.

[43] Onley, "The Politics of Protection."

[44] Ibid., p. 29; see Peter Lienhardt, "The Authority of Shaykhs in the Gulf: An Essay in Nineteenth Century History," *Arabian Studies*, Vol. 2 (1975), pp. 61–75; see also James Onley and Sulayman Khalaf, "Shaikhly Authority in the Pre-Oil Gulf: An Historical-Anthropological Study," *History and Anthropology*, Vol. 17, No. 3 (2006), pp. 189–298.

[45] Sulayman Khalaf, "Settlement of Violence in Bedouin Society," *Ethnology*, Vol. 29 (1990), pp. 225–42; Paul Dresch, *Tribes, Government, and History in Yemen* (Oxford: Oxford University Press, 1989); H. R. P. Dickson, *The Arab of the Desert: A Glimpse into Badawin Life in Kuwait and Saudi Arabia* (London: George Allen & Unwin, 1949).

[46] Onley, "The Politics of Protection."

in effect to annex them, enabling a British-run oil company, Petroleum Development (Trucial Coast), to explore and dig wells there."[47]

Thus, the British, represented by their Political Resident, entered into protector–protégé agreements with rulers to secure oil exploration as their interests moved inland. The introduction in 1951 of the British-backed security force, the Trucial Levies (later renamed "Scouts"), pacified hinterland tribal disputes, and drastically altered territorial power structures in favor of the rulers. The British Political Agent P. J. Tripp writes in his 1957 report that "With the approval and support of Her Majesty's Government ... The Rulers have become increasingly more powerful; their territories have become more profitable and their internal frontiers be completely settled. Their control over and knowledge of their outlying domains have been extended."[48]

The rulers' position had been strengthened internally as well. In the 1930s, the end of the pearling industry interrupted the tacit governing agreement between Trucial rulers and their merchant classes.[49] This occurred for two reasons. First, while sectors of the merchant classes and the *majlis* were involved in port and regional distribution activities,[50] most of the merchant class wealth throughout the region was based on profits from pearling. Once this ended, they no longer controlled the rulers' public purse strings, and thus there was a shift in the balance of power established during the pearling era that benefited Trucial rulers. Second, this shift also occurred because of concessions for oil exploration and air use.[51] The British signed these concessions directly with the rulers, beginning in the early 1930s with Trucial States Ras-al Khaimah and Sharjah, and then again in 1937 with Sheikh Said in Dubai.[52] As British territorial interests moved from sea to land and air, regional political balances established during the pearling era between merchant classes and rulers shifted. Successful reform movements launched by merchants in Kuwait and Bahrain were direct responses to these power shifts, but similar rumblings

---

[47] Ibid., p. 36.

[48] Tripp, "Political Agency," p. 77.

[49] The introduction of the Japanese cultured pearl in the early twentieth century devastated Gulf pearling. See Fatma Al-Sayagh, "Merchants' Role in a Changing Society: The Case of Dubai, 1900–90," *Middle Eastern Studies*, Vol. 34, No. 1 (1998), pp. 87–102.

[50] *Majlis* loosely translates as legislative council.

[51] Rupert Hay, "The Persian Gulf States and their Boundary Problems," *Geographical Journal*, Vol. 120, No. 4 (1954), pp. 433–43.

[52] Ibid.

among the Trucial merchant classes were contained with the help of British military presence.[53]

The British territorial project for the Trucial States involved destabilizing and pacifying tribal power structures so as then to be able to reconstitute territorial organization. Territorial boundaries, brokered and administered by empowered rulers, would subdivide what had been a more fluid territory, and in so doing weaken tribal power and their grazing livelihood. Sheikh power was further strengthened from economic revenue that came from oil concessions, which weakened the *majlis*, and the pre-oil consensual negotiation decision-making process. The quid pro quo relationship, then, secured territorial oil exploration rights, free and safe passage of goods by sea and air, and the swift expedition of negotiated needs through only one partner, in exchange for their support and protection of ruling sheikhs. The British required stricter territorial demarcation and definition to endorse legal claims on whatever future oil was discovered. In the following section, I explore the British border negotiation process in the Trucial States in the 1950s.

Surveying the Sand

Andrea Mubi Brighenti's work on territory and legality underscores the roles of actors, technology, and law in the construction of territory:

> Territory is regarded as an activity of boundary-drawing and as a process which creates pre-assigned relational positions, both of which are key concerns for law. From this perspective, law is an inherently territorial endeavour. The focus of enquiry is consequently shifted to the actors who, by building and shaping their social relationships, draw different types of boundaries, on the technologies they apply, and the aims they attempt to achieve through boundary-drawing.[54]

While the claim does not seem hard to accept, the challenges among the British and the Gulf regional actors during this period—Saudi Arabia in particular—centered precisely around which legal system of territorial sovereignty would hold sway: Islamic law, which determined territory through *zakat* tax payment and personal loyalties; tribal *dar* for grazing, which could require large expanses of territory; or the Western-defined "international law,"

---

[53] Christopher M. Davidson, *Dubai: The Vulnerability of Success* (New York: Columbia University Press, 2008); Al-Sayegh, "Merchants' Role in a Changing Society."

[54] Andrea M. Brighenti, "On Territory as Relationship and Law as Territory," *Canadian Journal of Law and Society*, Vol. 21, No. 2 (2006), p. 65.

to be adjudicated through institutions such as the International Court of Justice.[55] The issue was further complicated by the challenge of how to coordinate the multiple bilateral territory discussions into a larger territorial framework that would be agreed upon by all.[56] As oil exploration moved throughout the region, territorial domain took on a much greater significance for Gulf rulers and further precipitated border conflicts. For example, when oil concessions were signed with both Dubai and Abu Dhabi in the late 1930s, an initial disagreement on territorial boundaries was sparked. The Second World War temporarily halted explorations, but when they resumed in 1945, a border dispute flared in 1948 when a Dubai raiding group killed fifty-two Manasir allies of Abu Dhabi in a border battle.[57] Dubai and Sharjah had fought over similar issues in 1940, and required leaders from Ras al-Khaima to help broker a truce.[58] British political intervention addressed these conflicts by drawing up territorial boundaries for the region, but territorial boundaries would remain a point of contention among the emirates through federation in 1971. The Anglo-Saudi Buraimi oasis incident of 1949 made it clear to the British that development and modernization projects could not happen until territory was more predictably ordered and assigned.[59] As mentioned, they established the Trucial Scouts in 1951 for security and peacekeeping in the subduing of the many contentious Bedu factions,[60] and it is under these antagonistic circumstances that the British sent land surveyor Julian Walker to the Trucial States to negotiate, organize, and delineate boundaries among Trucial sheikhs, so as to establish clearer and more precise territorial boundaries, and essentially insist on what it had enjoyed up to that point. Walker was then largely responsible for mapping the Trucial territories throughout 1959 and early 1960.[61]

[55] Krista Wiegand, "Resolution of Border Disputes in the Arabian Gulf," *Journal of Territorial and Maritime Studies*, Vol. 1, No. 1 (2014), pp. 33–48; Gwenn Okruhlik and Patrick Conge, "The Politics of Border Disputes on the Arabian Peninsula," *International Journal*, Vol. 54, No. 2 (1999), pp. 230–48.

[56] Wiegand, "Resolution of Border Disputes"; Wilkinson, *Arabian Frontiers*; Schofield and Blake, *Arabian Boundary Disputes*, Vol. 25.

[57] Peck, *The United Arab Emirates*.

[58] Khalifa, *The United Arab Emirates*; Hay, "The Persian Gulf States."

[59] Tripp, "Political Agency," p. 76.

[60] Tripp, "Political Agency."

[61] Walker drew the borders between Sharjah, Dubai, Umm al Quwain, as far as Khor Fakkan. He did not participate in Abu Dhabi border-drawing. See Tahira Yaqoob,

Walker later spoke of the fundamental challenge of imposing British borders within this system: "The imposition of frontiers meant the rigidification of the traditional ebb and flow of influence between families of the coast at a chance point in history."[62] Walker managed to get nearly all sheikhs to agree, at least temporarily, over boundary disputes, with the recourse of lacunae-like "neutral zones" when no clear solution was possible.[63] It was during this period when Walker was surveying on behalf of the British that the ruler of Ajman took more official sovereignty over Mananmah and surrounding areas.[64] Sheikh Rashid of Dubai also promulgated the Land Law of 1960, which was structured specifically on the Sudanese land law, recently completed after Sudanese independence in 1956.[65] The law was essentially a homestead declaration giving land ownership to those Dubaians who could prove that they had lived on their property for a certain period of time. All other land belonged to the ruler, land could not be owned by those who were not Dubaians, and if the municipality needed private land for infrastructural purpose, it was committed to paying the appropriate price.[66] Clearly, the rulers could foresee what Walker's activities signaled, in terms of cadastral registration and a shifting in understandings of territorial organization, and they took pre-emptive action by establishing their own, more official forms of territorial law. In Dubai's case, there was precedent. In reviewing the British Agency communication from 1937 throughout the Trucial States, Zahlan highlights that the British land agent found that:

> The rulers had admitted that they had no fixed frontiers with their neighbors, but that they had given him instead details of what they considered their *ihram* (sacred passion, and therefore inviolable). The only ruler who was absolutely sure of the

---

"A Return to the Country he Drew," *The National*, 25 November 2008, http://www.thenational.ae/news/uae-news/a-return-to-the-country-he-drew

[62] Walker, "Practical Problems of Boundary Delimitation in Arabia," p. 110.

[63] Qasimi sheikhs of Sharjah and Ras al-Khaima did not reach agreement with the Sultanate of Muscat and Oman. See Schofield, "Borders and Territoriality in the Gulf"; Walker, "Practical Problems of Boundary Delimitation in Arabia"; and Schofield and Blake, *Arabian Boundary Disputes*, Vols. 7 and 25. See also Wilkinson, *Arabian Frontiers*, pp. 267–70, for his discussion of "neutral zones."

[64] Walker, "Practical Problems of Boundary Delimitation in Arabia."

[65] Balfour-Paul, *The End of Empire in the Middle East*; K. Hamza, "Dubai: The Pearl of the Coast," *Al-Massaref* magazine (Beirut, 1968).

[66] Gabriel, *The Dubai Handbook*.

extent of his territory was Sa'id of Dubai. Sultan of Sharjah, by contrast, was the only one who refused to state what territory he claimed.[67]

Territorial boundaries were brokered among the Trucial States through the British, and the role of infrastructure in establishing these boundaries was central. For the British relationship with the Trucial States, infrastructure would eventually serve as a mediator and techno-scientific knowledge (both technology and *techne*) for the domestication of territory, beginning with maritime routes, and subsequently with oil extraction, trade, and circulatory infrastructure. Indeed, as I have argued elsewhere, a great deal of the entire city-making enterprise for the UAE was infrastructural, but I focus now on Julian Walker's account of his mapping work for the British as it illustrates an essential nexus for the translation of infrastructural semantics across cultures.[68] Anthropologist Brian Larkin describes the concept of infrastructure as language; and within colonial and post-colonial circumstances, a kind of colonial language to be learned locally.[69] While this too occurred in the Trucial States, with Walker I am referring to his interview work, and the local "language" interpretation that he carried in his map-making. Recalling Wilkinson's quote above, tribal territorial logos was centered around:

> nodes of intensive land use where inputs and labour and capital had created agricultural land, permanent wells, towns, etc. Such nodes of intensive settlement, gave rise to usufructuary rights in the surrounding areas, both on the coast and in the desert. In these peripheries it was the use of resources that mattered.[70]

The argument underscores the importance of mobility, and suggests that infrastructure—exceptional, precious—defined the territorial meaning, ownership, and power. Walker used these signifiers in his map-making to help him identify and establish territorial boundaries and ownership: "[I]n the desert areas it was useful to know who had cemented desert wells, and, in agricultural

[67] Zahlan, *The Origins of the United Arab Emirates*, p. 148, cited in George Joffé, "Concepts of Sovereignty in the Gulf Region," in Schofield, ed., *Territorial Foundations of the Gulf*, pp. 78–93.
[68] For complete documentation of Walker's work, see Julian Walker, *Documentary Studies in Arab Geopolitics: UAE: Internal Boundaries and the Boundary with Oman*, 8 volumes (Cambridge: Cambridge University Press Archive Editions, 1994).
[69] Brian Larkin, "The Politics and Poetics of Infrastructure," *Annual Review of Anthropology*, Vol. 42 (2013), pp. 327–43.
[70] Wilkinson, "Britain's Role in Boundary Drawing in Arabia," 97.

areas, who maintained the water channels and taxed the farmers for the provision of irrigation water."[71]

Again, infrastructure marks territory, and identifies ownership and political relationship based on its use as a clientelistic medium. The infrastructural logos preceded the map, but the map promulgated these political relationships. Wells were used as identifiers of territorial ownership, dividing points where one tribe's territory ended and another began, and monuments for patronage,[72] in an otherwise unstable territorial field. In his accounts, though trying to represent as faithfully as possible the "local way of life" in his imposition of territorial "straight lines" in his surveying, Walker repeatedly underscores the fixity, dependability, and order in his work as giving transcendence and legacy to an otherwise (to his eye) chaotic territorial organization.[73] He concludes that while memories can fade, and natural features are "mutable," the British, and his particular work, scripted the very code of national definition that would make subsequent nation-building in the UAE possible. Interviewed fifty years later, Walker suggests that his greatest legacy was "achieving and agreeing the UAE. The fact speaks for itself."[74] In the Buraimi incident only a few years before Walker's expedition, the Saudi army occupied an oasis village deliberately as a claim to it, and the wider area that its resources served, as a fundamental claim on territorial rights. Walker's use of infrastructural elements such as wells engaged in a larger British reconstitution of territorial configuration by resignifying the infrastructural logos through his cartography project.

In the next section, I explore how this territorial infrastructure signification influenced territorial negotiation and inter-Trucial State relationships as the British announced withdrawal from the region in 1968, and in the subsequent formation of the United Arab Emirates.

UAE Federation and Infrastructural "Ostentatious Duplication"

In the UAE, territory is power, as a post-1971 nation-state standard; and power is territorial, as an inheritance of tribal legacies that continue to constitute much of the inter-emirate dynamics. On 18 February 1968, just after the

[71] Walker, "Practical Problems of Boundary Delimitation in Arabia," p. 114.
[72] Ibid.
[73] Ibid., p. 116.
[74] Yaqoob, "A Return to the Country he Drew."

British announcement to withdraw from the region, Sheikh Zayed of Abu Dhabi met with Sheikh Rashid of Dubai at Al-Sameeh, near their mutual border,[75] to begin preliminary federation talks. Before discussing their possible political partnership, they first had to resolve onshore and offshore territorial conflicts that remained between Dubai and Abu Dhabi, in spite of British arbitration from 1949. Sheikh Zayed agreed to cede the contested areas to Dubai, including the site of the future Jebel Ali port, industrial area and free zone, along with an offshore Gulf area that included "Fateh South," which would produce generous oil supplies for the future.[76] They also agreed that while Abu Dhabi would temporarily be the capital, a new capital city was to be built on the Dubai–Abu Dhabi border.[77] These negotiations were reflected in the UAE Constitution, where it states that the UAE Supreme Council "shall exercise sovereignty on all territories and territorial waters" of the UAE, but that member states were to exercise this territorial sovereignty with respect to all other issues not explicitly discussed in the Constitution.[78]

The negotiation details and intrigue among the emirates in the period between January 1968 and December 1971 are outside the scope of this chapter,[79] but it is clear that with over 80 per cent of the territorial area, and approximately the same proportion of oil production and reserves, Abu Dhabi was the core emirate around which the Union was to be built. Territorial expanse, and the associate odds for more oil production possibilities, clearly translated into political heft and an elite position for Abu Dhabi in the new Union. Indeed, its capital status would go unchanged. This also meant that Abu Dhabi carried more of the fiscal responsibility for federal economic development, and as

[75] Graeme Wilson, *Rashid's Legacy: The Genesis of the Maktoum Family and the History of Dubai* (Dubai: Media Prima, 2006); Ibrahim Al-Abed, "Formation and Evolution of the Federation and its Institutions," in Ibrahim Al-Abed and Peter Hellyer, eds, *United Arab Emirates: a New Perspective* (London: Trident Press, 2001), pp. 145–60; Rodman R. Bundy, "Maritime Delimitation in the Gulf," in Richard Schofield, ed., *Territorial Foundations of the Gulf* (New York: St Martin's Press, 1994), pp. 176–86.
[76] Al-Abed, "Formation and Evolution of the Federation and its Institutions."
[77] Ramos, *Dubai Amplified*; Al-Abed, "Formation and Evolution of the Federation"; Khalifa, *The United Arab Emirates.*
[78] Ibid., p. 89.
[79] Christopher M. Davidson, *The United Arab Emirates: A Study in Survival* (Boulder, CO: Lynne Rienner, 2005); Abdullah Omran Taryam, *The Establishment of the United Arab Emirates, 1950–85* (London: Croom Helm, 1987); Zahlan, *The Origins of the United Arab Emirates.*

Khalifa points out, for those poorer northern emirates without oil wealth, "once in the federal fold, these emirates could translate what used to be an Abu Dhabian charitable support into a moral and political obligation."[80]

If Abu Dhabi was able to contribute disproportionately to the Trucial States Development Office with the help of early oil largesse in the 1960s to fund regional infrastructure projects,[81] the federal UAE context focused more on helping those poorer emirate associates through economic development projects with the objective of a more balanced federal structure. But even when other emirates discovered fossil resources within their territories—oil and/or natural gas—the virtually unchangeable territorial sizes, and associate territorial resources, still maintain Abu Dhabi's political and economic prominence and leadership.[82]

For both the Trucial State Development Office and subsequent UAE economic development, funds transferred from oil-producing emirates to their partners were precisely for infrastructure investment that would duplicate, and aspire to compete with, their own. As a result, the process of territorial signification through infrastructure continues among the emirates after federation, in what Khalifa terms as "'ostentatious duplication,' or the inclination of some emirates to build infrastructure just because a neighboring one has done so."[83] Khalifa suggests that these rivalries are "embedded in the now fading tribal rivalries."[84] He identifies airport construction as the most egregious example of this kind of infrastructure rivalry, but he also includes seaports and cement factories as infrastructures that would not achieve economies of scale due to over-supply.[85] He identifies motivations that are political rather than economic as the cause of this duplication, and hopes that the UAE Federal Planning Board, with more power, would correct this dupli-

---

[80] Khalifa, *The United Arab Emirates*, p. 155.
[81] Taryam, *The Establishment of the United Arab Emirates*.
[82] While crude oil and natural gas reserve estimates for the UAE have changed over time, the proportion is generally constant, with Abu Dhabi possessing 90 per cent of each, and the remaining 10 per cent divided among the remaining emirates, particularly Dubai and Sharjah. In 1986, Peck estimated UAE oil reserves at 32 billion barrels; and in 2009, the UAE web page estimates 98.2 billion barrels. See: http://www.opec.org/opec_web/en/about_us/170.htm.
[83] Khalifa, *The United Arab Emirates*, p. 158.
[84] Ibid.
[85] See Ramos, *Dubai Amplified*, for other duplicated infrastructures during this period in the region.

cation. As demonstrated in the amount of federal funds used for these infrastructure projects, it is clear that they were, in part, simply redistributive acts
to allow the "poorer" emirates that had not yet discovered oil or gas to have
the elite, mega-infrastructure projects that their rich brethren did. Abu Dhabi
received almost none of these federal funds.[86] But until that time, Khalifa
believes that the emirates' "preoccupation with the wasteful spectacular over
the economically sound may well continue."[87]

Echoing Khalifa's concern, Fatima S. Al-Shamsi's work on UAE industrial
policy of the late 1970s warns that:

> Given the characteristics of Gulf state economies, the drive for industrial develop-
> ment will remain restricted unless it acquires a real [Gulf] regional dimension. ...
> Adherence to a regional strategy may lead to a more efficient resource allocation
> through reducing the cost of duplication and excess capacity of industrial projects.[88]

But, as Mary Ann Tétreault suggests, when looking at the UAE's overall
investments at this time, project duplication had a specific logic:

> UAE investments, particularly those made by Dubai, have been criticized as egregious
> examples of differential accumulation at the expense of regional partners. This is
> disputed by analysts who cite disparities in exchange rates, pricing policies and taxa-
> tion across the GCC [Gulf Cooperation Council formed in 1981], which though
> they are diminishing, are the chief culprits blocking the growth of regional trade.
> Indeed, such impediments make duplicate investment economically rational.[89]

Along with political distributive logics for a new, unevenly federated nation
in the 1970s and the regional economic rationale, perhaps equally important
was the legacy of infrastructural territorial demarcation as the true signifier of
political power, and ownership was a vestige carried over from the transitional-
modern moment of contested British territoriality. The construction of the
Jebel Ali port and industrial area on the Dubai–Abu Dhabi border is perhaps
the most spectacular of these projects.[90]

---

86 Ibid.
87 Khalifa, *The United Arab Emirates*, p. 159.
88 Fatima Al-Shamsi, "Industrial Strategies and Change in the UAE during the 1980s,"
    in Abbas Abdelkarim, ed., *Change and Development in the Gulf* (New York: St
    Martin's Press, 1999), p. 102.
89 Mary Ann Tétreault, "The Economics of National Autonomy in the UAE," in Joseph
    A. Kechichian, ed., *A Century in Thirty Years: Shaykh Zayed and the United Arab
    Emirates* (Washington, DC: Middle East Policy Council, 2000), p. 138.
90 Ramos, *Dubai Amplified*.

While the territory agreement between Dubai and Abu Dhabi was struck at Al-Sameeh in 1968, the border definition had previously been disputed and had caused bloodshed for both emirates. The British withdrawal meant that neither had the endorsement or protection of the Royal Navy to protect previous border agreements. This helps explain the motive of Dubai's Sheikh Rashid to punctuate the territory agreement with the world's largest port construction project. In addition, such an ambitious port project so close to their shared border could help give Dubai a competitive edge over any future Abu Dhabi port facility, and could potentially offer regional port services to both emirates. Knowing that Dubai itself had already chosen to duplicate the Bahraini Arab Shipbuilding and Repair Yard Company with its own dry dock facilities, Sheikh Rashid certainly knew that the same duplication could and would be employed by Dubai's neighbors, even after the 1971 federation of the UAE. Jebel Ali port is the monumental trade infrastructure clarifying *dar*, very close to a border that had been disputed, which was more solidly encoded into the territory than a "scrap of paper" or "straight line" could ever be.[91]

Conclusion

Larkin demonstrates that in political regimes, particularly in colonial and post-colonial circumstances, infrastructures are not driven underground into invisibility, but rather that "infrastructures are metapragmatic objects, signs of themselves deployed in particular circulatory regimes to establish sets of effects."[92] This was particularly true for the UAE during its transitional period from a pastoral, itinerant territoriality to a more fixed territory based on oil extraction and, subsequently, real estate development. Territory and infrastructure were each negotiated from Trucial State quasi-colonial circumstances through emirates nation-building processes as a jagged, fractured series of events and processes of transitional modernity.[93] Infrastructure carried a colonial logos to establish power relationships of territorial organization, but also recoded existing infrastructural elements as a way to define stricter territorial borders. In this way, Julian Walker's interviews and discussions with

[91] Walker, "Practical Problems of Boundary Delimitation in Arabia."
[92] Larkin, "The Politics and Poetics of Infrastructure," p. 336.
[93] Rhys A. Jones, "Mann and Men in a Medieval State: the Geographies of Power in the Middle Ages," *Transactions of the Institute of British Geographers*, Vol. 24, No. 1 (1999), pp. 65–78.

Trucial rulers make him both Anthropologist and Cartographer, knowing—if mildly lamenting—that British territorial objectives, under the guise of modernization, would prevail until UAE federation in 1971. UAE rulers were somewhat reluctant to give up British protection in 1971, but clearly their subsequent reliance on infrastructure, and its duplication, for territorial competition carries over from before.

Urbanism and architecture continue to be infrastructural elements that serve UAE territorial demarcation interests, and it is precisely for this that territory is the appropriate scale to discuss the emirates' urbanization and development. Desert wells are not exactly synonymous, of course, with contemporary ports and airports in the UAE, but each occupies the role of replenishment and respite during longer journeys. Usufructuary rights for their uses—now owned by global shippers and airlines—continue to signify territorial and political ownership. This shift away from Bedu territorial conceptualization occurred slowly, and with British influence once their interests moved inland for oil exploration. UAE federation completed the shift in territorial demarcation, and the infrastructural logos that constituted it.

5

GULF URBANISM

THE SEMANTIC FIELD OF A CATEGORY SPACE

Ahmed Kanna

The urbanization of the Gulf region, with its large and flashy development projects, has attracted increasing scholarly and journalistic attention in the past decade.[1] The amount and rate of knowledge, scholarly and journalistic, that is being produced around urban questions in the region, I argue in this chapter, warrants that we step back and ask some metacritical questions about the contours and conditions of this knowledge production, and reflect on what such questions suggest about the politics of urban knowledge for the region.

[1] I would like to thank Mehran Kamrava, Zahra Babar, and the participants of "The Evolution of Gulf Global Cities" working group hosted by the Center for International and Regional Studies, Georgetown University School of Foreign Service in Qatar, for their critical engagement with the chapter; the Arab Crossroads Program at New York University Abu Dhabi, and in particular Nathalie Peutz, Justin Stearns, Nils Lewis, and Steve Caton, have been warm hosts and critical interlocutors whose engagement has helped sharpen the argument.

The current conditions of knowledge production on Gulf urbanism are reminiscent of larger issues in metageography, for example, around the category of space. In his seminal 2004 lecture "Space as a Key Word," David Harvey notes with some frustration that the term "space" has eventuated in a theoretical crisis in the social sciences. Harvey notes that the application of the term to empirical research has not produced any clarity or rigor. Harvey finds particularly vexing the fact that the term "space" seems inevitably to "elicit modification," to "indicate a variety of contexts that so inflect matters as to render the meaning of space contingent upon the context."[2] The sites where the term is deployed seem infinite.[3] What, theoretically, he asks, do we gain from the category of space? Something like this is going on, if at a more modest scale, and with more modest theoretical and political stakes, in the current discourse of Gulf urbanism. Adapting Harvey, what, theoretically, can we gain from the analytical category of "the urban Gulf"? Or, approaching the question from another angle, what kinds of claims does the category make possible, and what kinds less possible?

The reader should not perceive this as a conventional research article. I will rarely offer any conclusive statements on what or how Gulf urban processes are or have been taking shape. Indeed, a critical analysis of the assumptions embedded in such questions makes up the substance of the chapter. This study seeks to contribute or provoke questions for further research which have seldom been posed in what I am calling here "Gulf urbanism discourse." I begin by tackling the category of the urban per se, but shift in the concluding section of the chapter to what I believe is a related question: the so-called anthropocene. We now know that urban questions and environmental questions are complexly entwined, yet to my knowledge not a single study has taken as its subject the relationship between the urban and the issue of the human–environmental in the Gulf. This is in spite of the fact that the scholarly literature on Gulf urbanism is becoming vast, the journalistic one even vaster. As I suggest in the conclusion to the chapter, as scholars, it is urgent that we begin to connect the Gulf, a valuable resource extraction zone in the neoliberal economy—indeed, a region whose entry into the neoliberal economy is fundamental to the shape that that the neoliberal project would take over the past four decades—to issues under the broad rubric of the anthropocene.

---

[2] David Harvey, *Spaces of Global Capitalism: Towards a Theory of Uneven Geographical Development* (New York: Verso, 2006), p. 119.

[3] Harvey, *Spaces*, p. 120.

Against Naïve Realism

Even when I first began my research in the region in 2002, it was obvious how much change, at least morphologically, cities such as Dubai, Abu Dhabi, and Doha were undergoing. In Dubai, every area from shipping to trade to the built environment and real estate projects seemed to be rapidly expanding. Superlatives seem to fall effortlessly from commentators' lips as they struggle to grapple with a seemingly novel phenomenon. It is no surprise that the urban condition in the region has become a focus of so much attention in this contemporary period. Even casual observers will leap to the conclusion that the cottage industry of urban writing on the Gulf in the first decade and a half of the twenty-first century is obviously a consequence of the kinds of economic and urban development undertaken by the various countries of the region according to the so-called visions of the dominant actors in cities such as Abu Dhabi, Doha, and Dubai.

A recent popular article voices, from an Emirati perspective, a view that very much reflects this *Zeitgeist*. In a piece titled "Gulf Cities Emerge as New Centers of Arab World," Sultan Sooud Al Qassemi, a frequent blogger for the US online daily *Huffington Post* and, according to his Wikipedia page, a "widely recognized" Twitter user based in Dubai, writes the following:

> Over the past few years, as these traditional Arab capitals (Cairo, Beirut, and Baghdad) became more embroiled in civil strife, a new set of cities started to emerge in the Gulf, establishing themselves as the new centers of the Arab world. Abu Dhabi, its sister emirates of Dubai and Sharjah and the Qatari capital, Doha, have developed as the nerve center of the contemporary Arab world's culture, commerce, design, architecture, art and academia, attracting hundreds of thousands of Arab immigrants, including academics, businessmen, journalists, athletes, artists, entrepreneurs and medical professionals. While these Gulf cities may be unable to compete with their Arab peers in terms of political dynamism, in almost every other sense they have far outstripped their sister cities in North Africa and the Levant.[4]

This construction of the Gulf city as a forward-looking crossroads of culture was typical of how people talked about Dubai during my fieldwork between 2002 and 2007 and what I have witnessed in media coverage since then. Indeed, Al Qassemi seems here to be quoting almost verbatim many of my own interlocutors during my years of field research in the UAE—or maybe

---

[4] Sultan Sooud Al Qassemi, "Gulf Cities Emerge as New Centers of Arab World," *Al Monitor*, October 2013, http://www.al-monitor.com/pulse/originals/2013/10/abu-dhabi-dubai-doha-arab-centers.html.

they are quoting him and other members of the intelligentsia like him. More plausibly, such a discursive construction of the city, I believe, is deployed in situations when the seemingly non-political appears as in fact political, and starts causing some anxiety among the ethnocractic elites of the region. To adapt a phrase from anthropologist James Ferguson, in contexts of real life contestation over the urban in the Gulf, the discourse of the city becomes an anti-politics.[5] I do not think that it is an accident that we witness a member of the Gulf intelligentsia being dispatched in the wake of the Arab uprisings to produce for the outside world such vivid and unambiguous renderings of the Gulf as a prosperous, modern, and stable island in a larger, more volatile and impoverished region.[6]

In this chapter, I do two things. First, I invert the common-sense notion that the proliferation of urban knowledge production on the Gulf over the past fifteen years is a consequence of the urban projects that have been undertaken

---

[5] James Ferguson, *Anti-Politics Machine: Development, Depoliticization, and Bureaucratic Power in Lesotho* (Minneapolis, MN: University of Minnesota Press, 1994). Ferguson argues that development discourse, posing as technocratic "good" or "common sense" solutions to problems of poverty and underdevelopment, in effect acts as a mechanism for "translating" problems inextricably entwined with politics into purely technical issues.

[6] Many of the "experts" who emerge in moments of political crisis, to remind us about how progressive the Gulf is, are the same experts who suddenly appear when politics raises its head at more local scales. Thus, in response to a major construction worker demonstration in Dubai in 2005, local academics made the media rounds to denounce worker militancy, one even going as far as to recommend the criminalization of acts or words that might shine a less than attractive light on the reputation of the state. Such a recommendation, one notices with melancholy, has become realized, for example in the draconian internet law promulgated in the United Arab Emirates in the aftermath of the Arab uprisings. I had a nearly identical personal experience with a locally-based Arab expatriate colleague in the early months of 2011, as my book on Dubai was going to press. I had asked the colleague whether they would feel comfortable if I thanked them in the acknowledgments section, given that my book could be read as politically critical. I had asked numerous other colleagues, both within the UAE and without, the same question. While the majority had no problem being thanked, some were hesitant and politely asked to remain unmentioned. The response of my Arab-expatriate colleague, however, took me aback. Why, they asked, if my critiques were true, did hundreds of thousands of foreigners, Arabs, Asians, Westerners, and so on, leave home to flock to Dubai's promise of opportunity? In connection to this, I note with interest that what applies to larger regional and global politics also applies to local politics.

during the contemporary period. This assumption betrays a naïve realism that goes from the referent to the sign, a theory of signification that linguistic anthropology has long ago advanced beyond. Rather, I will try to show that the situation is more complicated and may in fact be the reverse: that, to extend the linguistic analogy, the sign "city" and the semantic field in which it is situated help to constitute the arena in which certain forms are built and certain kinds of urban spaces take shape. The second part of my agenda here has to do with knowledge more specifically. Categories such as "the urban" and "urban space" are vague and do not lend themselves to precise analytical interventions. In spite of this, the proliferation of urban studies on the Gulf has tended to assume that such categories are self-evident. But in fact, we need first to ask what such categories specifically mean in different contexts, what kinds of analytical and political work they do in a given context. As I think is evident from my discussion above of Al Qassemi's essay, we cannot take such categories at face value. They can be made to signify different things. Rather than assuming we know to what "urban" or "city" refers, or asking "what is a city?" (only ostensibly an improvement), a better way of thinking about urban questions, I argue, is to ask: what does a category such as "the city" do? And how does it operate in contexts of cultural politics and historiography?[7]

Journalistic and Scholarly Discourses: A Semantic Field

Dwelling a little longer on Al Qassemi's essay, we begin to appreciate some assumptions worth noting here. Al Qassemi says, for example, that while the more "traditional Arab capitals" may be more politically dynamic than cities of the Gulf, the latter are outpacing these traditional capitals in the areas of culture and development. In other words, Al Qassemi sets politics on one side, and culture (in the common-sense understanding related to the arts, rather than an anthropological sense) on the other. Politics, he implies, is best left to elites or experts or to some other "responsible" authority. Urbanism and questions of urban life, which are deeply intertwined with questions of politics, become "translated" into issues of supposedly apolitical technical expertise.[8] What, after all, he seems to suggest, has the "political dynamism," the more

---

[7] Not being a historian, I will obviously restrict my comments to the issue of cultural politics, but I think that the question of the historiography of the category of the urban in the Gulf is a very interesting one.

[8] Ferguson, *Anti-Politics Machine*.

participatory and quotidian engagement with the political by everyday people in the traditional Arab capitals, brought except chaos and misery? Second, and as I analyze in more detail below, there is an explicit binary, "tradition/ traditional Arab" vs. "Gulf," a binary that has proven highly useful in highlighting the ways in which the Gulf is superior to the rest of the Arab region. Third, Al Qassemi's formulation begs the question: to whom does the city belong? In Al Qassemi's and so many other writings, the Gulf city is explicitly a city for professionals: the Gulf city as "the nerve center of the contemporary Arab world's culture, commerce, design, architecture, art and academia, attracting hundreds of thousands of Arab immigrants, including academics, businessmen, journalists, athletes, artists, entrepreneurs and medical professionals."[9] One might call these the "good subjects" of neoliberalism. Who gets excluded is obvious: the majority of the population who look after the children of these good subjects, drive them around, build and clean their homes, and serve their other needs.

Al Qassemi's comment on politics and Arab cities betrays another exclusion as well. The implication that Gulf cities are politically quiescent may align with some Western media stereotypes about wealthy sheikhs buying their subjects' loyalty with petrodollar handouts, but even a superficial glance at the events of the Arab uprisings, let alone a serious engagement with the history of the past century in the region, easily undermines this assumption. How are we to reconcile this stereotypical representation of politically quiescent Gulf cities, for example, with the Arab uprisings-era protests and encounters across the region? Moreover, why assume that "politics" is an activity that only the citizens of a state participate in? Why exclude non-citizens? Protests by non-citizens have been going on for a long time, the UAE being an excellent example.[10] The demands of citizens and non-citizens may be different, but calls for reform, along with the day-to-day politics of protests, worker militancy, and urban unrest have been a regular feature of Gulf life for almost a century, if not longer.[11]

A fourth aspect worth remarking on is implied by passages such as this one: "a new set of cities started to emerge in the Gulf, establishing themselves as the

[9] Al Qassemi, "Gulf Cities."

[10] Ahmed Kanna, "A Politics of Non-Recognition? Biopolitics of Arab Gulf Worker Protests in the Year of Uprisings," *Interface*, Vol. 4, No. 1 (2012), pp. 146–64.

[11] Christopher Davidson, *Dubai: The Vulnerability of Success* (New York: Columbia University Press, 2008); Robert Vitalis, *America's Kingdom: Mythmaking on the Saudi Oil Frontier* (Palo Alto, CA: Stanford University Press, 2007).

new centers of the Arab world. Abu Dhabi, its sister emirates of Dubai and Sharjah and the Qatari capital, Doha ... While these Gulf cities may be unable to compete with." The construction is only apparently common-sensical. What is interesting about it is the shift between "city" and "emirate" or "state." This is a common writing convention in Gulf urbanism, one with which I have struggled myself. What scale underpins our analysis of Gulf urbanism? Are we really talking about the city when we refer to the state, or vice versa? This is a question to which I have no ready answers, and would like to propose it as an avenue of future research. Are the city and the state the same thing? Or are we writers on Gulf urbanism simply being unsystematic or sloppy? Or is the conflation between city and state more politically determined? My sense is that this last question is both more interesting and more accurate.

There is a vagueness in the way we use the category of the urban when we write about the Gulf, and this is, I suggest, conditioned by our situation as we produce knowledge. Let me discuss some examples before offering tentative conclusions. Expert settings, such as academic and professional conferences, writings, and visual representations on and of Gulf urbanism are a useful kind of field site for the study of knowledge production, and specifically the schemas and systems of assumptions that we specialists deploy in our analytical work. In my first book, I explored similar questions, specifically the ways in which local Gulf monarchs and other land-owning notables hire foreign spatial experts, such as architects, planners, and real estate entrepreneurs, to develop consumer or prestige urban projects in different cities of the UAE.[12] I argued that in the context of the contemporary Gulf, the expert, and especially the Western expert carrying the cachet of Western cultural capital, becomes an important player in local cultural and spatial politics. The conventional story told about such actors is that they supply rising Gulf cities and their ambitious monarchs with the prestige and built iconicism necessary for global urban competition. This is the global "place wars" or "urban entrepreneurialism" argument about globalizing cities, familiar from the work of scholars such as Sharon Zukin, David Harvey, and Anne-Marie Broudehoux.[13]

---

[12] Ahmed Kanna, *Dubai, The City as Corporation* (Minneapolis, MN: University of Minnesota Press), pp. 77–104.

[13] Anne-Marie Broudehoux, "Spectacular Beijing: The Conspicuous Construction of an Olympic Metropolis," *Journal of Urban Affairs*, Vol. 29, No. 4 (2007), pp. 383–99; David Harvey, "From Managerialism to Entrepreneurialism: The Transformation in Urban Governance in Late Capitalism," *Geografiska Annaler. Series B, Human*

While there is much to recommend this theory, it tends to represent local actors as somewhat passive recipients of homogeneous neoliberal and Western-style global urban forms. What we see in fact is a more complex and ambiguous situation, in which global experts and local elites shape each other's agendas and, in turn, co-constitute Gulf urban space. I take so-called starchitects such as Rem Koolhaas and Zaha Hadid as exemplary of this process, not to argue that they are the most important or the only international experts participating in Gulf urbanism, but because they are symptomatic in a particularly striking way of these co-constitutions of Gulf space. Ultimately, what I have tried to show in my earlier work was that while these international experts consistently and explicitly spoke and wrote about the Gulf being an unprecedented "laboratory" that allowed them to enact their most daring aesthetic projects—in other words, to live the long dream of unfettered architectural formal experimentation in a real world setting—they unwittingly participated in the politics of legitimization of local elite, monarchical/dynastic claims on space and historiography.

While subject to less direct political and economic pressures, more academic attempts to grapple with the urban question in the Gulf are also excellent settings in which to examine our basic assumptions about space, the urban, and knowledge production. One example was the highly informative and generally excellent conference "Gulf Cities: Space, Society, Culture," which I attended at the American University of Kuwait (AUK) in March 2013.[14] The conference abstract begins in a typical way:

Geography, Vol. 71, No. 1 (1989), pp. 3–17; Sharon Zukin, *Loft Living: Culture and Capital in Urban Change* (New Brunswick, NJ: Rutgers University Press, 1989).

[14] The conference featured papers ranging over a broad spectrum of topics. Across dozens of papers, presenters covered topics such as port cities of the Gulf; debt, capitalism and land tenure in the Indian Ocean; "the urban growth machine of the Gulf"; corporate transit cities in the Gulf; public works; contested spaces; "militarized and ethnocratic" urban governance; "urban governmentality"; migration and urban commodification; "rhetorical relationships" between Gulf cities; higher education enclaves; oil and urbanism; and many others. Kuwait is particularly interesting, as it is characterized by a more robust open academic climate than is the case in the other Gulf countries. Nevertheless, readers assuming that I am strictly referring to official policies on academic research or juridical sanctions, such as censorship, when I speak of semantic fields or discourses are missing the point. As an anthropologist I am interested in the deeper, more unspoken discursive formations that constitute the ideological substrate through which categories such as the urban find their conditions of generative semantic possibility.

The Gulf region ranks among the most urbanized in the world, with an average of 84% percent [*sic*] of the population living in urban areas (this figure increases to 91% excluding Saudi Arabia, Iraq, and Iran) ... The region's distinctly urban identity is hardly a new phenomenon. For centuries before the advent of oil the coasts of both sides of the Gulf waters were dotted with prosperous port cities that served as vital entrepot and transnational hubs within the Indian Ocean trading network. These ports were cosmopolitan centers of human contact and cultural exchange, much like the Gulf's skyscraper cities of the 21st century.[15]

The introduction goes on to note that a rigorous scholarly focus has been largely missing in the literature on the region and that its urban histories and rapid contemporary urban growth invite new and exciting research.

I find in this little that is controversial, and much that is agreeable and even laudable. There is clearly something interesting going on in the urban Gulf and a closer look at it will very possibly contribute important new advances to urbanism scholarship. My aim here is neither to minimize this nor to argue that there is something uniquely diffuse or vague about academic conferences on the Gulf. It is to point out that, in spite of the apparent variety of the topics covered by conferences such as the AUK meeting, patterns become apparent and point in the direction of a possible semantic field of the urban.

A review of recent scholarly literature in the fields of Gulf urban planning and development reveals, for example, some basic assumptions that echo the more journalistic discourse of which the Al Qassemi piece cited above is symptomatic. For example, change in the Gulf city is often (indeed, usually) framed as proceeding through phases, even teleologically. Such scholarship is underpinned by a historiography that tracks the development of the Gulf city, for example from the "tribal" village or society to the "global city," from "localism" to "cosmopolitanism," from "endogenous" to "exogenous" development, and similar variations.[16] This echoes, probably unwittingly, the foundational narratives of the modern Gulf monarchies. Often, indeed, the story of the *telos* of urban modernity is one and same as that of the supposedly visionary, modernizing prince who, against great odds, gave the "gift of modernity" to his

[15] Gulf Studies Symposium, "Gulf Cities: Space, Society, Culture" Conference, 22–24 March 2013 (Kuwait City: American University of Kuwait), p. 5.

[16] Abdul-Khaleq Abdulla, "*Dubai: rihlat madina arabiyya min al-mahalliyya ila-l-alamiyya*," *Al-Mustaqbal al-Arabiyy*, Vol. 323 (2006), pp. 1–28; Mustapha Ben Hammouche, "The Changing Morphology of the Gulf Cities in the Age of Globalisation: The Case of Bahrain," *Habitat International*, Vol. 28, No. 4 (2004), pp. 521–40; Agatino Rizzo, "Metro Doha," *Cities*, Vol. 31 (2013), pp. 533–43.

people.[17] Another strand of literature, not unrelated to (and often underpinned by the same assumptions of) the first, frames the Gulf city as a mainly or even purely technical site: the city as a node for investment or development, excised from politics—for example, those around wages or working class labor and migration conditions; or the city as a node for various kinds of flows, financial, ideological, human—the city, in other words, as a site in which complex kinds of activities that do not resolve themselves so easily into the metaphor of "flows" have tended to be de-emphasized.[18] Finally, representing perhaps the most voluminous subgenre of gulf urbanism discourse, there is the discourse of "culture," specifically: spatializations of the urban as coterminous with a supposed cultural essence termed "Arab" or "Islamo-Arab," or vice versa. Such constructions inevitably, and almost without exception, conflate the identity of the ruling family with that of the entire society or urban space in question.[19]

[17] For example, Will Hunter, "Urbanism," *Architectural Review*, Vol. 229, No. 1371 (May 2011), pp. 72–7. The myth of the "great man" in Gulf historiography is discussed and critiqued in great detail in Robert Vitalis, *America's Kingdom: Mythmaking on the Saudi Oil Frontier* (Palo Alto, CA: Stanford University Press, 2007); and in Kanna, *Dubai, The City as Corporation*. Both of these works were anticipated by the pioneering work of historian Nelida Fuccaro. See, for example, the seminal "Visions of the City: Urban Studies on the Gulf," *MESA Bulletin*, Vol. 35, No. 2 (2001), pp. 175–87.

[18] Edward J. Malecki and Michael C. Ewers, "Labor Migration to World Cities: With a Research Agenda for the Arab Gulf," *Progress in Human Geography*, Vol. 31, No. 4 (August 2007), pp. 467–84; Michael Murray, "Connecting Growth and Wealth Through Visionary Planning: The Case of Abu Dhabi," *Planning Theory and Practice*, Vol. 14, No. 2 (June 2013), pp. 278–82; Agatino Rizzo, "Rapid Urban Development and National Master Planning in Arab Gulf Countries: Qatar as a Case Study," *Cities*, Vol. 39 (August 2014), pp. 50–57. For a critique of the metaphor of "flows" as applied to processes of transnational mobility, see James Ferguson, "Governing Extraction: New Spatializations of Order and Disorder in Neoliberal Africa," in Ferguson, *Global Shadows: Africa in the Neoliberal World Order* (Durham, NC: Duke University Press, 2006), pp. 194–210.

[19] One recent article is a good example: its authors argue that their Doha architectural "projects are successful because MZ Architects understands the underlying importance of cultural infrastructure"; the recognition of this "underlying cultural infrastructure," the authors argue, is important because "cities are slippery things, never really cut and dried. They are too diverse, take too long to construct and inhabit for anybody to easily think about them in one go." Diversity seems to be set against cultural essence in a binary opposition, with the former representing or

Much of contemporary scholarly literature on the urban Gulf, to summarize, raises the same issues as those in more journalistic literature: To whom does the city belong? Does urban discourse translate questions that are deeply political into technical questions? In other words, does the category "Gulf city" and its connotations represent an anti-politics of the urban? And does this discourse conflate the urban with the state in the service of such anti-politics? What much of this literature suggests is, at least, that it does not critically engage such questions. Unwittingly, it tends to reinforce a discursive field in which the city becomes a space of technocracy, both as a problem or object of study and as a space for apolitical technocrats; the bearer of a teleological march of development guided by a genius ruler; and a space whose essential cultural identity is coterminous with that of the ruling family. Wrinkles, tensions, and so-called contradictions—the real existence of politics, diversity, and uneven development—are marginalized, erased, or rendered unthinkable by this discursive field.

Mediation

Let us consider, moreover, how this scholarship is mediated—how its object of study is represented and what techniques are employed to represent this object. Maps, both representational and non-representational, were central to the papers delivered at the AUK conference. Representational maps, depicting urban plans, neighborhoods, demographics, and other kinds of data, produced an image of the city as a specific kind of object of expertise. This was an image of the city as an arena of surgical intervention, or as a demographic research problem, or as a spatial relation between built forms. But it was non-representational mapping that was particularly interesting: the given city or urban space represented as a space associated with qualities more ambiguous than can be captured by a representational map, such as a certain mood or a kind of memory. Such papers described the passing of certain kinds of urbanity, such as the city in which public parks and accessible spaces were common, and the emergence of a city in which highways and skyscrapers are dominant. Some papers discussed the aesthetics of public monuments and their connec-

---

indexing the fleeting and ephemeral; the latter, solidity, a place's core identity, *genius loci*, etc. See MZ Architects, "City Scale," *Architectural Review* (March 2013), pp. 6–9. See Kanna, *Dubai, The City as Corporation*, pp. 77–104 for a detailed discussion and critique of cultural essentialism in urban Gulf literature.

tions to collective memories, while others evoked even deeper histories and memories of urbanity, such as those connected to the pre-oil Indian Ocean arena or to the frontier cultures of early oil cities. Such non-representational geographies can refer to a past, but they can also refer to a future, or to a utopia. The most vivid example from the AUK conference was the silhouette image on the conference brochure's cover and in its logo: a blending of the shadows of iconic skyscrapers from the region's major cities, Doha, Dubai, Riyadh, and Kuwait, to create an image of overwhelming high-rise urbanity. In the foreground we see a darker gray silhouette referencing these cities specifically, in the background a lighter gray shadow of more anonymous buildings. The effect is one of Manhattan-like high modernism, an image resonant with the sometimes subtle, sometimes not-so-subtle, teleology underpinning the contemporary discourse of Gulf urbanism.

Binaries

The research workshop hosted by the Center for International and Regional Studies at Georgetown University's Qatar campus, which was the jumping-off point for this chapter and the present volume, and which I attended in October 2013, approached the urban in a similarly fascinating way. Entitled "The Evolution of Gulf Global Cities,"[20] the Center for International and Regional Studies' website explains the agenda of the research group thus:

> Within the GCC, an average of 88 percent of the total population live in cities, while on average only 56 percent of Yemen, Iraq, and Iran's population live in urbanized spaces. The tempo and *spatial ethos of urbanization* in the Gulf *differ markedly from patterns of traditional urbanism* in other developing countries. Within a matter of decades, *Gulf port cities* have rapidly evolved from *regional centers of cultural and economic exchange to globalizing cities deeply embedded within the global economy.* Exponentially evident features of Gulf cities such as international hotel chains, shopping centers, and entertainment complexes have classified these *cities as centers of consumption.* Other urban trends, such as *exhibition and conference centers, media and knowledge cities,* and branch campuses of Western universities have integrated Gulf cities within numerous global networks. ... While oil urbanization and modernization direct much of the scholarship on Gulf cities, understanding the evolution of the *urban landscape against a social and cultural backdrop* is limited within the academic literature. For instance, within the states

---

[20] We note here the ambiguity in the juxtaposition of the terms "Gulf" and "Global," as if the scale of the object of knowledge is indeterminate.

of the GCC, the citizen-state-expatriates nexus has largely geared the vision and planning of urban real-estate mega-projects. These projects reflect the increasing role of expatriates as *consumers and users of urban space*, rather than as mere sources of manpower utilized to build the city. Other state initiatives, such as the construction of cultural heritage mega-projects in various Gulf cities, reveal *the state's attempts to reclaim parts of the city* for its local citizens in the midst of a growing expatriate urban population. ... In addition to issues of class, nationality, and identity, gender and mobility within the city are vital to *understanding urbanizing Gulf societies in relation to the demographic imbalance*. The *political economy of urban development* is an emerging area of inquiry in the scholarship of Gulf cities. For instance, the spectacular architectural design of cultural heritage mega-projects is indicative of increasing *cosmopolitanism* of urbanized Gulf cities and their aim to cater to global audiences. A particular area of interest is the extent to which the state engages with *international consultants, local planners and architects* in *constructing cosmopolitan heritage projects* that solidify both national and transnational identity. Other sites in the city, such as the presence and use of public space in the urban landscape, can help in understanding processes of social interaction and the form and function of authority in the city. Some spaces, such as the Pearl Roundabout in Bahrain, have become symbolic sites of *political contestation*. Other seemingly less securitized sites and features of Gulf cities, such as Souqs (traditional marketplace), seek to reinvent traditional forms of urbanism by reconciling culture and the *creation of public space*.[21]

I have italicized in this passage terms that strike me as both common to discourses about the Gulf city and rich in connotation and therefore hold potential theoretical insight. There have been some attempts to render the reality of Gulf urbanism in a more theoretically compelling light, from the dismissive—such as in the writings of Mike Davis and David Harvey along with many other less known writers—to more serious attempts.[22] The latter

[21] See https://cirs.georgetown.edu/research-cirs/research-initiatives/evolution-gulf-global-cities/background-and-scope-project.

[22] Mike Davis and Daniel Bertrand Monk, eds., *Evil Paradises: Dreamworlds of Neoliberalism* (New York: New Press, 2011); David Harvey, "The Right to the City," *New Left Review*, Vol. 53 (Sept.–Oct. 2008), pp. 23–40; compare these dismissive accounts, and those discussed above, to the far more locally grounded and theoretically nuanced following works: Claire Beaugrand, Amelie Le Renard, and Roman Stadnicki, eds, "Villes et dynamiques urbaines en péninsule Arabique," *Arabian Humanities*, Vol. 2 (2013); Michelle Buckley and Adam Hanieh, "Diversification by Urbanization: Tracing the Property-Finance Nexus in Dubai and the Gulf," *International Journal of Urban and Regional Research*, Vol. 38, No. 1 (Jan. 2014), pp. 155–175; Nelida Fuccaro, ed., "Histories of Oil and Urban Modernity in the Middle East," *Comparative Studies of South Asia, Africa, and the Middle East*, Vol. 33,

group of scholars are producing work that is both empirically compelling and theoretically exciting. However, little attention has been paid to the issue of the semantic field of the urban in the Gulf, and I think that an anthropological perspective is well-equipped to address such a question. While hoping not to sound simplistic, I would like to ask a seemingly simple question: what do we mean by "the city" in the context of the Gulf? Might we begin to think productively of a project to theorize the Gulf's urban condition by surveying what we have inherited from the particular disciplines in which we have been trained, to see if there are not already conceptual tools that have proven useful? Though I hesitate to dredge up the ancient history of anthropology, it does seem to me that the paragraph I cited just above—a passage that is typical of the debates currently taking place in relation to Gulf urbanism—almost demands to be analyzed using proven, if dated, linguistic anthropological categories such as "codes," "binary schemas" and, as mentioned, semantic fields. Specifically, the following schema jumps out of the passage:

- GCC vs. Yemen, Iraq, Iran
- Gulf urbanism (which seems here to be the marked category) vs. MENA urbanism (the unmarked)
- Global vs. regional
- Cosmopolitanism vs. regionalism/localism
- Rulers and experts/consultants vs. non-rulers, non-experts
- Construction/agency or agentive construction vs. passive/constructed population/public space
- Heritage vs. demographic imbalance

Reading the passage above as a code of some kind, or better, as underpinned by a code, can offer a start to a theoretically more interesting approach than has generally prevailed in the discourse of Gulf urbanism thus far. It does not go far enough, however. One of the major problems of such semiotic or structural analysis is its Cartesian view of human behavior as primarily involving

No. 1 (2013); Pascal Menoret, *Joyriding in Riyadh: Oil, Urbanism, and Road Revolt* (New York: Cambridge University Press, 2014); Robina Muhammad and James D. Sidaway, "Spectacular Urbanization amidst Variegated Geographies of Globalization: Learning from Abu Dhabi's Trajectory through the Lives of South Asian Men," *International Journal of Urban and Regional Research*, Vol. 36, No. 3 (May 2012), pp. 606–27; Stephen Ramos, *Dubai Amplified: The Engineering of a Port Geography* (Burlington, VT: Ashgate, 2010).

the "act" of cogitation; the main human conundrum, in turn, appearing to consist in trying to fit all experience into the aforementioned pre-existing cultural "codes." But codes, as we know from the work of at least two generations of scholars in the humanities and human social sciences, cannot be extricated from their contexts of codification.[23] Structures cannot be detached from the everyday practices in which they are interpretively enacted, nor semantic fields from the generative lived situations of their effectivity. What does that context of codification look like in the Gulf? While I have no definitive answers yet, and while different parts of the Gulf are obviously not identical to each other, it is still valuable to venture some preliminary thoughts and generalizations, if only as invitations to future, more grounded and contextually sensitive, research.

What I suggest going forward should not be read as applying transhistorically or cross-culturally across the entire Gulf region. It is meant, rather, to be taken as a provocation to conduct future research with alertness for the need to grapple with Gulf urbanism as a critical theoretical project. As I have suggested elsewhere, my strong sense is that the category of "the city" has become central in state and capitalist projects—both ideological and discursive—in the Gulf over the past fifteen to twenty years.[24] Although the Gulf has been part of global political and symbolic economies (of oil, urbanism, and knowledge) for much longer—and different parts of the Gulf earlier than others—it is really only since the 1990s that states in the region, especially the UAE and Qatar, have been making a compelling case for their "cosmopolitanism." Reinforcing this idea have been various urban and economic projects, from prestige or iconic built environments, special economic zones and other enclave developments like "knowledge villages," "education cities," and collaborations with foreign, especially US higher education; to foreign aid politics and attempts to influence regional MENA politics through other means, both diplomatic and military. We can probably add many other items to the list.

Running through and organizing much if not all of this is a central thread, "the city." The Gulf, we are constantly told, is an "urban" region. Conferences and symposia proliferate during this period and consciously or unconsciously deploy the same symbolic pattern, which I schematized above: the city is an

23 Sidney W. Mintz, *Sweetness and Power: The Place of Sugar in Modern History* (New York: Penguin, 1987).
24 Ahmed Kanna, "Speaking of the City: Establishing Urban Expertise in the Arab Gulf," *International Journal of Middle East Studies*, Vol. 46 (2014), pp. 169–71.

object of knowledge, it stands for cosmopolitanism, it is a space to whose production and on whose behalf only experts, under the aegis of a wise and generous ruler, are entitled to act and to speak; it stands against the "non-modern" MENA ("Iran, Iraq, Yemen" etc.), it is afflicted with problems lending themselves to authoritarian solutions—the "demographic imbalance," for example.

Moreover, what are we to make of the fact that such conversations tend to occur in highly controlled environments, in the seminar rooms and auditoriums of Gulf universities increasingly operating, whether officially or unofficially, under Western, particularly US, for-profit paradigms along with local structures of patron–client relations? As I have written elsewhere:

> What kind of urban knowledge object is produced in this [context]? Is it one that highlights and naturalizes, for example, consumption of global commodities as a source of well-being, or one in which rights discourses organize (and contain) the politics of labor, or one that closes off possibilities for alternative modes of urbanism, etc.? Who invokes "the city", in what contexts, and how are they acting to frame and transform reality by this? Does it matter that a region long stereotyped as "archaic" or "Bedouin" is suddenly stereotyped as hyper-urban and super-modern? What kinds of legitimacy are conferred by "urbanizing" the Gulf in this way?[25]

Political theorist Timothy Mitchell proposes a useful formulation in his justly celebrated recent book, *Carbon Democracy: Political Power in the Age of Oil*. Referring to what he calls "logics of distribution," Mitchell advocates a non-referential approach to categories such as "democracy" or "the economy." Rather than simply describing reality "out there," such categories act to carve up the world, to frame it as an object of specific kinds of intervention. The boundaries such categories deploy function to demarcate

> certain areas as matters of public concern subject to popular decision while establishing other fields to be administered under alternative methods of control. For example, governmental practice can demarcate a private sphere governed by rules of property, a natural world governed by laws of nature, or markets governed by principles of economics. Democratic struggles become a battle over the distribution of issues, attempting to establish as matters of public concern questions that others claim as private ... or ruled by the laws of the market.[26]

Applying Mitchell's insight to the examples of Gulf urbanism discourse I have been discussing here highlights the fact that the question of the urban in

---

[25] Ibid.

[26] Timothy Mitchell, *Carbon Democracy: Political Power in the Age of Oil* (New York: Verso), p. 9.

the Gulf operates as a logic of distribution, organizing political and intellectual perceptions of, interventions into, and analytical approaches to, many other issues, from modernity to labor to heritage to national, ethnic, gender, and normative urban identities, and of course, to material resources.

Toward a Critique of the Category "Urban" in the Gulf

Let me close by shifting gears and addressing another, related issue. Recent anthropological research into the so-called anthropocene, an optic that takes human ecological impacts at a global scale, suggests another fascinating implication of the semantic field approach to Gulf urbanism, and alerts us to the ways that such a semantic field can shape and limit spatial knowledges and discourses in the region. That cities are major energy consumers and carbon emitters, and that the Gulf (especially the UAE) is an astonishingly high per capita energy consumer, are well-known facts. Moreover, the idea of economic growth itself emerges in the form with which we are familiar only in the middle twentieth century, as the Arab/Persian Gulf extraction states enter the US-dominated post-war order.[27] The notion that the economy is something that has the capacity for theoretically infinite growth is obviously a contested one, and, as Mitchell has shown, these contestations themselves correlate with the rise of neoliberalism. Nevertheless, growth is both an idea that continues to underpin authoritative state discourses and governmental projects into the twenty-first century, and one that aligns well with much deeper Western Protestant assumptions about the separation between the human and the natural, assumptions that, with the rise of the US imperial project, come to inform the development agendas and governmentalities of very different cultures.[28] The category of the anthropocene seems to take particular salience in this period of "late growth" capitalism, let us call it, in which a discursive field is beginning to arrange itself around as yet inchoate alternatives to the "fuel economy" of infinite growth.[29] As anthropologist Amelia Moore puts it, the anthropocene "refers to the pervasive influence of human activities on planetary systems and biogeochemical processes. Devised by Earth scientists, the term is

---

[27] Mitchell, *Carbon Democracy*.
[28] Melissa Caldwell sheds light on Western Protestant logics of nature in her comparison to Russian cultural views of nature in *Dacha Idylls: Living Organically in Russia's Countryside* (Berkeley, CA: University of California Press, 2010).
[29] Mitchell, *Carbon Democracy*, pp. 109–43.

poised to formally end the Holocene Epoch as the geological categorization for Earth's recent past, present, and indefinite future."[30]

The Gulf region has often been described as a place where urbanism takes no account of the earth's depleting resources and the environmental damage that is caused by intensive oil consumption. Whether this is accurate or a stereotype—the truth is probably somewhere in between—it is incorrect to assume that we can extract the Gulf from analyses organized around the category of the anthropocene. Even in the early 2000s, local concerns were often voiced in the media and by my own interlocutors about what the kinds of urbanism—the high-rises, the golf courses, the land reclamation projects, the car-centric cities—meant for the environment, locally and globally. Like many North Americans, Gulf people often expressed feeling torn between the impersonal forces that have shaped the society in which they lived and their own desires for what they too called "sustainability." The discourse of sustainability, of course, is highly problematical and rather conveniently aligned with neoliberal logics. That is a topic that has been addressed by many others, and I cannot do this critical work justice here.

I would like here to raise a more discrete issue as, again, an invitation for future research. I return to Al Qassemi's argument, with which I opened this chapter, and his assertion that the Gulf city is "the nerve center of the contemporary Arab world's culture, commerce, design, architecture, art and academia, attracting hundreds of thousands of Arab immigrants, including academics, businessmen, journalists, athletes, artists, entrepreneurs and medical professionals."[31] This is a summary of what I have been calling the semantic field of the urban in the Gulf, and I would like to suggest that in establishing the conditions by which we think of the Gulf city as a city of neoliberal professionals, this field limits the ways in which the Gulf engages the question of the anthropocene. In so privileging the neoliberal professional and expert, what sorts of engagements with the anthropocene are made thinkable and what sorts are made far less likely thinkable? What productive avenues for new kinds of urbanism are anticipated, for example, by Norman Foster's Masdar (should it ever be completed)? Or the other less celebrated interventions into the problem of the anthropocene that occur in the various knowledge-production settings I have discussed here?

---

[30] Amelia Moore, "Anthropology and the Anthropocene," *Anthropology News*, Vol. 54, No. 9 (September 2013).

[31] Al Qassemi, "Gulf Cities."

Here, I cite some pertinent and incisive comments from Amelia Moore:

I would ... like to caution against potentially unhelpful uses of the Anthropocene idea. The term should not become a brand signifying a specific style of anthropological research. It should not gloss over rigid solidifications of time, space, the human, or life. We should not celebrate creativity in the Anthropocene while ignoring instances of stark social differentiation and capital accumulation, just as we should not focus on Anthropocene assemblages as only hegemonic in the oppressive sense.[32]

Does the emergence of the anthropocene as both a source of concern and knowledge production in the Gulf avoid or go beyond the temptation to brand, to which this notion, as Moore rightly warns us, is all too susceptible? Are Gulf engagements posing fresh and productive responses to the "rigid solidifications of time, space, the human, or life," as Moore puts it, or do they simply ignore stark social differentiations and promote the agendas of capital accumulation?

On the other hand, to quote Moore again, "we should be cautious with our utilization of the crisis rhetoric surrounding events in the Anthropocene, recognizing that crisis for some can be turned into multiple forms of opportunity for others."[33] Representations of the Gulf as symptomatic or symbolic of the apocalyptic *telos* of capitalism, as exemplified by Mike Davis' notion of "evil paradises" and David Harvey's comment about the "criminally absurd" urbanism of the region, should be avoided.[34] These kinds of rhetoric traffic in the kinds of arid apocalyptic "crisis" discourse identified by Moore, and to which both the anthropocene and the Gulf seem to lend themselves. We should, rather, see the Gulf as very much engaged in the anthropocene, in ways shaped by its historical legacies of empire, dynastic politics, resource extraction, and its own locally inflected versions of global and neoliberal capitalism, as well as the more impersonal factors of its geology and physical geography. We should avoid falling into the trap of employing anthropocentric discourses to exoticize the region or to impose on it a zombie capitalist logic supposedly predetermined by the past, let alone (and worse) by the putative moral character or cultural personality of its peoples.

The Gulf remains a marginalized, even unfashionable, area of research in the Western Middle East academy. In spite of—or maybe because of—this

32 Moore, "Anthropocene."
33 Ibid.
34 See note 19.

marginality, the region offers an interesting vantage point for reflecting on the production of knowledge about generally ignored questions in the wider regional literature, such as those pertaining to the related arenas of urbanism and the anthropocene. Every discipline is organized around both the legitimacy and prestige of its objects of knowledge, which in turn constitute a precondition of the given discipline's process of knowledge production. The frame of knowledge production casts into relief discourses of "the city" in Middle East, and particularly Gulf, studies over the past decade. The marginality both of the Gulf and of the question of the urban in the wider Middle East field contrasts strikingly with the emphasis on the urban in Gulf studies, and invites a number of questions: why is the urban so central in Gulf studies? How and when does it become so central? How does it organize, focus, and distribute power and resources, historiography, cultural capital, and other arenas of public concern such as the environment and the anthropocene? The question of knowledge producton also helps us wrap our heads around seemingly unwieldy and metaphysical questions: what do we mean when we use the term "city" and how does this category operate politically and intellectually? In that, grappling with knowledge production of and within Gulf cities can help us to clear away a lot of the theoretical morass around questions of urbanism in the social sciences, and opens possibilities for engaging larger questions of urbanism in the global south and beyond.

6

THE EMERGING URBAN LANDSCAPE IN THE SOUTHERN PERSIAN GULF

Ashraf M. Salama

This chapter examines the state of contemporary urban environments in the Gulf, and aims to explore the phenomenon of global flows and their impact on regional urbanism and architecture. The key characteristics of contemporary urbanism are identified through a critical analysis of three main aspects. These include the development of "bespoke" infrastructure to accommodate "global flows"; the decentralizing of urban governance and decision-making to entice investment in the urban environment; and the resulting chaotic but emotionally detached urban scene characterized by exclusive development projects, high-rise agglomerations, and social segregation. As architectural innovation is an integral component of the urban landscape of emerging cities in the Gulf, I classify contemporary endeavors into two categories: the overt and subliminal agenda to construct an iconic and cultural architectural identity, coupled with the resultant evolution of "multiple modernities" as reflected in a strikingly vibrant plurality of trends. Case examples demonstrate the rush to brand art and culture into a comprehensive and admired identity supported by a rigid agenda to encourage and sustain educational and environmental awareness. After exploring these issues, the chapter concludes with key challenges relevant to the competitive nature of various emerging cities in the Persian Gulf.

The Urban Gulf: Global Flows and Emerging Cities

Since the early 1990s, urban theorists, historians, and geographers have been taking note of the trailblazing phenomenon of globalization and its impact on consequential "global flows." These flows, which represent movements of people, capital, information, and knowledge, emerged in the last two decades and have profoundly influenced interconnectivity in singular new ways. Currently, not only are they occurring at unprecedented rates and contributing to an increased connectivity between places, cultural integration, and economic interdependence, but they are also triggering the vibrant restructuring of urban forms and cities.[1] The revolution in communication technologies and transportation prompted by the commercialization and availability of information and communication technologies has radically changed not only how users experience time, but, most significantly, has decelerated the limitations of distance. This spearheading characteristic of the globalization era is referred to as "time–space compression,"[2] which has expedited the integration of social, cultural, economic, and political processes and systems around the world, resulting in a vibrant cross-migration of what is termed "global flows."

The notion of "space of flows" was introduced by Manuel Castells, who maintains that contemporary societies are structured around flows of capital,

[1] David Held and Anthony McGrew, eds, *Governing Globalisation* (Cambridge: Polity Press, 2002); Ulf Hannerz, *Transnational Connections: Cultures, People, Places* (London: Routledge, 1996). I have addressed the notion of flows in my earlier writings within the overall context of the urban Gulf. See Ashraf M. Salama, "Identity Flows: The Arabian Peninsula, Emerging Metropolises," in Luis Fernández-Galiano, ed., *Atlas Architectures of the 21st Century: Africa and Middle East* (Madrid: Fundacion BBVA, 2011), pp. 175–221. Other scholars, however, have addressed these flows in specific contexts. Hussam Salama discussed such a notion in the context of the emirate of Dubai, while Yasser Mahgoub discussed it in the context of the city of Kuwait. See Hussam Salama, "Dubai in a World of Flows," *ArchNet-IJAR*, Vol. 7, No. 2 (2013), pp. 136–45. See also Yasser Mahgoub, "Tracing the Evolution of Urbanism in Kuwait," *Open House International*, Vol. 38, No. 4 (2013), pp. 80–89.
[2] See David Harvey, *The Condition of Postmodernity: An Inquiry into the Origins of Cultural Change* (Cambridge, MA: Blackwell, 1990).

information, technology, images, sounds, and symbols.[3] While the existence and impact of such flows can be examined and validated, his additional claim that the global city is not necessarily a place but a process has not proven true. His premise is clearly refuted in the rise of emerging globalizing cities, such as Abu Dhabi, Doha, and Dubai in the Gulf region, which are witnessing continuous urban development and rapid growth processes. In effect, the revolutionary changes in the ways in which people communicate and interact have dramatically impacted and influenced trends in urban development. While it is true that some of these changes can impact negatively on local cultures and identities, they also offer unlimited opportunities for rapid modernization and change to these developing cities through easy access to global capital and knowledge. These vibrant new and emerging urban landscapes have primarily been instigated by the constant and unceasing exposure to global flows. Cities like Abu Dhabi, Doha, Dubai, and Manama are generally referred to as "global" cities since they are exposed to more flows than cities like Jeddah, Kuwait, Muscat, or Riyadh.[4] I refer in this context to Arjun Appadurai who has labeled global cities "scapes of flows," made up of five types of flows: Ethnoscapes, Mediascapes, Financescapes, Technoscapes, and Ideascapes.[5]

When mapping these scapes of flows onto the current general profile of Gulf global cities, the key features of globalization and global flows become evident. The first scape of flows is Ethnoscapes, which are created by the need for an international workforce and the ensuing interaction of various cultures where expatriate professionals, as well as skilled technicians and skilled or unskilled laborers, may live in, work in, or visit those cities. Travellers and tourists, migrants and immigrants, and refugees and exiles are perpetually moving from one place to another, and their stay, whether short or long, invariably contributes to the shaping of urban landscapes. This cross-cultural impact is clearly

---

[3] See Manuel Castells, *The Rise of the Network Society, The Information Age: Economy, Society and Culture* (Oxford: Blackwell, 1996).

[4] See Ashraf M. Salama, "Identity Flows: The Arabian Peninsula, Emerging Metropolises," in Fernández-Galiano, ed., *Atlas Architectures of the 21st Century: Africa and Middle East*, pp. 175–221.

[5] While the earlier writings of Arjun Appadurai have introduced the "scapes of flows," discussions of these flows were elaborated and articulated in his later writings. See Arjun Appadurai, "Disjuncture and Difference in the Global Cultural Economy," *Public Culture*, Vol. 2, No. 2 (1990), pp. 1–24; and Arjun Appadurai, *Modernity at Large: Cultural Dimensions of Globalization* (Minneapolis, MN: University of Minnesota Press, 1996).

manifested both in the population profile of Gulf global cities and in the rising numbers of travellers and temporary visitors.

Mediascapes, the second scape of flows, are generated by the expanding role of media, which can be seen as a concomitant result of the information technology revolution. Media cities, the internet, and TV news channels such as Al Jazeera of Doha and Al Arabia of Dubai, are major sources of disseminating local, regional, and international news, information, and knowledge. The creation of such globally acclaimed channels and news networks are a clear manifestation of the import and role of media in these emerging globalized cities. Dubai has even developed its own "Media City" for foreign and locally-owned media corporations to compete on the global level.

The third scape of flows is Financescapes. These are landscapes created by the flow of capital and the establishment of transnational and multinational financial corporations, stock exchanges, and currency markets. The very fact that many of the regional banks, investment companies, and real estate agencies now operate branches in places such as New York, London, Paris, Rabat, and Geneva are testament to Gulf financial organizations' inroad into the world of international finance and markets. Another type of scape, Technoscapes, reflects the ongoing onslaught and impact of telecommunication technologies, emerging high-tech industries, and the establishment of free trade zones (FTZs) on contemporary urban life in many cities of the Gulf. Free trade zones such as Masdar City in Abu Dhabi and Jebel Ali free zone in Dubai offer facilities such as warehouses, factories, and offices, as well as licensing and documentation services; all provide an attractive tax-free, foreign-ownership environment with a ready pool of cheap labor for foreign investors.

The fifth scape of flows is Ideascapes. These are landscapes that have been developed from the spread of various educational ideologies and counterideologies. Education City and the Qatar Science and Technology Park in Doha, and Knowledge City in Dubai, in addition to international branch campuses of well-known universities in Abu Dhabi, Doha, Dubai, and Manama, are clear examples of the transformative power and influence of Ideascapes. Every Gulf country now boasts foreign branch campuses of prestigious universities: the Sorbonne in Abu Dhabi, London Business School and Middlesex University in Dubai, and Weill-Cornell, Georgetown University School of Foreign Service in Qatar, and Texas A&M in Doha are just a few of the myriad universities now offering undergraduate and graduate degrees in the region. By and large, these "scapes" are important influences in the shaping of new and far-reaching social and professional practices and major impacts on the resulting spatial environments that accommodate them. They articulate and accentuate the pivotal role that global flows play in shaping contemporary development processes and trends.

The notion of flows as delineated by Castells and Appadurai has resulted in a new international discourse about the global knowledge economy.[6] This type of economy is characterized by three components: international services and banking institutions, high-tech industries, and knowledge-creating institutions, such as universities and research establishments. Such an economy has been identified as one of the key drivers for spatial development processes. It is frequently argued that the rapidly evolving global knowledge economy is continuously both reshaping spatial development and directly impacting on the urban environment in a wide variety of ways.[7] In the context of the global knowledge economy, some of these newly emerging cities around the world have been actively challenging established networks; indeed, influential cities in the Arabian Peninsula and the Persian Gulf coast have gained a new geostrategic importance.[8]

---

[6] Discourse about knowledge economies as a worldwide phenomenon can be seen in recent writing in several contexts. In the context of Europe, see Alain Thierstein, Stefan Lüthi, et al., "Changing Value Chain of the Knowledge Economy: Spatial impact of intra-firm and inter-firm networks within the emerging mega-city region of northern Switzerland," *Regional Studies*, Vol. 42, no. 8 (2008), pp. 1113–31. In the context of the Gulf, see Alain Thierstein and Elisabeth Schein, "Emerging Cities on the Arabian Peninsula: Urban Space in the Knowledge Economy Context," *ArchNet-IJAR*, Vol. 2, No. 2 (2008), pp. 178–95.

[7] Ibid.

[8] The research findings of Globalization and World Cities—GaWC Research Network at Loughborough University—demonstrate how Gulf cities are gaining international attention. A longitudinal study in 2000 and 2010 was conducted on world city networks showing that the global urban hierarchy is pioneered by a small group of cities, namely London, New York, Hong Kong, Tokyo, and Paris, that are well connected to each other. Published in 2000 the first ranking of Gulf cities shows seven emerging cities from the Gulf, with Dubai as the most connected city globally and regionally. Classified from the highest to the lowest rank, the cities are Dubai (UAE), Manama (Bahrain), Jeddah (Saudi Arabia), Riyadh (Saudi Arabia), Abu Dhabi (UAE), Kuwait (Kuwait), and Doha (Qatar). In 2008, however, minor changes appear when Muscat, the capital city of the Sultanate of Oman, enters the total ranking, while Doha raises its position within the Gulf city ranking from the last position to the 5th position in 2010. See Globalization and World Cities—GaWC, Loughborough University, 2009, http://www.lboro.ac.uk/gawc/, last accessed 26 May 2016. Recent studies have offered interpretations of these rankings. See Ben

Gulf cities such as Abu Dhabi, Doha, and Dubai have developed into central hubs for air traffic, cargo-shipping, leisure pursuits, and business and financial centers in geographical locations right in-between developed Western nations and the rising economies of Asia.[9] As a consequence, the import and impact of a number of cities and urban spaces in the Gulf in global knowledge economy networks have grown rapidly. This has resulted in development projects designed to accommodate and represent these new economies, giving form and meaning to their significance and a new position on the world stage. Accordingly, architecture and urbanism in the region continue to be viewed as a crucial catalyst for cities to sustain their position in the milieu of a global knowledge economy. Dubai has come to set the stage as an exemplar of a global city, and, in their desire to supersede Dubai's international appeal, other Gulf cities have been inspired to challenge and compete through their architecture and urban environment. This has resulted in the construction of iconic new "cities with cities," such as the Pearl in Qatar or Palm Island in Dubai, and large-scale urban regeneration projects like Msheireb Downtown Doha or Al Bastakia Dubai. Many other such new projects throughout the region are now in their final completion phases.

Key Characteristics of Gulf Urbanism

The predicted decline in the oil and natural gas reserves coupled with a worldwide reduction in energy sources from oil and natural gas suggest grave concern to Gulf governments. The trend toward using alternative energy sources such as hydroelectricity, wind energy, and solar energy is having profound repercussions on the economies and societies of most Gulf countries, which are still highly dependent on the export of fossil fuels and their by-products. In consequence, concerned and concerted reactions to global flows in the form of economic diversification have become an integral component of most

Derudder, Peter Taylor, et al., "Pathways of Change: Shifting Connectivities in the World City Network, 2000–08," *Urban Studies*, Vol. 47, No. 9 (2010), pp. 1861–77; and Ashraf M. Salama and Alain Thierstein, *Final Research Report: Investigating the Qualities of the Urban Environment in Emerging Regional Metropolises: The Case of Doha* (Doha: Qatar National Research Fund, 2014).

[9] See Elisabeth Schein, *Built on Sand? Emerging Cities on the Arabian Peninsula in the Knowledge Economy Context*, doctoral dissertation supervised by Alain Thierstein and Ashraf M. Salama, Technical University of Munich, 2009.

national development strategies.[10] Although efforts to build an economy independent of oil had already begun in the 1970s, major steps toward developing alternative economy service hubs have only been carried out in the last decade. Due to their limited oil resources, Bahrain and Dubai began investing in their future some years earlier than other Gulf countries, whose abundance of natural resources reduced the pressure to develop and encourage economic diversification.[11] However, since the beginning of the new millennium, all GCC countries are actively involved in promoting and developing oil and gas-independent economies, particularly in sectors such as trade, finance, banking, and tourism. The most important and most visible catalyst of recent urban developments has been the liberalization of regulations governing local real estate markets, as well as major public investments in large-scale projects that have initiated and sustained the recent surge in construction activities and infrastructure development. These latest developments are clear evidence of specific emerging qualities or attributes unique to the urban environment in cities characterized by emerging knowledge economies.[12]

Accommodating Global Flows

Astute regional rulers recognize and exploit the vast potential and extensive opportunities to develop their major cities further into viable and expansive trading hubs for commerce between Asia, Europe, and Africa. All along the Gulf coast, a number of deep water harbors have been built in order to increase import, export, and transit capacities for global trade. Additionally, existing international airports have been expanded and iconic new airports launched in order to enlarge and bolster air cargo services and to accommodate increasing passenger traffic in these transit hubs. The focus on trade as an essential part of a future economy has rapidly accelerated as a result of the introduction of free trade zones in the Gulf by the emirates of Dubai and Abu Dhabi.

[10] See Ashraf M. Salama and Florian Wiedmann, *Demystifying Doha: On Architecture and Urbanism in an Emerging City* (Farnham, Surrey: Ashgate, 2013); and Florian Wiedmann, Ashraf M. Salama, and Alain Thierstein, "Urban Evolution of the City of Doha: An Investigation into the Impact of Economic Transformations on Urban Structures," *JFA/METU Journal of the Faculty of Architecture*, Vol. 29, No. 2 (2012), pp. 35–61.

[11] Florian Wiedmann, *Post-oil Urbanism in the Gulf: Case Study: Kingdom of Bahrain*, doctoral dissertation supervised by Eckhart Ribbeck, Stuttgart University, 2010.

[12] Florian Wiedmann, *Post-oil Urbanism in the Gulf: New Evolutions in Governance and the Impact on Urban Morphologies* (Stuttgart: SVH Verlag, 2012).

In 1985, the first FTZ was established in Jebel Ali, which was then far beyond the outskirts of Dubai. This novel development attracted the attention of many local and international companies due to its minimal or no taxation policies and its modern, sophisticated infrastructure. Additionally, reduced bureaucratic requirements and less restrictive labor legislation have garnered the interest of international financiers and have encouraged them to establish profitable businesses in Dubai, neighboring Abu Dhabi, and, most recently, Ras Al Khaimah. Similarly, over the following decade, other FTZs were founded in the state of Kuwait, the kingdom of Bahrain, and, most particularly, in other emirates such as Ras Al Khaimah and Ajman in the UAE. The size of these FTZs, which are usually located near airports or harbors, varies from single port facilities as in Manama, or airports such as Sharjah International Airport, to large industrial areas such as Jebel Ali in Dubai.[13] Such developments and investment projects that promote the idea of a "service hub" can be regarded as important strategic actions to accommodate global flows. For example, the emirate of Dubai—no more than a sleepy backwater fishing and pearling harbor fifty years ago—has now become the most important financial center of the United Arab Emirates, gaining in recent years both regional and global attention and major investments. It stands out amongst its neighbors as the fastest growing and most attractive investment hub in the Middle East, despite its difficulties during the short-lived but disastrous world economic crisis of 2008.

Over the past decade, tourism has also played a major role in the economies of Oman and the other smaller Gulf countries of Qatar and the kingdom of Bahrain. Since the 1990s, the emirate of Dubai has been busy reinventing and developing itself into an international and sophisticated tourist destination, offering world-class hotels and entertainment venues, pristine beaches, and sophisticated, branded shopping facilities. In addition to attracting international tourists from North America and Eastern and Western Europe, Dubai has also established itself as a major tourist destination for regional tourism where travellers from neighboring countries regularly visit the city for short or prolonged holidays. The high number of visitors from the region can be partially attributed to certain social restrictions and a general lack of entertainment and leisure facilities in countries such as the kingdom of Saudi Arabia and Iran. In addition, the physical attraction of Dubai Creek, its extensive and exclusive malls with shops to rival those in London and Paris, and its

---

[13] Ibid.

dedicated preservation of authentic heritage buildings are big drawing cards for regional visitors. Huge numbers of international hotels, large themed shopping malls, dedicated sport and entertainment venues for international events, and themed amusement parks have sprung up to meet this growing regional demand.

Following Dubai's example, other Gulf cities have started imitating this successful income diversification strategy. This has had a direct impact on attracting major investments from the private sector and international promoters. Sport events such as Formula 1 in Bahrain and the 2006 Asian Games in Doha have marked an exciting new stage and focus in terms of providing iconic and architecturally novel venues for quality art exhibitions, theatrical events, and entertainment, recreational, and leisure centers which have subsequently attracted both regional and global attention and patronage. More recently, there have been major investments designed to create and forge a sustainable and identifiable local cultural identity and fabric, primarily by revitalizing old city center cores and establishing internationally acclaimed museums and art centers. These developments and projects have helped turn Gulf cities into promising international cultural destinations. This is clearly evident in the construction of new signature museums such as the Museum of Islamic Art in Doha, and branches of the Louvre and Guggenheim Museum on Saadiyat Island in Abu Dhabi.[14]

Decentralizing Urban Governance

The contemporary urban landscape in the Gulf is currently characterized by a new generation of dynamic desert and coastal cities supplied with expansive and costly state-of-the-art infrastructure, as evidenced by the growing number of extensive multi-lane highways and freeways, elaborate flyovers, massive deep-water ports, iconic airports, and cutting-edge metro and railway projects. These are partially designed to attract global investment and the highly skilled expatriate residents who will help transform these newly built shells into vibrant and desirable urban hubs. Importantly, it should be noted that urban governance in Gulf cities has been the initiator and enabler of space for evolving such vigorous economic interaction, as, for example, recent public investment in the development of infrastructure and the promotion of attractive marketing strategies and perks to garner international attention. This concerted campaign has resulted in the cities themselves becoming brands for

[14] Salama, "Identity Flows."

investment; today's regional rulers have found themselves in the role of CEOs managing urban development as a "business idea."[15] However, the majority of transnational corporations which initially relocated to the Gulf in connection with the execution of these "business ideas" have mostly been investment banks and construction industries.

In the region, a so-called "temporary society" with an ever-changing and exchanging population of migrant workers and expatriate professionals has emerged. This constant movement of residents, workers, and visitors has significantly impacted on Gulf cities over the past two decades. Consequently, policymakers and planners, with the full support of Gulf rulers, have had to plan and devise viable development strategies for entire cities with the aim of fostering urban consolidation and cohesion. In order to develop new economic strategies, various independent authorities have been created, including organizations such as the EDB (Economic Development Board) in Bahrain, the DED (Department of Economic Development) in Dubai, and, more recently, the GSDP (General Secretariat for Development Planning) in Qatar.[16] As a result, these changing development goals have led to a new form of urbanism and a new globalized cultural and investment role for cities in the Gulf.

While rapid modernization and the development of major infrastructure through public investments were given priority during the prosperous period of oil production in the 1980s, 1990s, and early 2000s, in vivid contrast the past decade of the twenty-first century has been dominated by the growing impact of private investments and semi-public authorities in urban development. This concerted effort to attract more investors, both foreign and domestic, has led to a new phase of investor-driven urbanism in the Gulf, resulting in the creation of major real estate holding corporations and development agencies. The interest of the private sector in investing in the building of cities in the region has been particularly influenced by changing investment conditions in the West, and expectations of high future revenues in GCC countries as important centers for emerging and up-and-coming global markets. Regional investors in particular have recently started to invest in local projects instead of focusing their investment interests abroad.[17] The result has been a dramatic shift in, and impact on, urban development.

---

[15] Mike Davis, "Sand, Fear and Money in Dubai," in Mike Davis and Daniel Bertrand Monk, eds, *Evil Paradises: Dreamworlds of Neoliberalism* (New York: New Press, 2008), pp. 49–67.

[16] Salama and Wiedmann, *Demystifying Doha.*

[17] Wiedmann, *Post-oil Urbanism in the Gulf.*

Major development companies have also started to operate as managers of large-scale developments and blueprints in the form of new housing districts, business parks, and mixed-use projects, which is a clear indication of the growing role of the private sector in urban development. One interesting development is the fact that the public sector has now taken over the government's former function of organizing and developing the infrastructural supply of these projects. Nonetheless, all decisions related to the major planning of developments and the distribution of land remain in the hands of regional rulers and their top officials, many of whom are or have become direct or indirect associates and sponsors of these developments.[18] While planning authorities still remain in control at the helm, real estate developers have far fewer restrictions than in the past; they now have more freedom and increasing opportunities to design and implement project development master plans individually. This new decentralized form of urban governance, based on case-by-case decision-making, has led to new dynamics in urban developments and rapid growth on the one hand, and an increasing lack of infrastructural consolidation on the other. In essence, for most cities in the Persian Gulf, the decentralization of governance and the liberalization and opening up of markets driven by a global hub agenda, in combination with large-scale public investments, have resulted in, and heavily impacted on, a radical new and dynamic urban transformation process.

Between Exclusive Developments and Social Segregation

The effects of some of the new planning strategies that have resulted from various responses to adapt to global flows are clearly visible in the urban scene of most Gulf cities. One of the far-reaching effects of decentralizing urban governance and decision-making has been the emergence of a new urban project phenomenon, known as "cities within the city," or CiC, which can be observed in all major cities in the Gulf.[19] While such cities are usually client-

---

[18] Mohammad al-Asad, *Contemporary Architecture and Urbanism in the Middle East* (Gainesville, FL: University Press of Florida, 2012).

[19] The phenomenon of projects known as "cities within the city" (CiC projects) can be observed in many cities around the world. It can be attributed to the diminishing ability of public authorities to deliver efficient urban environments or to renew existing fragmented urban fabric. However, I would argue that it is primarily attributable to privatization and decentralization within urban governance, which took place since the end of the twentieth century in many countries. This argument can

particular due to their large-scale developments, spatial quality, iconic design, exclusivity, and the fact that they stem from public–private partnerships; unfortunately, these new cluster developments in actuality have a negative impact on urban growth. This is due to the fact that their very exclusivity generates disengaged urban fragmentation which in turn promotes social segregation (as discussed in Chapter 4 of this volume). In the past fifteen years, the oil-impoverished emirate of Dubai has been pioneering such types of exclusive development, beginning with its early initiative in 1999 to intro-duce freehold property rights for its first large-scale project, "Emirates Hills," in the northern suburb of Jumeirah. The project was developed by the newly founded real estate company Emaar, 33 per cent of whose shares are actually owned by the government of Dubai.[20] In the following decade, a number of new real estate development companies were established, many of which are subsidiaries of public holdings, in order to initiate iconic and unprecedentedly ambitious urban development projects. One such example, the private island and holiday destination project "World Islands," launched in 2009, is an archi-pelago consisting of man-made islands resembling a map of the world. After several years of inactivity, the luxury property project is now being revived and construction work has already begun on the Heart of Europe island project.

In vigorous competition with Dubai, other Gulf cities have introduced similar urban growth strategies encouraged by policies liberalizing markets and the establishment of real estate development companies with public shares. Despite the fact that several luxury construction projects launched in Dubai have not yet been sold (Figure 6.1), this has not deterred property developers from launching comparable projects in cities such as Doha and Abu Dhabi in terms of branding and scale. Today, three main types of CiC

---

be supported when looking at several studies relevant to contemporary urbanism and the specific role of the private sector and its large-scale developments. In this respect, Michael J. Dear has analyzed recent liberalization tendencies in urban gov-ernance which had a significant impact on understanding cities as branded corpo-rate entities. See Michael J. Dear, *The Postmodern Urban Condition* (New York: Wiley, 2001). Other authors, such as Nan Ellin and Jason Hackworth, have traced the phenomenon of "cities within the city," its roots and its various causes. See Nan Ellin, *Postmodern Urbanism* (Princeton, NJ: Princeton Architectural Press, 1999); and Jason Hackworth, *The Neoliberal City: Governance, Ideology, and Development in American Urbanism* (New York: Cornell University Press, 2006).

20 Christopher Davidson, *Dubai: The Vulnerability of Success* (New York: Columbia University Press, 2008).

6.1: Sheikh Zayed Road in Dubai
Source: Salama and Wiedmann, *Demystifying Doha*.

projects can be identified: mixed-use projects, tourism projects, and FEZ projects. While mixed-use CiC projects integrate commercial facilities in the form of retail districts and malls, tourism projects typically provide areas for resorts, marinas, theme parks, and promenades. A very recent phenomenon is the newly established satellite cities that usually consist of several CiC projects. While tourism projects are mainly located at waterfronts, where they are often developed on reclaimed land or man-made islands, FEZ projects are typically located at the junctions of main infrastructural networks. One of the most significant characteristics of these development types is their planning process, which is usually carried out independently from general master planning strategies adopted and approved by local authorities and the public sector. Consequently, despite the reliance on public infrastructure, many projects developed by major real estate companies actually formulate their own building and planning controls and guidelines. This laissez-faire approach has resulted in unprecedentedly rapid and sometimes shoddy urban and suburban growth. Additionally, the overall consolidation of new and existing urban structures has become a major challenge for contemporary urban planning in most Gulf cities.

The new development strategies formulated and endorsed by Gulf states have had a significant impact on both urban structure and architectural development. The decentralization of planning decision-making has led to the increasing influence of private and semi-public developers and wealthy property tycoons. These have initiated master-plan projects in the form of exclusive man-made islands, attractive but isolated new suburban districts, and mixed-use cities and residential enclaves within the primary city, such as Palm Island in Dubai or Pearl Qatar. While newly initiated master-developers launched impressive and eye-catching large-scale development projects, high-rise agglomerations were also being built along the urban periphery. These peripheral projects have resulted in new purpose-designed business districts, as ancillary support hubs, emerging along main growth corridors, like Sheikh Zayed Road in Dubai, West Bay in Doha, or King Faisal Highway in Manama.[21] Due to disinterested laissez-faire policies, areas previously designated as low-rise, low-density residential districts were subjected to unbridled development and are now frequently characterized by disparate clusters of mixed-use residential and commercial high-rises often populated by unattractive, closely packed tower blocks. This energetic construction activity has been fueled by the exponential need for housing and commercial establishments due to the rapid influx of migrant labor and expatriate workers as well as investment pressures. In addition to high-rise clusters and master-plan development projects, urban sprawl in the form of low-rise housing projects has continued at the periphery of major cities. In spite of concerted efforts to revitalize old or historical center cores, the focus of the development has primarily been on the urban periphery due to lower land prices and higher accessibility, and along waterfronts dramatically expanded by land reclamation.[22]

Another important characteristic of urbanism in most Gulf cities is the presence of certain segregation patterns due to new real estate typologies and the extensive inflow of a medium- to high-income expatriate workforce and their families.[23] The residences of higher-income expatriate groups were initially

---

[21] Salama and Wiedmann, *Demystifying Doha*.

[22] Wiedmann, Salama, and Thierstein, "Urban Evolution of the City of Doha."

[23] For an expanded discussion on segregation aspects, migrant communities in the Gulf, and the qualities of the environment in which they live, see Andrew Gardner, "Why Do They Keep Coming? Labor Migrants in the Gulf States," in Mehran

located on the fringes of the historic center cores, where the first compounds were usually built as gated communities, and thus, as a rule, maintained the existent segregation patterns preferred by Gulf citizens. However, the recent surge in construction activities has given rise to new locations for this type of housing on the peripheries of cities where established local communities and neighborhoods already exist. In addition to compounds geared toward well-paid expatriates, a new residential typology—the service apartment and apartment hotels—has emerged. Such high-rental apartments are generally located in residential high-rises and tower blocks built on key sites within cities, often close to business areas or service locations.

The city of Doha clearly exemplifies this growing phenomenon where, immediately, certain segregation patterns are revealed. For instance, in order to prevent overcrowding in Doha's central areas and residential neighborhoods as well as to maintain prevalent segregation patterns, low-income groups and laborers are often housed in insalubrious areas located on the southern periphery of the city. One such locale is the industrial area where low rentals encourage employers and sponsors to house their technical staff and laborers in cheap accommodation. These inadequate, crowded, and substandard accommodations have recently attracted international scrutiny and negative commentary. The lack of affordable accommodation for this employee sector is a growing problem which some property companies have tried to address.[24] While such initiatives are an attempt to provide appropriate and affordable housing for laborers and low-wage earners, the peripheral location of such housing reinforces extant residential segregation patterns.[25] As such, these prevailing patterns of segregation have resulted in "island" communities of expatriate workers that only serve to increase residential fragmentation. In effect, accommodation segregation is practiced deliberately in order to maintain the status quo by reserving housing areas for certain groups of the popula-

---

Kamrava and Zahra Babar, eds, *Migrant Labor in the Persian Gulf* (New York: Columbia University Press, 2012), pp. 41–58.

[24] For example, in order to increase the capacity of labor housing for low-income classes, Barwa, a major real estate player, in cooperation with the public sector, has launched a 1.8 square kilometer low-income housing development known as Barwa Al Baraha. It is currently expected that around 50,000 laborers will be housed in this worker community in Doha's industrial zone.

[25] Ashraf M. Salama, "Navigating Housing Affordability Between Transdisciplinarity and Lifestyle Theories," *ArchNet-IJAR*, Vol. 1, No. 2 (2007), pp. 57–76.

tion. This segregation is partially based on exorbitant property prices, as well as a keen desire to keep neighborhoods that are primarily populated by local citizens as separate as possible.

On the other hand, while high-income groups mainly reside on the north and west peripheries of the city, low- to medium-income groups generally live in marginalized shabby or derelict housing in congested city core neighborhoods or, as mentioned above, in substandard and often appalling accommodation in peripheral industrial areas to the south.[26] Furthermore, as the local population is only a small minority of the total population (approximately 15 per cent), there is no coherent majority within Doha's society apart from the extremely diverse groups of expatriates. The most well represented groups of expatriates are South Asians from India, Pakistan, and Bangladesh. But constantly, segregation patterns between nationals and expatriates are zealously maintained. Furthermore, constraints to developing a less anonymous and more integrated society are also reinforced by the continuous labor movement patterns and exchange of most of the expatriate workforce.[27]

As a result of the desire of the decision-makers to maintain the existing status quo, possibly due to the morbid fear of "cultural contamination" and negative influence, little effort has been made to develop more integrated environments and public realms as platforms for an emerging society. Nevertheless, there is some, very limited, mixing in the cultural venues and shopping malls which are the most frequently used leisure and entertainment spaces for higher-income groups; low-income groups, however, usually shop and stay close to their residences, a clear indication of social and income demarcation which extends beyond residential patterns. This shopping pattern is partly due to unavailability of public transport, as most low-income workers depend on the inadequate and infrequent bus service provided by Karwa, the sole public transportation company in Qatar. Most bus routes require two or three transfers, a further discouragement to venturing too far away from the familiarity of home. Of course, many of these low-paid workers can rarely hire taxis, which are expensive and hard to find. In view of these exclusionary residential policies and practices, it can be seen that the contemporary society and social fabric of Doha is built on a plurality of parallel socie-

---

[26] Sharon Nagy, "Making Room for Migrants, Making Sense of Difference: Spatial and Ideological Expression of Social Diversity in Urban Qatar," *Urban Studies*, Vol. 43 (2006), pp. 119–37.

[27] Salama and Wiedmann, *Demystifying Doha*.

ties living in various segregated environments in very different living conditions and standards. It should also be noted that the spatial context of such social segregation remains typical in the whole of the Gulf, as can be witnessed by housing development patterns in other countries in the region: for example, similar patterns of segregation, in various forms, can be readily found in Abu Dhabi, Sharjah, Dammam, and Manama.

Identity Crises and Multiple Modernities

At the dawn of the new millennium, regional rulers, decision-makers, and top government officials started to take a keener and more attentive interest in historic buildings, architecture, development projects, and real estate investment. This focused interest and attention has resulted in a new, highly influential phase firmly impacting on the development of architecture in the Gulf cities. With such a vested interest and high investment in property, many cities in the Gulf are currently experiencing rapid growth coupled with fast-track urbanization processes. This growth spurt is marked by large-scale projects, new educational and residential environments, and a wide variety of mixed-use developments. New large-scale interventions are on the rise, from Abu Dhabi's Saadiyat Island Development to Bahrain's Financial Harbor, and from Kuwait's City of Silk to Qatar's Lusail, City of the Future. Moreover, the engagement of prominent internationally acclaimed architects and the often marginal participation and input of local architects have heavily impacted on the design focus, image, and urban development of most Gulf cities. As a result, contemporary architecture in the Gulf has thus developed as an extraneous architecture detached from the region's traditional roots, which follows Western postmodernist trends. Recent attempts to integrate traditional forms and images in various cultural and architectural contexts to create a more visual and visceral connection to the local culture have resulted in a somewhat half-hearted struggle to both foster and retain cultural identity amongst Gulf citizens. As such, architecture itself has now become a major factor in marketing and labeling Gulf cities as future global hubs reacting to global flows. This sort of judgmental labeling has subsequently led to experiencing cities that house this type of architecture as vacuous "no-places."[28] This is particularly the case regarding the

---

[28] The notion of "no-places" has been articulated by Edward Relph in 1993 and Juhani Pallasmaa in 2008. Relph introduced the concept of "existential outsideness," which involves conscious un-involvement, an alienation from people and places, a sense

6.2: Saadiyat Island Development
Source: http://saadiyatculturaldistrict.ae/en/saadiyat-cultural-district/saadiyat-island/, 2013.

construction of superlative and soaring iconic landmarks, such as the Burj Khalifa in Dubai and the Burj Qatar in Doha, among others. Thus, the goal of urban design and architecture has changed focus and is now moving in a new direction of fostering international recognition to attract highly-skilled workers, well-heeled residents, and affluent local, regional, and foreign investors as well as sophisticated tourists, rather than making an effort to reconnect to traditional and cultural values mandated by contextual requirements.

Struggling for Constructing Identity

The narrative of expressing cultural identity through architecture and urban form has been typically represented on the map of architectural and urban

of unreality in the world. Pallasmaa elaborated on the concept as it relates to the architecture of place, and introduced "existential homelessness" with reference to mobility and travel. See Edward Relph, "Modernity and the Reclamation of Place," in David Seamon, ed., *Dwelling, Seeing, and Designing: Toward a Phenomenological Ecology* (Albany, NY: SUNY Press, 1993), pp. 25–40. See also Juhani Pallasmaa, "Existential Homelessness: Placelessness and Nostalgia in the Age of Mobility," in Sigurd Bergmann and Tore Sager, eds, *The Ethics of Mobility: Rethinking Place, Exclusion, Freedom and Environment* (Farnham, Surrey: Ashgate, 2008), pp. 143–56.

discourse, not only in the Gulf region but also throughout the Arab world. Examination of the notion of identity in contemporary literature reveals divergent interpretations; for example, while some theorists see the quest for identity as a human need,[29] others regard it as a process of constructing meaning on the basis of giving priority to a set of cultural attributes over other sources of meaning.[30] However, in architecture, identity can be further envisioned as the collective aspect of a set of characteristics by which a building or a portion of the urban environment is definitively recognizable.[31]

Issues that pertain to identity and character in Gulf architecture have been the topic of fervent debate for the past few decades, the more so because of this region's contradictory state of both cultural exclusivity and plurality. However, it is this very cultural uniqueness that has made the debate a tough pursuit and has, in many cases, culminated in a type of overt and occasionally crass symbolism that is painful to comprehend. Some critics question the seeming necessity to use cultural or religious symbolism in architecture to reflect or maintain a specific identity, while others argue that Gulf architecture should embody the collective aspirations of societies in this region. Still others query the seeming need to debate architectural identity at all, claiming that such debates merely display a lack of "self-confidence" as a region or as a group of nations. In effect, the ongoing debates in the contemporary architectural scene show that we still seem to be at odds with the issue of identity.[32] Charles Correa defines identity as a process, not a found object, and not a self-conscious process. He posits that our search for identity could give us a much greater sensitivity not only to our environment, but also to ourselves and to the society in which we live.[33] Hall similarly argues that "cul-

---

[29] Yuswadi Saliya, "Notes on the Architectural Identity in the Cultural Context," *MIMAR* 19: Architecture in Development (1986), pp. 32–3.

[30] Manuel Castells, "The Relationship between Globalization and Cultural Identity in the early 21st Century" (Barcelona: Forum 2004), http://www.barcelona2004. org/www.barcelona2004.org/eng/banco_del_conocimiento/documentos/ficha-faec.html?IdDoc=1628, last accessed 26 May 2016.

[31] See Ashraf M. Salama, "Architectural Identity in the Middle East: Hidden Assumptions and Philosophical Perspectives," in D. Mazzoleni et al., eds, *Shores of the Mediterranean: Architecture as Language of Peace* (Napoli: Intra Moenia, 2005), pp. 77–85; and Ashraf M. Salama, "Doha: Between Making an Instant City and Skirmishing Globalization," *Middle East Institute—Viewpoints* (Washington, DC: American University, 2008), pp. 40–44.

[32] Salama, "Architectural Identity in the Middle East."

[33] Charles Correa, "Quest for Identity," in Robert Powell, ed., *Architecture and Identity*

tural identity is a matter of 'becoming' as well as of 'being' and it belongs to the future as much as to the past."[34] Two polar qualities in Hall's position reflect a more in-depth understanding of identity. One relates to similarity and continuity, while the other recounts difference and rupture.[35] In actuality, contemporary architecture in the Gulf vividly exemplifies this contrasting yet somehow complementary duality. In essence, identity can be represented by three cogent underlying characteristics: a) the permanence over time of a subject unaffected by environmental changes below a certain threshold level, b) the notion of unity, which establishes the limits of a subject and enables us to distinguish it from the others, and c) a relationship between two elements, which enables us to recognize them as identical. Together these characteristics suggest permanence, recognition and distinction, and determine the presence of identity in a physical object, a work of architecture, or a portion of a built environment.

In attempting to construct architectural identity in the Gulf, it should be noted that identities can be invented and endorsed, in some cases, by the various, cultural, social, and political institutions that decision-makers impose and decree, which are often self-indulgent schemes and realizations of key personal preferences. In other instances, identities are created by property developers whose main interest is based on economic concerns, market logic, and market demands rather than social needs or environmental concerns. Within this tightly controlled context, some architects are in continual conflict, constantly criticizing and evaluating their own versions of modern and postmodern architecture against prevailing contemporary practices and discourse. This may suggest and promote the recycling of traditional architecture and its elements as a way of establishing and imposing a more meaningful character in the contemporary city.[36] One such approach is the refurbishing of representa-

---

(Singapore: Concept Media/The Aga Khan Award for Architecture, 1983), pp. 10–13.

[34] Stewart Hall, "Cultural Identity and Diaspora," in R. Rutherford, ed., *Identity: Community, Culture, Difference* (London: Lawrence & Wishart, 1990), pp. 223–37.

[35] See Yasser Mahgoub, "Architecture and the Expression of Cultural Identity in Kuwait," *Journal of Architecture*, Vol. 12, No. 2 (2007), pp. 165–82.

[36] More recently Ashraf Salama addressed the dimension of geocultural politics as part of the discussion on the struggle for constructing architectural identity. See Ashraf M Salama, "Architectural Identity Demystified: Visual Voices from the Arab World," in Paul Emmons, Jane Lomholt, and John Hendrix, eds, *The Cultural Role*

tive structures such as old palaces, public buildings, and traditional settlements, or involvement in conservation projects like the old Bastakia quarter in Dubai or innovative reconstruction efforts like those carried out in Souq Waqif in Doha.

Another approach is to establish cultural visual references borrowed from the past, either real or imagined, and to utilize these in contemporary buildings. Historical architectural revivalism is one of the paradigms that characterize such schemes. With a view to constructing a recognizable architectural identity, some architects adopt and adapt a selection of historic features derived from Arabic and Islamic heritage. They believe that simulating or even fabricating history in contemporary buildings can help establish a sense of belonging and forge strong emotional ties between society, place memory, and contemporary interventions. Mina Al Salam at Jumeirah Beach in Dubai and the Barzan Tower in Doha are just two structures that manifest this composite approach, further examples of which can be found in many other Gulf cities. Underpinning these two approaches in order to boast and boost the profile of their capital cities, Gulf rulers, governments, and officials typically adopt projects promoting traditional imaging to impress local society with a carefully contrived reconstruction and reimagining of their origins and traditions.[37]

Addressing and visually representing tradition and modernity is another paradigm that requires international architects to construct architectural identity as they or their clients conceive it. Tradition in this respect can be seen either as an internal action or as a reaction to external forces. In essence, the result of the interaction between internal influences and external forces creates and fosters a perceived, if not necessarily authentic, identity. While the discourse continues on the dialectic relationships between tradition and modernity, the contemporary and the historic, and the global and the local, a number of important projects either recently built or currently under construction exemplify the acknowledgement, presence, and incorporation of such multiple identities.

---

of Architecture: Contemporary and Historical Perspectives (London: Routledge, 2012), pp. 175–84.

[37] Scholars argue that as many nations are resorting to heritage preservation, the reinvention of tradition, the rewriting of history as forms of self-definition, and the questioning of the role of tradition and heritage in the shaping of architectural identity have become a necessity. See Nezar Al Sayyad, ed., *Consuming Tradition, Manufacturing Heritage* (London: Routledge, 2001).

6.3: Examples of conservation and reconstruction projects: Souq Waqif, Doha (top);
Al Bastakia, Dubai (bottom)

Source: Salama and Wiedmann, *Demystifying Doha*.

6.4: Examples of integrating traditional elements in new projects: Mina Al Salam at Jumeirah Beach, Dubai
Source: Salama, "Architectural Identity Demystified".

One such building is the satellite engineering college branch of Texas A&M University at Qatar, established under the aegis of Hamad bin Khalifa University, in Education City in Doha. In his monolithic and visually stunning structure, architect Ricardo Legoretta's striking application and adaptation of pre-Colombian and post-Colombian Mexican architecture dramatically represents this wider global context. Legoretta uses traditional Mexican architectural elements in his work, including earth tones, plays of light and shadow, and features such as central patios, courtyards, and porticos, as well as massive solid volumes. The design concept is based on two independent but adjoining masses linked by a wide, spacious atrium: the Academic Quadrangle and the Research Building. The overall expression of the building demonstrates a masterful integration of solid geometry with a skillful use of color and tone values, resulting in a visually pleasing conceptual dialogue between tradition and modernity. Such a dialogue is also evident in his latest intervention, the Hamad bin Khalifa University Student Center, a striking building that acts as a catalyst for a vibrant and welcoming environ-

143

6.5: Texas A&M Engineering College (top) and Student Center (bottom), Education City, Doha, by Ricardo Legoretta

Source: Salama and Wiedmann, *Demystifying Doha.*

ment, with a cinema, bookshop, art gallery, gymnasium, black-box theater, and even a crèche and nursery. Such user-friendly accoutrements are likely to foster dynamic social and cultural interaction.

In the Central Market in Abu Dhabi, world-renowned architect Norman Foster has offered another type of dialogue between tradition and modernity, with a different expression and purpose, and for a different kind of clientele. The project has replaced the traditional souk, or market, on one of the oldest mercantile sites in the city, substituting low-rise retail centers with roof gardens to form a new public park with three tower blocks for offices and residences. In a bold attempt to avoid the feel of a universally generic shopping experience, the functional design blends local vernacular with contemporary global aspirations. Despite these design innovations, the place has a rather desolate atmosphere, in stark contrast to the once vital and popular marketplace that previously occupied the space. Inevitably, the project raises questions around the justification for a reinterpretation of local vernacular that has so unequivocally replaced a bustling and thriving traditional marketplace with a new, less user-friendly commercial environment that targets the elite and the affluent and thus excludes a major segment of Abu Dhabi's populace—the very people who used to frequent the original site. Similarly, the huge Msheireb urban regeneration project in Doha, conceived by AECOM in partnership with Mossessian and Partners and Allies and Morrison Architects, is another example of a once vibrant urban commercial landscape frequented by low-income office workers, employees, and laborers which will soon be catering to a more affluent sector of society. Already some of the massive fortress-like buildings under construction give the impression of distinct class barriers and exclusivity. Interestingly, in an attempt to balance global contemporary aspirations and the reinterpretations derived from traditional environments, such projects endeavor to recount spatial and visual language concerns in an integrated yet highly selective manner. The considered selection and/or rejection of appropriate/inappropriate architectural elements are crucial to the success of such designs and projects.

Manifested discourses addressing tradition and modernity are clearly evident in the work of Ehrlich Architects' design of the Federal National Council (FNC) parliament building in Abu Dhabi. On the one hand, with passive solar and energy efficiency qualities at the core of Ehrlich's work, the design provides users with an exotic artificial microclimate. This is achieved through the introduction of a dome structure that covers the main assembly building and its surrounding courtyard. On the other hand, in contrast, the Emiri

6.6: Abu Dhabi Central Market, Abu Dhabi by Foster and Partners (top); and Msheireb urban regeneration project (bottom)

Sources: top: http://www.fosterandpartners.com/projects/aldar-central-market/; bottom: courtesy of Msheireb Properties, 2012.

Diwan quarter of the much larger Msheireb urban regeneration project in Doha attempts to create an intervention that is not just a glass or metal greenhouse but a structure that is ostensibly rooted in perceived, if not actual, Qatari culture. Al Barahat Square by Mossessian and Partners is another intervention and a central element of the larger project. Drawing on traditional Qatari architecture as a main feature of the surrounding buildings, it is intended to act as an urban lung for the development.

Plurality of Trends and Multiple Modernities

Gulf rulers and governments are actively advocating and supporting design innovations that utilize advanced technology in construction systems in conjunction with concessions to certain local expressions. However, some of the designs are solely intended to attract the interest of the global community rather than pique the interest of the actual populace. A considerable number of current undertakings address the global city condition and the narrative of "scapes of flows," setting out to establish the branding of an iconic city with signature buildings. Recent projects that mark the presence of exploratory novelties range from impressively tall plate-glass office towers to large-scale public buildings.[38] One of the most extraordinary new buildings in Qatar is the new Ministry of the Interior head office, located opposite the huge Grand Doha Park, currently being landscaped. This massive monumental fortress-like building is reminiscent of an Aztec pyramid and is certain to become a signature Doha landmark.

From novelty at the concept and structural innovation levels to the confident display of high-tech material technologies,[39] and in a deliberate attempt to stamp strong impressions and images on the minds of local residents, expatriate professionals and international visitors, such iconic structures and

[38] Notable office towers in Gulf cities include the Burj Khalifa by Adrian Smith of SOM, Tower 014 by Reiser & Umemoto, Signature Towers by Hadid and Schumacher, the Gateway Building for RAK by Snøhetta, all in Dubai. Other examples are the Burj Qatar of Nouvel, and Jeddah's Kingdom Tower designed by Adrian Smith and Gordon Gill Architecture, to name a few. See Kheir Al-Kodmany and Mir Ali, "Importing Exceptional Buildings: Transforming Urban Arabian Peninsula into Skyscrapers Cities," *Open House International*, Vol. 38, No. 4 (2013), pp. 101–10.

[39] See Kheir Al-Kodmany, "Green Towers and Iconic Design: Cases from Three Continents," *ArchNet-IJAR*, Vol. 8, No. 1 (2014), pp. 11–28.

6.7: Competing high-rise towers in West Bay, Doha
Source: Salama and Wiedmann, *Demystifying Doha.*

projects all exemplify avid regional competition and sustained superlative aspirations between Gulf cities to be the best, the tallest, the biggest, or the first. These examples only serve to reinforce the premise of Gulf urban tech-noscapes, abetted by the transfer of advanced technology, in a concerted effort to express themselves into what can be called "multiple modernities."[40] The term "multiple modernities" refers to the various socio-economic trans-formations, characterized by vested economic interest and secularism, and bound together in a profound determination to claim ownership of advanced construction technologies. As a concept, multiple modernities inherently

---

[40] Sadria, Mojtaba, ed., *Multiple Modernities in Muslim Societies* (London: I. B. Tauris, 2009).

suggests that certain forces of modernity can be received, perceived, reacted to, and developed in a variety of different ways and in different contexts. In essence, this response eventually results in creating an architectural and urban heterogeneity that goes beyond the dualisms of east/west, history/contemporaneity, and local/global to address the notion of a universalism in architecture that attends and responds to the needs of a universal client and/or a universal user within a universal value system.[41] Concomitantly, the notion of what it means to be modern can be thoroughly examined and thereby establish an open-ended debate on "critical regionalism" and its impact and influence on Gulf architecture.[42]

Branding art and culture is one of the contemporary manifestations that succinctly illustrates the presence of multiple modernities. Governments in the Gulf are actively encouraging and promoting mutual cultural flows, where cultural traffic between east and west, after having been a one-way flow for centuries, is exchanged, modified, adapted, and reformulated to embrace a budding new cultural context. Key building types such as museums and cultural facilities have gained immense attention and interest at the local, regional,

[41] Juxtaposing urban heterogeneity and homogeneity is discussed in recent writings of several scholars, including that of Nezar Al Sayyad. See Nezar Al Sayyad, "Neither Homogeneity Nor Heterogeneity: Modernism's Struggles in the Muslim World," in Mojtaba Sadria, ed., *Homogenization of Representation* (Geneva: Aga Khan Award for Architecture, 2012), pp. 87–96.

[42] The term "critical regionalism" in architecture was coined by Kenneth Frampton and elaborated upon by Suha Ozkan, Alexander Tzonis, and Liane Lefaivre. Broadly defined, critical regionalism is an attempt to synthesize the rooted aspects of a region, including physical and cultural characteristics, with appropriate contemporary technology. It is the search for a contextual architecture; a content that is meaningful within its context and at the same time participates in the more universal aspects of a contemporary society. Critical regionalism is an architectural position that calls for reading the history of a region and extracting its essence while adapting it to suit the spirit of the times. It can be regarded as a way to manifest cultural, economic, and political independence. See Kenneth Frampton, "Towards a Critical Regionalism: Six Points for an Architecture of Resistance," in Hal Foster, ed., *The Anti-Aesthetic: Essays on Postmodern Culture* (Port Townsend, Washington: Bay Press, 1983), pp. 16–30. See also Alexander Tzonis and Liane Lefaivre, *Critical Regionalism: Architecture and Identity in a Globalized World* (New York: Prestel, 2003); and Suha Ozkan, "Introduction—Regionalism within Modernism," in Robert Powell, ed., *Regionalism in Architecture* (Singapore: Concept Media/The Aga Khan Award for Architecture, 1985), pp. 8–16.

and international level from both officials and the public. Dedicated to reflecting the full vitality, complexity, and multiplicity of the arts of the Islamic world, the Doha Museum of Islamic Art designed by I. M. Pei collects, conserves, studies, and exhibits masterpieces spanning three continents (Africa, Asia, and Europe) from the seventh to the nineteenth centuries. The museum building is the result of Pei's comprehensive tour of the Islamic world to understand the diversity of Islamic architecture. Profoundly influenced by the architecture of the Ahmad Ibn Tulun Mosque in Cairo, the museum is composed of two cream-coloured limestone buildings: a five-storey main building featuring a large open-air courtyard on the left, and a two-storey education wing, linked by a covered and arched passageway. The main building's angular volumes recede as they rise around a five-storey domed atrium, concealed from outside view by the walls of a central tower. An oculus at the top of the atrium captures and reflects patterned light within the faceted dome. In addressing the notion of receptacle and spectacle, the building has both a strong exterior presence and a dramatic interior. I would argue that the building is a conscious and deliberate attempt to translate the cultural aspirations of a tiny but extremely ambitious country, anxious to be a major player on the world cultural stage, into a unique and iconic manifestation that speaks to world architecture while at the

6.8: Museum of Islamic Arts, Doha, by I. M. Pei
Source: Salama, 2013.

same time addressing the specific contextual demands placed on the design by the regional culture and local environment.

By contrast, in the cultural district of Abu Dhabi's Saadiyat Island, there has been a surge in the construction of fabulous and costly museum buildings, which go beyond being elegant receptacles for art, to being artistic spectacles in and of themselves. Despite the intriguing conceptual design drivers of Ando's Maritime Museum, Gehry's Guggenheim, Foster's Zayed National Museum, Jean Nouvel's Abu Dhabi Louvre, or Zaha Hadid's Performing Arts Centre, they all yield to an inclination and preference for creating architectural "spectacles" over constructing locally relevant "receptacles." In this context, I would argue that this "spectacular" approach to building design has instigated an extraordinarily competitive interface between the public presence of museum architecture and its implicit order. In essence, balancing the interests of the artist, the architect, the curator, and the visitor is indeed a challenge, especially where it is crucial to harmonize the sense of institutional responsibility with conventional expectations.

Building on the real and perceived memory of Doha, Jean Nouvel's Qatar National Museum reflects an ingenious endeavor to retain a visual connection to the desert and to Bedouin culture. The building is a series of interconnected pavilions interfacing with outdoor terraces enclosed by a large open-air courtyard. In an attempt to create a dramatic contrast with the existing 1920s Emiri Palace, the pavilions are covered with circular roofs, which are intended subtly to echo the texture of shifting desert sands and the grainy desert rose, which allegedly provided the inspiration for Nouvel's design. In this context, I would argue that this concept is a disguised attempt to establish and insinuate a rather flashy dialogue between architectural "receptacle" and architectural "spectacle." Notably, Nouvel adopts a strikingly contrary attitude by focusing on the spectacle rather than receptacle in his flamboyant and extravagant Dubai Opera House.

Incorporating education and environment is another indicator of the presence of "multiple modernities" wherein global knowledge flows contribute to the creation of place and space typologies that attract flows of knowledge; nowhere is this more strikingly evident than in the overall regional context of the Gulf. Within this vibrant new framework, key ideals relevant to the environment and new types of learning are actively promoted and disseminated, and stimulating discussions are generated with reference to the role that architecture can play as both a "substance" and "sustenance."[43] While substance

---

[43] Paul Emmons offers a concise discussion of architecture as substance and sustenance, and the cultural aspirations involved, in "Architecture as Substance and

6.9: Guggenheim Museum by Frank Gehry, Saadiyat Island Development, Abu Dhabi
Source: Salama and Wiedmann, *Demystifying Doha*.

here refers to both the tangible and intangible aspects related to its meaning
and essence, sustenance signifies the act of sustaining and nourishment. Two
examples of large-scale interventions have been selected to reflect this notion
of architecture in Gulf cities, as having inherent qualities of both substance
and sustenance.

Many of the built interventions in various Gulf cities address particular
environmental concerns and thus establish certain exemplars, while at the
same time promoting specific or specified cultural or religious ideologies. In
this instance, I refer here to two important examples. The first is the work of
Norman Foster in Masdar City in Abu Dhabi, a comprehensive project that
incorporates a number of the traditional architectural design features of the
region. Masdar City is conceived as a pedestrian-oriented development with
narrow streets and walkways shaded by window overhangs, high exterior walls,
and thick-walled buildings, and dotted with hierarchical courtyards, patios
and wind towers, and luxuriant vegetation. A considerable number of sustain-

Sustenance: Cultural Desires and Needs," in Paul Emmons, Jane Lomholt, and John
Hendrix, eds, *The Cultural Role of Architecture: Contemporary and Historical
Perspectives* (London: Routledge, 2012), pp. 79–83.

6.10: The architecture of Masdar City, Abu Dhabi, by Foster and Partners
Source: Salama and Wiedmann, *Demystifying Doha.*

able planning and design strategies at the core of the development include the use of ecological and recycled materials for construction of all buildings in the city as well as the adoption of sustainable transportation strategies wherein vehicles within the city are powered by renewable energy sources.

The second intervention, Qatar Foundation for Education, Science and Community Development in Doha, is another important example. This was one of the first regional knowledge-based initiatives and testifies to the commitment of the rulers to promoting and supporting educational endeavors and research. From its inception, the mission of the Qatar Foundation has been to provide world-class educational opportunities and to improve the quality of life for the people of Qatar and the region. This vision includes a higher education campus under the umbrella of the Hamad bin Khalifa University (HBKU), an education city adopting the branch campus concept, where world-class universities offer some of their most prestigious programs to HBKU as full-fledged partners of Qatar Foundation. This cooperation is unique both in the history of education and in the history of architecture, and is claimed to be the first such project worldwide with many international architects working on buildings on the same site and at the same time. These well-known figures include Isozaki, Legoretta, I. M. Pei, and OMA, all of

153

whom have contributed their ideas, expertise, and visual concepts to create vibrant and stimulating environments for learning, nurturing, and research.

The preceding two examples of place typologies represent striking evidence that "global flows" can effectively produce a type of architecture that goes far beyond market logic and market demand. With and along these flows, modern architecture has the opportunity and capacity to address the multifaceted nature of contemporary urban conditions in the Gulf as exemplified by growing environmental concerns, hands-on and research learning, and knowledge production. Through and from such projects, architecture can continue to play its traditional role, as well as a more contemporary, more definitive, and more encompassing role, as a provider of both substance and sustenance.

Conclusion

Currently, the Gulf region is considered to be one of the largest and most expansive construction sites in the world. The resulting transformation of the built environment has led to a new, more dynamic and more functional type of city in the form of the emerging service hub. Creating a knowledge economy in the Gulf states has led to a new and different way of understanding and investing in cities as future assets that can sustain and increase the economic prosperity of the region. The main effect of these efforts to create well-facilitated service hubs has been to open strategic new markets and to interweave with global business. Dubai has been the major trend-setting center for this new movement, because of its visionary schemes to introduce new methods for creating and maintaining vast urban growth, thus attracting international attention. Not to be left behind, other Gulf cities, such as Doha, Abu Dhabi, Manama, and more recently Kuwait, have also followed suit. Notably, these cities have embraced policies to develop similar far-reaching and globally important new development projects and business and market strategies. In recent years, the growing economic and cultural competition between Gulf countries has increased the speed and extent of new urban development as each Gulf city vies to outdo and outshine the others.

Notably, the dramatic urban development strategy introduced by Dubai during the 1990s has become the imprint model for the new rulers of Abu Dhabi and Qatar, which has enticed them to embrace modern urbanism and in doing so establish their capitals as important international service hubs. Bahrain can also be considered one of the pioneers regarding economic diversification strategies, stimulated by a decline in oil reserves which in turn reduced oil production and refining. A causeway to Saudi Arabia built during the 1980s and more liberal investment policies and strategies in the financial sector have been major factors in progressive economic developments within the service sector in Bahrain. Plans are in the offing for Bahrain to build a new causeway to connect it to Qatar and a further causeway with rail link to Saudi Arabia. In the case of Dubai, the introduction of freehold property laws in the late 1990s was a catalyst for exponential growth in recent years. However, as we have noted, the rapid growth of Gulf cities is also characterized by continual urban fragmentation and divisive social segregation patterns which represent certain challenges to the environmental and social sustainability of those cities.

While cities such as Dubai, Abu Dhabi, Doha, and Manama represent main centers of emerging knowledge economies, other cities in the UAE, Oman, Kuwait, and Saudi Arabia have also been witnessing rapid urban transformation processes. Additionally, the rapid growth of Dubai has resulted in the establishment of dormitory settlements in the smaller, less affluent northern emirates of the UAE, due to lower land prices and service costs, which has helped boost their weaker economies. Furthermore, the successful marketing of Dubai as a branded international tourist destination and hub has led to improved tourism prospects for Oman, which promotes its unique cultural heritage and more diverse landscapes and climate zones. One recent consequence has been the initiation of large-scale real estate projects in the form of freehold development and tourist projects in Muscat and its environs. In the foreseeable future, Gulf cities will therefore face a variety of challenges in their race to become competitive stakeholders and players in their local and regional growth, while at the same time implementing the necessary measures to consolidate and develop more sustainable urban structures.

Hence, it is evident that the architecture of emerging cities in the Gulf is characterized by the drive to establish a sustainable identity and the need to react and respond opportunely to global flows. The question that now presents itself in this context is whether or not contemporary architecture in the Gulf region actually represents the culture in which it exists. One answer would be that with the notion of scapes of flows, there is no one culture on which the expansive concepts and plans are based; rather there is an ongoing ever-changing plurality and multiplicity that fundamentally invigorates and sustains the architectural footprint of the region. If indeed architecture is to sustain itself as a form of human expression that can characterize the physical environment of the region's past, a thorough examination of contemporary architectural schemes and developments in the Gulf and their capacity for symbolic representation in its fullest sense will require a more detailed study. Indeed, many of the projects and the emerging place typologies will undoubtedly succeed in responding to the global flows of the present era, but these successes will also raise many questions relevant to their sociocultural and environmental impact on the average citizen, the expatriate professional, and the migrant worker.

7

REAL ESTATE LIBERALIZATION AS CATALYST OF URBAN TRANSFORMATION IN THE PERSIAN GULF

Florian Wiedmann

Introduction

Recent globalization dynamics have led to increased competition between emerging cities in the Global South to successfully enter consolidated networks of capital flows.[1] Local decision-makers thus initiate new development visions and plans in order to position cities as main hubs for global services.[2] In this regard, as well as public investment in infrastructure to increase the connectivity of cities, the other key strategy commonly imple-

---

[1] Jonathan V. Beaverstock, Richard G. Smith, and Peter J. Taylor, "World City Network: A New Metageography?" *Annals of the Association of American Geographers*, Vol. 90 (2000), pp. 123–34.

[2] Jonathan V. Beaverstock, "World City Networks 'from below': International Mobility and Inter-City Relations in the Global Investment Banking Industry," in Peter J. Taylor, Ben Derudder, Pieter Saey, and Frank Witlox, eds, *Cities in Globalization* (London: Routledge, 2007), pp. 50–69.

mented is the liberalization of local markets, which is inevitably needed in order to attract more involvement of the private sector. One key market which usually undergoes rapid growth during the first years of liberalization is real estate.[3] The subsequent construction boom is in itself the major driver of economic growth in most emerging cities, due to extensive employment within construction-related sectors.[4] The resulting immigrant workforce has in turn led to an increasing demand for goods and services. Thus, the newly emerging market place is usually dependent on the continuous growth of the real estate sector.[5]

In the Gulf region, the emirate of Dubai and the kingdom of Bahrain were the first pioneers to follow the vision of establishing service hubs in the Persian Gulf by opening local markets. The main cause for the initiation of a new development direction was shrinking oil and gas revenues since the beginning of the 1970s. In addition to establishing the first free trade zones in Manama and Jebel Ali during the 1980s, the rulers recognized the large potential of initiating a construction boom by permitting foreigners to invest in local real estate. Due to various obstacles, freehold property markets for foreign investment were first introduced at the end of the twentieth century, which led to developments of unprecedented scale and speed. The two biggest factors in the exponential real estate investment in Dubai and Manama at the beginning of the new millennium are often said to be the flight of Saudi capital from the United States after the terrorist attacks of 9/11 and a widespread general recognition of the development potential of Gulf cities as major future hubs, due to their geopolitical location between major global markets.[6]

It can therefore be argued that in many cases of recent urbanization in emerging Gulf cities, real estate plays a key role in redefining development patterns.[7] Rising land prices, new forms of urban governance and an extensive

[3] Saskia Sassen, *The Global City. New York, London, Tokyo* (Princeton, NJ: Princeton University Press, 1991).

[4] Robin Cohen, "The New International Division of Labor: Multinational Corporations and Urban Hierarchy," in Michael Dear and Allen J. Scott, eds, *Urbanization and Urban Planning in Capitalist Society* (London: Methuen, 1981), pp. 287–317.

[5] Neil Brenner, "Between Fixity and Motion. Accumulation, Territorial Organization and the Historical Geography of Spatial Scales," *Society and Space*, Vol. 16 (1998), pp. 459–81.

[6] Christopher Davidson, *Dubai: The Vulnerability of Success* (New York: Hurst & Co., 2009).

[7] David Harvey, *The Condition of Postmodernity* (Oxford: Blackwell, 1989).

demographic change have led to completely new urban morphologies reflecting the immediate consequences of rapid urban growth. Harvey Molotch argues that cities worldwide became growth machines mainly driven by the link between the established global financial system and liberal land ownership rights.[8] Real estate has thus become one of the top commodities facing few restrictions regarding speculative tendencies. The rise and bust of real estate markets became a widespread pattern affecting local developments worldwide, as displayed in the case of the international financial crisis in 2008. Thus it can be argued that the extensive global trade with real estate and the merge of international capital have created a new basis for city networks, in which each city's objective is to become a major control center of international advanced producer service sectors playing key roles in initiating urban growth in strategic locations.[9]

One parallel of contemporary urbanism in the case of most Gulf cities is the distinctive role that real estate sectors have played in promoting both economic growth and a reinvention of the cities' identities.[10] The initiation of freehold property markets in combination with ambitious economic development visions as future global trading, finance, and tourism hubs have fueled one of the biggest construction booms in human history.[11] Speed and scale of developments can only be compared to emerging cities in China, which is a remarkable fact considering the comparatively small size of native populations, the missing hinterland, and the desert environment. While in 1950 around 400,000 inhabitants lived in small settlements along the Gulf coast, today more than 17 million inhabitants live in eleven cities, with a share of more than 60 per cent foreigners.[12] The still remaining wealth of fossil fuels in combination with a fortunate geopolitical location and a worldwide unique governance structure within city states led to urban agglomerations reaching more than 4 million inhabitants. Since the majority of new

---

8 Harvey Molotch, "The City as a Growth Machine: Towards a Political Economy of Place," *American Journal of Sociology*, Vol. 82 (1976), pp. 309–32.

9 Beaverstock, Smith, and Taylor, "World City Network".

10 John W. Fox, Nada Mourtada-Sabbah, and Mohammed Al-Mutawa, *Globalization and the Gulf* (New York: Routledge, 2006).

11 Elisabeth Blum and Peter Neitzke, *Dubai: ein Zwischenbericht über die derzeit größte Baustelle der Welt* (Dubai: a preliminary report on the largest construction site in the world) (Stuttgart: Birkhäuser Verlag, 2009).

12 Population data from the World Bank, http://data.worldbank.org/indicator/SP.POP.TOTL, last accessed 26 May 2016.

immigrants have been directly or indirectly engaged within the construction sector, the population growth has become highly affected by turbulences on real estate markets, as displayed in the case of the international financial crisis in 2008. While the general economic growth in countries and emirates with a remaining wealth of fossil fuels, such as the emirates of Qatar and Abu Dhabi, was less impacted by the crisis, the development dynamics in Dubai and Bahrain were severely affected due to the discontinuation of a large percentage of real estate projects.[13]

In order to understand the impact of real estate in redefining local urbanism, we need to survey the historic evolution of land ownership, then look more closely at the two case studies of Dubai and Bahrain in order to carry out a comparative assessment of the various forms of local real estate markets and their impact on urban structures.

The Historic Evolution of Land Ownership in the Gulf

Before oil production commenced and enabled the emergence of metropolises in the Gulf, the main economic basis of small and scattered settlements was limited to oasis agriculture, fishing, or trade, and the basic key to survival was the tribal organization of various clans under one leading sheikh. All knowledge of founding new settlements was based on the experience of previous generations, who had to adjust to harsh climatic conditions and limited water sources. Thus, major settlements such as Dubai and Manama could only be sustained in locations where oases allowed annual date tree plantations and where important trade routes intersected. The general rules of developing new settlements were dictated by climate and culture. This resulted in vernacular oasis towns with markets and mosques as central public realms surrounded by enclosed private residential districts inhabited by segregated clans and migrants.[14] The tribal sheikh had the last authority of arbitration in the case of any settlement development. It was his decision as ruler to decide the general distribution of land for residential areas as well as main settlement facilities, such as cemeteries, markets, ports, and mosques.[15] This tribal hierarchy

---

[13] Renaud Bertrand, "Real Estate Bubble and Financial Crisis in Dubai: Dynamics and Policy Responses," *Journal of Real Estate Literature*, Vol. 20 (2012), p. 51.

[14] Ibrahim Jaidah and Malika Bourennane, *The History of Qatari Architecture 1800–1950* (Milan: Skira, 2010).

[15] Besim S. Hakim, "Revitalizing traditional towns and heritage districts," *International Journal of Architectural Research*, Vol. 1 (2007), pp. 153–66.

was complemented by a *majlis* system, in which all leading figures of clans commonly agreed on major decisions.[16] Unused land remained under the authority of the leading tribe and no investments could be carried out by inhabitants to gain the right to its future use.

In contrast to other Middle Eastern regions, the Gulf underwent only marginal colonial influence before the discovery of oil, due to the harsh environmental circumstances.[17] The first significant transformation of the traditional form of urbanism within the Gulf region was caused by the emerging pearl trade during the nineteenth century, which led to larger settlements along the coast. The migration of large inland tribes, East African slaves, and merchant families from India and Persia led to new social structures. Subsequently, port settlements like Dubai and Manama reached populations of more than 30,000 inhabitants at the beginning of the twentieth century, and thus reached the size of other major inland settlements such as Riyadh.[18] Each migrant community lived in separate areas in order to prevent conflicts between various cultural and ethnic groups.[19] This tribal and ethnic segregation was the direct consequence of the land distribution schemes dictated by the leading tribe. It led to a distinctive variety of urban forms reflecting a certain level of self-governance of each community. The power of distributing land became the most important factor in sustaining the leading tribe's position, in spite of the fact that the tribe's share in the overall population was decreasing due to continuous immigration.[20]

While the pearl trade had limited influence on the traditional structures of settlements, the socio-economic change brought about by the production of oil meant the end of traditional urbanism. The first oil settlements of Aramco in the Eastern Province of Saudi Arabia during the 1940s introduced a new urban form based on Western technology and expertise.[21] The newly initiated modern ports and first airports permitted the large-scale import of building materials as well as equipment. Thus, the wealth derived from oil enabled the

[16] Saleh Al-Hathloul, *The Arab-Muslim City: Tradition, Continuity and Change in the Physical Environment* (Riyadh: Dar Al Sahan, 1996).

[17] Fred Scholz, *Die kleinen Golfstaaten* (The small Gulf states) (Gotha: Justus Perthes Verlag, 1999).

[18] Saleh Al-Hathloul and Muhammed A. Mughal, "Urban Growth Management. The Saudi Experience," *Habitat International*, Vol. 28 (2004), pp. 609–23.

[19] Hakim, "Revitalizing traditional towns and heritage districts."

[20] Al-Hathloul, *The Arab-Muslim City.*

[21] Al-Hathloul and Mughal, "Urban Growth Management."

newly emerging Gulf states of Kuwait, Bahrain, Qatar, and United Arab Emirates, which remained British protectorates until the 1970s, to introduce the first period of urban modernization.[22] During these three decades, tribal leaders were mainly concerned about raising living standards to maintain their position as key decision-makers.[23] Subsequently, the first infrastructural networks were introduced to enable electricity, sanitation, and water supplies, which led to rapidly expanding settlement areas. During this first modernization phase, any unbuilt land was treated as the private property of rulers, who distributed land to local citizens and public land use in accordance with infrastructural developments.

The rapid modernization of settlements was furthermore enabled by the immigration of thousands of guest workers from South Asia and other countries in the Middle East. The old traditional markets were replaced by clusters of large warehouses, and central residential districts were turned into multi-storey housing for labor, surrounded by informal commercial streets. Previous local neighborhoods were thus transformed overnight into dense mixed-use downtown districts, and local residents became landlords renting their former land and properties to companies and their foreign staff. Based on extensive public land distribution, local inhabitants moved to new suburban housing areas on the outskirts of cities. This led to a significant change in their way of life, which was previously grounded in the close proximity of extended families within traditional neighborhoods, known as *"fareej."*[24] Thus, the first period of modern urbanization caused scattered and fragmented settlements with low-rise peripheries beyond mixed-use centers with high urban densities. For the first time in Gulf history, subdivided land could be purchased, sold, or rented by local investors. The widespread interest in investing in land was supported by the first local banks and their interest-free loans.[25]

Consequently, the end of traditional forms of settlements was abrupt and irreversible. The former rural local population consisting of Bedouins, fishermen, and oasis farmers became dependent on public subsidies as well as revenues from renting or selling land. A new stage in the evolution of Gulf urbanism was fueled by independence from British protection, and accelerating oil production

[22] Scholz, *Die kleinen Golfstaaten*. Kuwait became independent earlier than the other countries, in 1961.

[23] Alexander Melamid, "Urban Planning in Eastern Arabia," *Geographical Review*, Vol. 70 (1980), pp. 473–77.

[24] Hakim, "Revitalizing traditional towns and heritage districts."

[25] Scholz, *Die kleinen Golfstaaten*.

during the 1970s and 1980s. The previous uncoordinated development was replaced by the first initiation of strategic plans implemented by newly founded public bodies and advised by Western consultants such as the British architect John Harris in Dubai. The newly introduced central administration in all Gulf countries led to a strong development emphasis on capital cities, with many inhabitants moving from rural to urban areas. Since the introduction of modern governance, central planning erased the previous practice of self-governed neighborhoods, and the extent of the local inhabitants' individual participation in urban development was therefore reduced.

Within less than three decades, the indigenous population found itself in a new kind of city designed by Western planners and built by mostly South Asian guest workers with imported construction materials and methods. The construction of tall walls around dwellings was one of the few elements introduced by local cultural habits, in order to protect the privacy of families. The biggest impact of the native population on urban development, though, was the habit of investing in land rather than accumulating wealth in bank accounts or stock markets, which led to a high percentage of vacant lots. In the case of Qatar's capital Doha, for instance, more than 55 per cent of lots remained unbuilt until the 1990s due to land speculation by local investors.[26] While in the past undeveloped land could not be possessed by any individual, the newly introduced form of property rights permitted any local inhabitant to invest in land. In addition, plots were distributed by newly introduced housing acts and strategies, such as the first public housing program in Bahrain in 1961,[27] in order to prevent a growing gap of living standards within local communities.

In addition to the implementation of land use regulations, the urbanization phase after national independence was marked by industrialization and economic diversification processes. Furthermore, landmark projects were discovered to be important tools to emphasize the new status of independent Gulf states and to raise national awareness of the population, which still remained segregated according to tribal affiliations. In addition to remaining social conflicts, some countries, such as Dubai, faced serious economic challenges

---

[26] Fadl A. Al-Buainain, *Urbanisation in Qatar: A Study of the Residential and Commercial Land Development in Doha City, 1970—1997* (Salford: University of Salford, 1999), p. 407.

[27] Florian Wiedmann, *Post-oil Urbanism in the Gulf: New Evolutions in Governance and the Impact on Urban Morphologies* (Stuttgart: SVH Verlag, 2012).

due to limited oil wealth. The favored development strategy in these cases was the initiation of large ports and airports to become regional trading hubs, in combination with the introduction of a progressive finance sector introducing Islamic banking.[28]

The emirate of Dubai and the kingdom of Bahrain were pioneers in establishing economies independent of public oil revenues. The initiation of economic free trade zones (FTZ), such as Jebel Ali in 1985 and Mina Salman in 1979, accelerated the emergence of the first service hubs in the region.[29] The particular geographic location between emerging markets in Asia, Africa, as well as the Middle East and already-established markets in the West led to the initiation of well-connected hubs based on the publicly funded extension of airports and ports as well as national airlines. The new role of cities as service hubs led to increased commercial developments and land ownership in key urban areas. These became the most important means of access to participate within the new central business districts and their growing trend of high-rise structures.

In most Gulf cities, plots within downtown areas had been owned by a large number of local investors since the first construction boom during the 1970s. In order to extend the urban area in proximity to the first business centers, land was added via reclamation, which was enabled by shallow coasts. Any reclaimed land became official public property and therefore under the direct control of rulers and their development visions. Due to oil and gas revenues there was no need to sell public land in order to finance infrastructure. The public sector thus initiated joint ventures with the private sector to develop large-scale projects along the coasts. In many ways the newly founded holdings operated as private profit-orientated entities in spite of the large public share. This new phenomenon of semi-public holdings as major land owners and developers has flourished, particularly since the liberalization of local real estate markets in the Gulf and the subsequent second major construction boom at the beginning of the new millennium. The main initiator of this new development model has been Dubai, whose rulers were the first shareholders of large-scale real estate developers in the Gulf.

[28] A. L. M. Abdul Gafoor, *Islamic Banking and Finance* (Groningen: APPTEC Publications, 1999).
[29] Scholz, *Die kleinen Golfstaaten.*

LIBERALIZATION AND URBAN TRANSFORMATION

Dubai as Pioneer of a New Form of Urban Governance

The emirate of Dubai achieved rapid global awareness when its rulers introduced a new strategy to promote the Gulf region by establishing tourism and liberalizing local real estate markets for regional and foreign investors. The Dubai Shopping Festival, launched in 1996, created a new trend of expanding local retail markets by attracting regional tourists. Subsequently, Dubai reinvented itself as an emerging entertainment attraction in addition to being a major regional trading center. Heiko Schmid described this as the initiation of an "Economy of Fascination," which can be best compared to the phenomenon of Las Vegas in the United States.[30]

The end of the twentieth century was marked by a period of rapid urban expansion, with the total urban area of Dubai increasing at a rate of more than 3 per cent per year. The population grew from 370,788 in 1985 to 862,387 in 2000.[31] This was due to a huge influx of expatriate migrants, who constituted about 53 per cent of the total population in the year 2000.[32] At the end of 1999, the construction of the Burj Al Arab hotel was completed, and along with it the beginning of a new era of iconic landmarks in Dubai. The Burj Al Arab and other landmark projects, funded by the public sector or leading figures, became key elements of a new marketing strategy to brand Dubai. An important basis for this new direction in development was the entrepreneurial foresight of Emir Mohammed bin Rashid Al Maktoum. Dubai's economic strategy of developing as a regional tourist center was intended, on the one hand, to fill the vacuum of leisure and entertainment presented by the two large conservative countries of Saudi Arabia and Iran; and on the other hand, tourism itself was used to position Dubai as an emerging investment hub for real estate.[33]

The events of 11 September 2001 and the following US-led "war on terror" led to a new investment situation in the Gulf, wherein regional investors began searching for new nearby opportunities to replace Western markets.[34]

[30] Heiko Schmid, *Economy of Fascination: Dubai and Las Vegas as Themed Urban Landscapes* (Stuttgart: Borntraeger, 2009).
[31] Wiedmann, *Post-oil Urbanism in the Gulf.*
[32] Michael Pacione, "City Profile: Dubai," *Cities*, Vol. 22 (2005), pp. 255–65.
[33] Mike Davis, "Sand, Fear and Money in Dubai," in Mike Davis and Daniel B. Monk, eds, *Evil Paradises: Dreamworlds of Neoliberalism* (New York: New Press, 2007), pp. 49–67.
[34] David Commins, *The Gulf States: A Modern History* (London: I. B. Tauris, 2012).

Consequently, Dubai began to develop new free trade zones, and became the first of the Gulf states to officially open the local real estate market to foreigners. The consequence of this new strategy was an unexpected surge in investment in the development of freehold properties for foreign investors in distinct areas in inner city districts as well as the outskirts. In order to cope with the increasing investment pressure of developments being carried out, the old centralized urban management structure of one municipality allocating building permits according to the Structure Plan of 1993 had to be changed to a more decentralized and flexible approach.[35] This led to a significant change in urban governance wherein real estate companies, which were typically public joint stock companies, played a new role as the main developers shaping urban growth in Dubai.

In 1999, the Emirates Hills project marked the beginning of the real estate boom of the following years by offering properties for sale to foreign investors on a limited basis of lots on lease for 99 years.[36] Although this project contradicted existing laws in the UAE, under which only locals could possess property, it became the precursor to many subsequent developments in the entire Gulf region. The first project of this kind that attracted more widespread international recognition was the Palm by Nakheel, which was proposed in 2001 and developed over the following years with overall completion in 2010. The project consisted of a palm-shaped island on the coast in Jumeirah, which constituted a new benchmark in real estate developments sold as freehold properties. The Palm was a new landmark showing the future possibilities of property developments in the Gulf by using large-scale forms as pictorial branding for successful marketing.

Furthermore, many new free trade zones were either planned or built in order to increase economic diversification and attract future investors. In 2000 and 2001, the FTZs of Dubai Internet City and Dubai Media City were established as new economic sub-centers of Dubai. Both "cities" were constructed within the area of many new developments in Jumeirah, which became the first large-scale city extension in the new millennium, including the housing developments of Dubai Marina, Emirates Hills, and Jumeirah Islands. A characteristic of the new FTZs has been their set-up as "cities" within the city, where each has its own particular theme and specialization in an economic sector,

---

[35] Ahmed Kanna, *Dubai, The City as Corporation* (Minneapolis, MN: University of Minnesota, 2011).

[36] Davidson, *Dubai: The Vulnerability of Success*, p. 129.

7.1: Emirates Hills, Dubai Marina, and the Palm, Jumeirah in Dubai
Source: Florian Wiedmann.

such as, ICT, media, or healthcare.[37] In many cases, however, the economic vision of branded new cities was mainly used to advertise integrated real estate projects, which usually cover a large percentage of the entire development area. While this phenomenon of initially branding major real estate developments as cities was not originally invented in the Gulf, the particular characteristics have led to new forms and dimensions of this kind of urbanism.[38]

The result of the construction boom was a remarkable rise in land prices due to growing speculation and a considerable shrinkage of unbuilt area in the small emirate. The consequence has been the development of several offshore projects, made possible by reclaiming land, and the construction of many multi-storey blocks and high-rises in order to create higher densities. Consequently, Dubai has become a laboratory of construction superlatives, such as the highest tower in the world, the Burj Khalifa. This skyscraper over 800 meters high was completed in 2010, and marks the center of the Downtown Dubai development located along Sheikh Zayed Road.

The three major real estate developers in Dubai—Nakheel, Emaar Properties, and the subsidiaries of Dubai Holding—have the special feature

[37] Yasser Elsheshtawy, *Dubai: Behind an Urban Spectacle* (London: Routledge, 2009).
[38] Yasser Elsheshtawy, *The Evolving Arab City* (London: Routledge, 2008).

of being under the control of the royal family, who initiated their founding and became either their largest shareholder, as in the case of Emaar, or a private owner of the whole company, as in the cases of Nakheel and Dubai Holding, by means of direct investments and the provision of land for developments (Figure 7.2). This semi-privatization of urban governance has caused Dubai's physical and economic development to become more entrepreneurial in nature, while the basic control and power of veto have continued to remain in the hands of the ruler.

In cooperation with other investors, the public joint stock company Emaar was founded in 1997 with an equity capital of 2.65 billion dirhams. Because of the allocation of land for the development of real estate, the Maktoum family became the biggest shareholder with 33 per cent of the stock. The Emir appointed Mohammed Al Abbar—a proven financial expert who worked on previous projects in Dubai—as chairman of Emaar. In 2007, the company had an annual net profit of more than 6.5 billion dirhams, which continued to grow over the following years due to the company's expansion within the

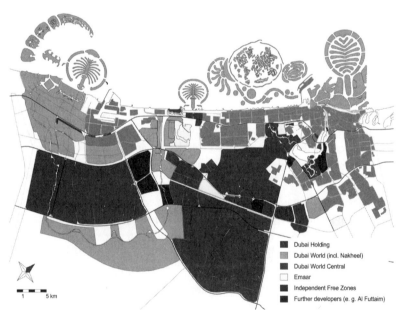

7.2: The various projects of Dubai holdings in 2007

Source: Florian Wiedmann.

region and globally.[39] In parallel with Emaar, Sheikh Mohammed initiated the establishment of a second large real estate company, Nakheel, or "palm", named after its signature project of reclaimed islands in front of Dubai's coast in the form of a palm tree. The maximum net profit of Nakheel was 4,688 billion dirhams in 2007, before the decline caused by the international financial crisis in 2008.[40]

Since the 1970s, although all ministries have been established in Abu Dhabi as the center of governing the major domestic and external affairs of the UAE, several governmental institutions that have played a major role in initiating the construction boom were founded in Dubai. The Dubai Municipality, established in the 1950s, was followed by the Department of Economic Development (DED) in 1992, the Dubai Ports Authority (DPA) in 1991, the Dubai Commerce and Tourism Promotion Board in 1989—later replaced by the Department of Tourism and Commerce Marketing (DTCM) in 1997—and the Dubai Development and Investment Authority (DDIA) in 2002.[41] The DED was developed to analyze the economy, unlike the DDIA, which was put in charge of executing the outcome of these analyses within the sectors of infrastructure development, project management, and investment raising.

Thus, the DDIA was one of the most important institutions, and was consequently put under the direct supervision of Sheikh Mohammed Al Maktoum, who appointed Mohammed Abdallah Al Gergawi as its chairman. In the following years, these public institutions were often reformed and restructured, particularly the DDIA. After four years of its existence it was privatized and subordinated to Dubai Holding (DH), which was developed in parallel as a private version of the DDIA at the beginning of the millennium. Due to DH's success and future prospects as a private cooperation, it was able to establish a strong position for itself.[42]

A further holding, known as Dubai World, was launched in 2006 in order to replace the Ports, Customs and Free Zone Corporation (PCFC), which was founded in 2001 as an umbrella organization covering the Jebel Ali FTZ and the Dubai Ports Authority (DPA). Because of its remaining public functions, the DPA, which had already been founded in 1991 as a public institu-

---

[39] Davidson, *Dubai: The Vulnerability of Success*, p. 129.
[40] Wiedmann, *Post-oil Urbanism in the Gulf*.
[41] Schmid, *Economy of Fascination*, p. 117.
[42] Ibid.

tion, did not become part of the holding Dubai World. This was despite the fact that it was financially independent and profit-orientated, unlike other companies that joined the new holding, such as for example Dubai Maritime City (DMC) and, most importantly, the real estate giant Nakheel. Today, the Dubai World conglomerate covers over thirteen different economic sectors with a focus on the maritime sector and large-scale real estate ventures.[43]

The former chairman of the PCFC, Sultan Ahmad Bin Sulayem, was also appointed as new head of the board of directors of the new Dubai World group. Furthermore, he remained chairman of Nakheel, Dubai Ports World (DPW), and the Jebel Ali Free Zone Authority (JAFZA) within the holding until 2010, when he was replaced by Sheikh Ahmed bin Saeed Al Maktoum. In addition, he was put in charge of the semi-public DPA and thus gained an important governmental role. However, he was not the only one to be appointed to a leading position within the public sector, as both Al Gergawi (DH) and Al Abbar (Emaar) were appointed to important public functions in addition to their chairmanships of the private corporations that played the most decisive role in initiating the construction boom. While Al Gergawi became Minister of State for Cabinet Affairs, the position of the General Manager of the Department of Economic Development was given to Al Abbar. Consequently, all three became important members of the Dubai Executive Council and thus some of the most politically influential persons in Dubai, while being leading figures in expanding the local real estate market.[44] The Dubai Executive Council (DEC) was founded in 2003 in order to create development plans for Dubai and to decide on the phrasing and implementation of new laws.

The Dubai Municipality itself has been reorganized into five sectors: namely the Corporate Service Sector, the General Service Sector, the Environmental and Public Health Services Sector, the Health Service and Environmental Control Sector, and the Planning and Engineering Sector. However, all central development decisions and initiatives originate from the Emir and his main economic leaders within the DEC. Thus, the governance of Dubai has been largely formed by corporate interests and the general

---

[43] Ibid.

[44] Heiko Schmid, "Dubai: Der schnelle Aufstieg zur Wirtschaftsmetropole" (Dubai: The Fast Ascent to an Economic Metropolis) in Elisabeth Blum and Peter Neitzke, eds, *Dubai—Stadt aus dem Nichts* (Dubai—City out of Nowhere) (Berlin: Birkhäuser, 2009), pp. 56–73.

growth and profit orientation of the newly emerging semi-public sector and its wide range of real estate projects. This new model of corporate-driven governance has led to a more efficient, but decentralized administration.

The transformation of the form of Dubai's urban governance from a centralized administrative form to an increasingly corporate-driven one introduced a new model of urbanism in the Gulf region. One of the first consequences of this transformation was the foundation of new governmental institutions intended to initiate strategies for rapid economic growth and diversification. Major public investments were needed to establish new economic sectors, such as the emerging tourist industry. In this context, landmark projects have become driving forces in the creation of new images of Gulf cities. Along with the already established connectivity to regional and global markets, tourism and growing international attention became important factors in attracting investments. The subsequent construction boom led to the influx of many international companies which benefited from the fast growth in the real estate sector, cheap labor, and shrinking restrictions. In a short period of time, real estate became the main factor in rapid economic growth.

The Impact of Liberalized Real Estate Markets in Bahrain

In the case of Bahrain, the various aspects of the economic and political background of urbanism need to be introduced before recent development tendencies caused by an emerging real estate market can be discussed. Although the economic diversification of Bahrain had started earlier than in many other Gulf states, the price decline of oil in 1986 had a major impact on the fall of the country's GDP, thus proving that it was still reliant on fossil resources at that time. Most of Bahrain's production industries, including the aluminum industry, depended on cheap energy. Apart from the fall in the price of oil, Bahrain's economy was seriously affected by Iraq's invasion of Kuwait, which led to major costs in the military sector and thus to a huge loss of public investment in infrastructural and industrial developments. In particular, joint industrial and infrastructural projects between Gulf states were either reduced or cancelled so that instead of a project volume worth about US$ 2.6 billion being carried out, only about 27 per cent of this volume, about US$ 700 million, was developed during the 1990s.[45]

---

[45] Scholz, *Die kleinen Golfstaaten*.

Apart from the attempt to diversify the industry of the country through public investments, economic development driven by the private sector became more important. One example of the growing privatization is BALEXCO, a company founded in 1977 by public investments, over 60 per cent of which was sold to private investors during the early 1990s after it had been transformed into a stock corporation. While in the mid-1990s the privatization of Gulf Air did not succeed, due to increasing financial problems and dependency on public subsidies, the private sector did carry out essential infrastructural projects such as a new energy plant. Furthermore, new privately owned companies such as Bahrain Leisure Facilities Company, Bahrain Gulf Course Company, and Al Jazira Tourism Company were founded in order to establish a tourism industry in Bahrain, which was mainly kick-started by the construction of the new King Fahad Causeway connecting Bahrain to Saudi Arabia. In 1994, more than 5.2 million people crossed the causeway, including an increasing majority of shopping and leisure tourists.

Since 2006, the Bahrain International Circuit and the annual Formula 1 race have led to wider regional and global awareness about Bahrain as a travel destination. In addition to the development of its tourism sector, Bahrain's role as an offshore banking center has become increasingly important for its economic diversification. Toward the end of the 1990s, about 47 offshore banks with an overall capital of about US$ 67.9 billion existed in Bahrain. Furthermore, the number of local commercial banks grew rapidly and more than 32 companies sold their shares on the local stock market, which was introduced in 1989. In order to attract more regional and international investors, the government decided to found Bahrain Development Bank in 1991, which provided low-priced loans and venture capital. Then the Bahrain Marketing and Promotion Bureau was introduced to support companies establishing their headquarters in Bahrain, in addition to supporting a public program since 1993 involving tax concessions, a reduction of costs with regard to rent and electricity, and subsidies in the case of the employment of Bahrainis. A further major change in Bahrain's economic development was the permission to found companies 100 per cent owned by foreign capital.[46]

While Bahrain's economic development was focused on increasing business possibilities for foreign and regional investors, a large share of the local population did not actively participate within these new economic sectors. Apart from limited public investment in the education of the local population, the

[46] Ibid.

speed and scale of new developments called for an immediate need for highly educated, mostly foreign, employees. In order to reduce the negative impact on the local Bahraini population, several government programs were launched in order to integrate the local workforce into the expanding private sector. Unlike in other Gulf countries, such as Qatar and Kuwait, the local population of Bahrain has been receiving fewer government subsidies, forcing many to accept low-paying jobs. The continuously increasing living costs, in addition to the general demand for more political rights and participation by the Shi'a majority, have led to public demonstrations and social unrest.[47]

After the death of the Emir Sheikh Isa in 1999, his son Sheikh Hamad became ruler of Bahrain and initiated a major change in the country's political system. In 2002, the state of Bahrain was proclaimed a constitutional monarchy, and the re-establishment of an elected parliament led to a certain degree of public participation. In the following five years the population grew from about 672,000 people to more than 1,046,000 in 2007, mainly caused by the immigration of around 250,000 guest workers, whose share in the overall population increased from about 38 per cent to almost 50 per cent.[48] This major growth was the direct consequence of newly introduced strategies to stimulate local real estate markets. This rapid rise of a construction boom in Bahrain was majorly affected by residential real estate, since Bahrain's cities were seen as ideal dormitory satellites for middle- to high-income expats engaged in the Eastern Province of Saudi Arabia, and as holiday homes for wealthy Saudi citizens.

In order to stimulate growth, the structure of urban governance, which had been shaped by a strict centralized administrative structure over the previous decades, needed to be reorganized. The development strategy to initiate extensive urban growth by liberalizing markets led to a more corporate and flexible form of governance through the introduction of new agencies and semi-public holdings. This particularly affected the urban planning sector, which was dominated by the Ministry of Housing (MoH) from 1975 to 2002. In addition to being responsible for housing developments, the Physical Planning Directorate and the Survey Directorate had been under the authority of the

---

[47] Ute Meinel, *Die Intifada im Ölscheichtum Bahrain* (The Intifada in the Oil Sheikhdom of Bahrain) (Münster: LIT Verlag, 2002).

[48] Mustapha Ben-Hamouche, "Manama: The Metamorphosis of an Arab Gulf City," in Yasser Elsheshtawy, ed., *The Evolving Arab City* (London: Routledge, 2008), pp. 184–217.

MoH until it was restructured in 2002. While the Physical Planning Directorate, which remained in charge of the overall physical planning, was moved to the Ministry of Municipalities and Agricultural Affairs, the Survey Directorate became an independent authority. Furthermore, the Ministry of Works was added to the MoH to establish a joint Ministry of Works and Housing, which was split again into two separate ministries five years later in 2007. In recent years, the first steps have been made to transform the various ministries into authorities, as is the case of the Ministry of Electricity and Water, which was changed into the Electricity and Water Authority in 2007.

Parallel to the reorganization of the ministries under the king's cabinet, Crown Prince Sheikh Salman initiated the founding of the Economic Development Board (EDB) in 2002. This new agency became a driving force within urban governance as a result of its introducing the Economic Vision 2030 and establishing several new committees such as the Urban Development and Housing Committee, which was put in charge of a large residential development called Northern New Town. The main goal of the EDB, however, is to diversify Bahrain's economy quickly by developing a comprehensive strategy and creating a climate that will attract direct investments from abroad. Consequently, several initiatives were established, including the Formula 1 Grand Prix, the liberalization of Bahrain's telecommunication industry, and bringing about the privatization law in addition to a Free Trade Agreement with the United States. Moreover, the EDB has functioned as a marketing agency of Bahrain as a future investment hub in the Gulf by promoting business opportunities in order to enforce foreign investments and the establishment of public–private partnerships.

In order to implement its Economic Vision 2030, the EDB took over much of the responsibility for key decision-making within urban governance, particularly regarding the creation of a new strategic plan for Bahrain. In this regard, the EDB engaged private consultants such as Skidmore, Owings & Merrill to design the new national strategic plan. Furthermore, the Housing and Urban Development Committee was created to develop a large-scale project on the north-western coast to solve Bahrain's growing social housing crisis. However, in 2008 this project was put under the authority of the Ministry of Housing. This incident is one of several examples where areas of responsibility have overlapped between the ministries and the EDB, which emerged as a new visionary entity within the traditional form of governance promoting privatization, particularly in regard to urban developments.

At the beginning of the twenty-first century, almost the entire territory of Bahrain was turned into a free zone offering a low tax environment, making it one of the most cost-effective locations in the GCC. In addition, there was no law that forced companies to assign a certain amount of shares or to engage a mediating agency. This liberalization led to the private sector's growing interest in Bahrain, particularly regarding the rapidly growing real estate market between 2002 and 2008. Since 2002, the development of the Bahrain Financial Harbor has been the embodiment of the new approach to re-establish Bahrain as a financial capital in the Gulf. While the real estate market was already open to GCC nationals by 1999, a 2003 law allowed foreigners to buy freehold properties and thus to receive a self-sponsored residence permit.[49]

The new legal situation and the general investment climate have led to a construction boom in the form of various projects, mainly on reclaimed land in the north and close to the urban centers. One of the first freehold property developments has been the Amwaj Islands in the north-east of Muharraq, which was announced in 2002. In the following years, the private sector launched several other projects on reclaimed islands, such as Reef Island and Bahrain Bay along the waterfront of Manama and the Durrat Al Bahrain development in the south of the main island. Beside the coastal developments, the freehold projects of Al Areen and Riffa Views were launched inland. All these developments are designed by a master developer of a private investor group or a semi-public holding. These are made up of mixed-use projects with integrated commercial districts, leisure facilities, and hotels, in addition to a large percentage of residential use.

Parallel to these master-planned projects, zoning plans for certain urban areas, such as the reclaimed coastal districts of Manama, known as the Seef District, the Juffair District, and the Seafront District, were modified to permit the development of freehold property developments. Based on the new regulations, multi-storey buildings and high-rises were built in order to make the available plots as profitable as possible. The consequent verticalization of the built environment has been an indicator of the profound change of urbanism in Bahrain, which has been increasingly dominated by real estate speculations. In addition, new landmarks, such as the World Trade Center Bahrain and the Bahrain Financial Harbor, were initiated to consolidate and stimulate the post-oil economic sectors. These investments, however, were in most cases directly or indirectly associated with adjacent real estate ventures.

---

[49] Maher Al-Shaer, *Real-Estate Developments for Economic Growth: Significance and Critical Role of Real Estate Developments in the Kingdom of Bahrain* (Saarbrücken: LAP Verlag, 2013).

While in previous decades most aspects of urban planning had been the responsibility of a single ministry, the decision to move the Planning Directorate in 2002 to another ministry and an increase in master-planned projects on the basis of case-by-case decisions led to the decentralization of urban planning in Bahrain. Due to increasing pressure from developers and real estate investors, the state's existing zoning plans were adjusted to accommodate growth rates and new development preferences. Based on Resolution No. 27, which was approved by the Council of Ministers in 2005, developments were less restricted regarding land use, maximum construction ratio, and building height. The highest densities are permitted in areas with the type "Investment Building B-A" (Figure 7.3), the construction ratio of which can be as much as 1,200 per cent of the total plot area, which is comparable to downtown Manhattan.[50]

The major share of developed real estate is located on reclaimed land along the northern and eastern shoreline of Bahrain's capital, Manama. In addition

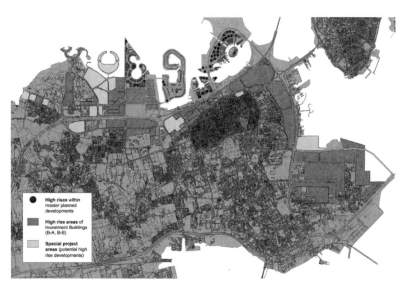

7.3: The distribution of zones in Manama permitted to be developed as Investment Buildings

Source: Florian Wiedmann.

[50] Wiedmann, *Post-oil Urbanism in the Gulf*, p. 126.

to the development of many former empty plots within the central business district along the King Faisal Highway in the north, the new centers of construction have been around the Seef District in the north-west and Juffair in the south-east. Because of the easy access provided by the main highways leading from central Manama to the causeway to Saudi Arabia, several shopping malls have been constructed in the Seef District. Thus, many banks and office buildings have relocated to this district, which was built on land that was reclaimed in the 1980s to create a new suburb. Because of the US Navy base and the immigration of many foreign guest workers in recent years, the Juffair district has witnessed a fast development of multi-storey apartment buildings and compounds (Figure 7.4). In 2007, the main property transactions by non-Bahrainis were carried out by Saudis with an overall share of 52.9 per cent, followed by Kuwaitis with 21.4 per cent.[51]

The recent development trend of focusing on new urban areas has led to the reclamation of about 170 hectares in the Seafront District, about 140 hectares in the Seef District, and about 80 hectares in Juffair since 1998. The overall urban area of Manama has expanded by more than 15 per cent, from around 2,700 hectares to almost 3,100 hectares (Figure 7.5). A further consequence of the recent construction boom has been an exponential increase in land prices, which has contributed to less investment in old parts of Manama due to low profit expectations. All in all, there has been a clear shift and transformation of urban development toward increasingly densely built areas along the coast, in addition to reclaimed island projects, with a still remaining high percentage of around 40 per cent of unbuilt land in the old urban areas of Manama.[52]

As in the other Gulf states, the international financial crisis of 2008 had a drastic impact on local developments in Bahrain. While before the outbreak of the crisis the annual growth rate of the real estate sector reached 24.7 per cent in 2007, the value of residential freehold properties decreased by an average of more than 25 per cent in 2010.[53] In 2013, investment in real estate remained below 50 per cent of its preceding peak in 2007.[54] Combined with social unrest in recent years, the investment climate has profoundly changed,

---

[51] Oxford Business Group, *The Report: Bahrain 2008* (Oxford: Oxford Business Group, 2008), p. 145.
[52] Ben-Hamouche, "Manama: The Metamorphosis of an Arab Gulf City."
[53] Oxford Business Group, *The Report: Bahrain 2008*, p. 143.
[54] Oxford Business Group, *The Report: Bahrain 2013* (Oxford: Oxford Business Group, 2013), p. 29.

7.4: Residential high-rise buildings in Juffair
Source: Florian Wiedmann.

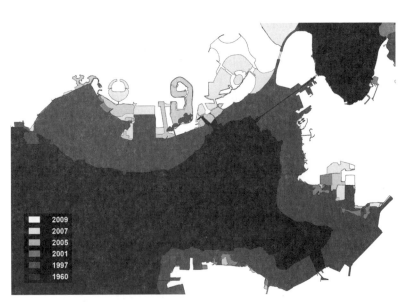

7.5: The extensive land reclamation in Bahrain's capital, Manama
Source: Florian Wiedmann.

leading to cancelled or delayed developments. The fast rise of the construction boom followed by the abrupt crisis together display the increasing dependency between economic stability and a flourishing real estate market. Growth expectations have been merely a consequence of speculative incentives, which, however, heavily rely on a stable environment to avoid major setbacks as in the case of Bahrain between 2008 and 2013.

Conclusion and findings

Gulf cities such as Dubai and Manama face various challenges to developing a sustainable form of urbanism in a region that is witnessing increasing competition regarding new economic sectors. Thus, on the one hand, liberalization strategies and extensive public investments are needed to establish growing hubs; while, on the other hand, diverse, efficient, and attractive urban environments are needed to become sustainable metropolises. In both cases recent urban development strategies have led to rapid urban growth fueled by emerging real estate markets. While in Dubai the local population has become a minority of less than 15 per cent, the native share of Bahrain's population shrank from over 80 per cent to about 50 per cent over the last ten years. However, it is important to put these figures into perspective, as a large majority of guest workers are employed on construction sites and will leave after the completion of their short-term contracts. In both cases, however, cities are built for a new form of socio-economic reality, which is dependent on future immigration.

The main parallel between Dubai and Bahrain is the fact that, in both cases, local oil and gas revenues have played a diminishingly significant role in economic development since the 1970s and after the first modernization period. Subsequently, rulers in both countries initiated alternative economic strategies to secure future prosperity. While Bahrain was one of the first offshore banking centers, Dubai became a major regional trading hub since its first economic free zone was launched in Jebel Ali in 1985. Simultaneously, both countries discovered tourism to be a major factor in their economic diversification during the 1990s. The newly launched shopping festival in Dubai and the construction of a causeway between Bahrain and Saudi Arabia led to a new chapter of local economic development driven by the expanding need for leisure in the region. The expansion of regional airlines in combination with large-scale tourism resorts led to new images of the city that attract the rising interest of investors and thus the pressure to liberalize local markets.

The major differences in impact of the recent construction booms in Dubai and Bahrain are mainly rooted in their particular political circumstances and social realities. While the emirate of Dubai is part of the United Arab Emirates with Abu Dhabi City as the capital, the kingdom of Bahrain has become dependent on Saudi Arabia for its economic development as well as its domestic concerns. The divide between Bahrain's rulers and a large share of Bahrain's Shi'a population is historically rooted, and during the outbreak of the "Arab Spring," social unrest demanding the end of monarchy led to a major intervention supported by GCC allies, particularly Saudi Arabia. Due to the existing inequity and lack of political rights, the consequent lack of social stability has become the key factor weakening Bahrain's position as a regional investment hub in recent years. Local real estate developments have therefore been mainly driven by local and Saudi investment interests.

In contrast to Dubai, semi-public holdings and their real estate developments are rejected by a large percentage of the local population in Bahrain. The newly emerging urban landscapes of high-rise agglomerations and artificial islands are often seen as antithetical to local culture and values. Thus, major projects are limited to areas that can be directly accessed by the main highway network, and certain measures haven been applied to develop gated and luxurious resorts detached from old urban areas. This has led to highly segregated urban landscapes in Bahrain displaying the conflict between the minority leading social classes and the majority of the population left out of the current development dynamics. One particular aspect has been the focus of new development areas along the coast due to the existing land ownership rights. In contrast to Manama's old urban districts, Dubai's downtown areas such as Bur Dubai and Deira have witnessed a gradual upgrading process. Strict physical planning by the Dubai Municipality and continuous public investment in infrastructure have prevented the deterioration of Dubai's historic center and ensured less isolation between old and new urban areas than can be witnessed in Manama.

While Dubai's real estate markets have rapidly diversified in response to the various interests of investors, Bahrain's real estate sector can best be described as conventional, since it is mainly focused on medium-sized residential properties in the form of serviced apartments along the coast in addition to exclusive villa developments on reclaimed islands and scattered commercial developments. One similarity is the use of iconic shaped islands in order to attract the attention of investors and the general verticalization of certain districts due to rising land prices. The general scale of development sites in

Bahrain is, however, reduced due to the limited size of project sites and the formation of relatively small semi-public real estate holdings.

In both Dubai and Manama, new urban typologies such as residential high-rises and island projects have led to the overall transformation of urban morphologies. The redefinition of urbanism due to stimulated real estate markets has led to a new chapter of local urban development trends. While the scale of Dubai's real estate markets has never been reached by Manama or any other Gulf city, most other GCC governments followed the general approach of liberalizing markets in order to attract foreign investment, extending public land via reclamation, and founding semi-public holdings as developers. Real estate projects became the most important factor in redefining the image of Gulf cities, replacing the stereotypical dullness of oil cities resulting from monotonous urban typologies with a modern globalized vision in the form of emerging skylines and themed urban landscapes. The Burj Al Arab in Dubai was one of the first pioneering projects that introduced a new city-branding strategy to attract global media attention. However, while in Dubai the new model of urban governance has completely reformed and replaced former conservative structures, cases like Bahrain display an increasing conflict between newly initiated development visions and the continuing social and economic realities on the ground.

The import of Dubai's strategy of rapid urban growth has led to increasingly severe division of urban structures in Bahrain and other Gulf cities. The deterioration of certain urban areas and the lack of infrastructural supply will further increase inequity in cases like Bahrain, where historic conflicts between social groups have remained. The segregation and isolation of new developments will exclude a large share of the population, and the liberalized local real estate market has thus become a catalyst for an increasing gap between income groups in a fragile political environment. The capital accumulation in real estate in the Gulf in recent years has yet to be seen and analyzed critically in terms of its impact on social, economic, and environmental sustainability. Short-term speculative interests have turned cities into growth machines with hardly any long-term perspective of consolidating economic growth within real estate independent sectors. Overrated growth potentials have led to high land prices, which are currently preventing a transformation from supply-driven to demand-driven development patterns. Thus, most tenants have to accept a limited variety of properties, increasing rental costs and low construction standards as well as a lack of integrated services, which diminishes the general attractiveness of Gulf cities.

The existing pressure on sustaining urban growth in order to prevent the collapse of real estate prices is mainly based on the fact that most economic sectors are directly or indirectly dependent on the construction boom. Today, it is difficult to predict how the real estate-driven form of contemporary urbanism in some Gulf cities will transform into a new stage of consolidation. In contrast to most of its neighbors, Dubai launched its model of real estate-driven urban growth after its establishment as a main regional trading, tourism, and finance hub. The imitation of its growth strategy and the increasing competition between Gulf cities to establish post-oil economic sectors to sustain urban growth will inevitably lead to major crises of real estate markets. This can be caused, for instance, by social unrest, infrastructural collapse, lack of public investment liquidity, and severe environmental problems.

Real estate can thus be identified as a conflicted catalyst of urban transformation in the Gulf, resulting in the phenomenon of "instant cities" based on speculative incentives rather than on actually existing and developing post-oil economies. While Dubai might manage to recover completely from the first severe real estate crisis of 2008 and preserve a dynamic real estate market due to its role as a major regional hub, several cities, including Manama, will face a variety of challenges to prevent the scenario of a non-recovering real estate bubble and subsequent long-term economic recession.

8

NEOLIBERAL URBANIZATION
AND SMART CITIES IN THE GULF REGION

THE CASE OF ABU DHABI'S MASDAR CITY

Remah Gharib, M. Evren Tok and *Mohammad Zebian*

This chapter provides a critical examination of the phases, spatialities, and temporalities of neoliberalism by looking at cities. Masdar City, a "smart cities initiative" in Abu Dhabi, constitutes the case study in this chapter. Neoliberalism can be considered a global transformative force that shapes urban governance in both public and private realms, and has been extensively employed to explain urbanization patterns. Masdar City is indicative of a trend in cities of the Persian Gulf which does not totally fit common neoliberal urbanization trajectories. The extent to which Masdar City represents the neoliberal experience can be understood by a comparison with common patterns of neoliberal urbanization, as well as an assessment of contested and divergent forms and what such forms mean for urbanization experiences in cities of the Gulf region. The chapter begins by situating the concept of smart cities with a conceptual discussion that delineates the relationship between neoliberalization and urban spaces and identifies major fault lines. The next section focuses on Gulf cities in general and then moves on to the criteria necessary for a city in the Gulf to be considered "smart." The third section concentrates on the case study of Masdar City as an example of a smart city in the making. As such, the project's evolving and ongoing nature makes its evaluation and critical analysis difficult. But the fact that Masdar represents an ambitious effort to construct a smart city, premised on new assumptions that are nothing short of paradigm shifts, cannot be denied.

Neoliberalization of Urban Spaces

Given the history and political economy of the region, state–market relations in the Persian Gulf region have developed in particular ways. A leading factor in their development is the aspiration to diversify economies away from oil. Decision-makers of the Gulf Cooperation Council (GCC) states need to deliver solutions for shaping new cities—cities that can safeguard the environment while being economically diverse and competitive. One option is initiating the development of smart cities that rely on inputs and outputs other than non-renewable resources—a smart economy, smart mobility, a smart environment, smart people, smart living, and smart governance.[1] In this sense, the interstices of neoliberalism, urbanization, and evolution of Gulf cities provide information about dynamics that necessitate strong states (or governments) as opposed to "minimized" neoliberal states. The evolution of Gulf cities illustrates that the dynamics of neoliberalism assign a vital role for states. The cases of Masdar City and other smart cities of the Gulf resemble common local forms of neoliberal experiences,[2] which rely heavily on state capacities to establish institutional and organizational mechanisms for markets to operate

---

[1] This chapter utilizes Dameri's definition of smart cities: "A smart city is a well-defined geographical area, in which high technologies such as ICT [information and communications technology], logistics, energy production, and so on, cooperate to create benefits for citizens in terms of well-being, inclusion and participation, environmental quality, intelligent development; it is governed by a well-defined pool of subjects, able to state the rules and policy for the city government and development." Renata Paola Dameri, "Searching for Smart City definition: a comprehensive proposal," *International Journal of Computers and Technology*, Vol. 11, No. 5 (2013), p. 2549.

[2] Jamie Peck and Adam Tickell, "Neoliberalizing Space," *Antipode*, Vol. 34, No. 3 (2002).

and integrate local economies with global neoliberal structures, but at the same time there are perceptions that these mechanisms help build more cohesive, sustainable local/urban/national institutional contexts.[3]

In general, neoliberalization refers to a range of policies whose intent is to extend market discipline, competition, and commodification throughout society. Its objective is to secure the vital cycle of economic growth in the current period. Neoliberal doctrines have brought about the deregulation of state control over industry and markets, assaults on organized labor, the downsizing and/or privatization of public services and assets, the dismantling of welfare programs, the enhancement of international capital mobility, and the intensification of interlocality competition. Their implementation has relied on the restructuring of projects by states,[4] while the dominance of competitive logic over redistributive objectives has opened up new spaces of collaboration among states, economic actors, institutions, municipalities, and civil society.

By understanding the increasing hegemony of neoliberalism in redesigning, restructuring, and reproducing urban spaces, it becomes possible to conceptualize this phenomenon as a state strategy for creating new conditions of capital accumulation. It would be misleading to assume that neoliberalism unfolds in a linear fashion. Neoliberal policies internalize two contradictory tendencies, which become explicit when the intersection between urbanization and neoliberalism as well as spatial implications are considered. The two tendencies are toward state capacity and market centrism, though there are some ambiguities. For instance, does neoliberalism mean that the state's functions are minimized, or is there still a large role for states to shape outcomes for their publics? Moreover, what kind of role is ascribed to the state when it comes to generating wealth? Approached from the perspective of these contradictory tendencies, the emergence of smart cities in the Gulf is indicative of a delicate balance between the two tendencies. State capacity appears to remain strong, albeit with varying scales and temporalities. The establishment of Masdar City in particular and the rise of smart cities in general can be better understood according to two axes that imply crucial trade-offs and sensitivities: (i) state capacity versus market centrism and (ii) oil/gas dependency versus diversification and sustainability.

---

[3] Jamie Peck, "Geography and public policy: constructions of neoliberalism," *Progress in Human Geography*, Vol. 28, No. 3 (2004), pp. 392–40.

[4] Jamie Peck, Nick Theodore, and Neil Brenner, "Neoliberal Urbanism: Models, Moments, Mutations," *SAIS Review*, Vol. 29, No. 1 (2009), pp. 49–66.

Figure 8.1 extends the aforementioned axes. As illustrated, the formulation and production of urban policies are simultaneously influenced by a top-down approach engineered by the state and a bottom-up approach that is primarily defined by the population.[5] With emerging urban spaces like Gulf smart cities on the rise, is it realistic to expect smart cities to address various policy challenges—finance, environment, technology and sovereignty support—as explicated in Figure 8.1? The answer depends on the characteristics of local neoliberal experiences and the way that institutional alignments and dynamics are constituted.

The establishment of smart cities and other direct forms of government-led intervention that promote innovation have been widely documented, particularly in Asian countries that have rapidly industrialized, such as Japan, South Korea, Taiwan, and Singapore, where advanced, diverse economic development is now a reality. Innovation drives in targeted industries were made possible by dramatic increases in government spending, as well as policies to promote research and development and participation in global alliances, which drove capacity/competency building and knowledge transfer. New technologies—in the cases of the Asian countries, electronic and automobile

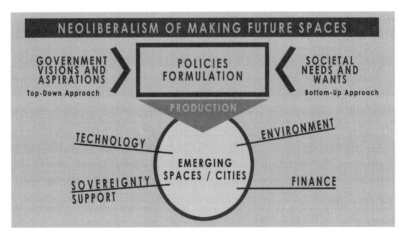

8.1: Model of neoliberalism in emerging urban spaces

[5] M. Evren Tok and Melis Oguz, "Manifestations of Neoliberal Urbanization: The Case of Sulukule/Istanbul," *Journal of Planning*, Vol. 23, No. 2 (2014), pp. 57–66.

components, as well as information and communications technologies—played a major role in export-oriented economic development.

Jacobsson and Bergek emphasize the importance of institutional alignment,[6] such as openness to new ways of thinking and political imaginaries that privilege market-based over redistributive mechanisms, as a driver of technological change and, subsequently, economic development. They argue that the legitimacy of neoliberal actors, their new technologies, their access to resources and the formation of markets is strongly related to a country's institutional framework. If the framework is not aligned with the new technologies, several economic functions may be blocked. Therefore, institutional alignment—and by implication institutional politics—is at the heart of the process whereby new technologies gain ground.

Institutional alignment is a multifaceted process. Supporting the formation of a new technological system involves a reformulation of science and technology policy in order to facilitate the development of a range of competing technological designs. Such knowledge creation may have to begin well in advance of the emergence of markets, but it also needs to be sustained throughout the evolution of the new technological system. Institutional alignment also involves market regulations, tax policies, and value systems that may enable the operations of specific firms. Institutional change is often required to generate markets for new technologies. Such change may involve, for instance, the establishment of regulatory standards.

Jacobsson and Bergek also outline the various stages of development that new technological systems go through. During the "formative" phase, policies are necessary to provide the right conditions for investment in new technologies, which cause a cluster of actors to form. The subsequent "change in gear" phase, which is characterized by a self-sustaining system that is far less reliant on state policies, whereby a market begins to develop positive feedback loops and more actors become involved across the value chain. To succeed, national development strategies must be built on a foundation of strong, responsive institutions, good governance and "openness"—or what some scholars refer to as the principle of neoliberalism.

Broad initiatives promoting economic development, the emergence of technology and innovation clusters, and investments in institutional capacity-build-

---

[6] Staffan Jacobsson and Anna Bergek, "Transforming the Energy Sector: The Evolution of Technological Systems in Renewable Energy Technology," *Industrial and Corporate Change*, Vol. 13, No. 5 (2004), pp. 815–49.

ing, education, and infrastructure are becoming increasingly prevalent in several GCC states. The UAE—Abu Dhabi in particular—is making significant efforts in this regard, which this chapter examines further by looking at the company Masdar, a state-owned subsidiary of the Mubadala Development Company. Regarding the UAE, various economic and social indicators based on data from the World Bank have tracked steady progress in terms of development since the 1990s.[7] The UAE has invested heavily in education as well as research and development, reflecting an ambition to build a more diversified knowledge-based economy.[8] This drive for knowledge and innovation is exemplified by Masdar, whose mission is to invest in, incubate, and commercialize new renewable energy and clean technologies both within Abu Dhabi and around the world. The extent of the UAE's commitment to economic development, institutional capacity-building, and the openness that underpins these processes becomes clear by examining Masdar and the degree to which the company represents the neoliberalism emerging in the GCC. But first, this chapter turns to an overview of neoliberal urbanization in Gulf cities.

Urbanization of Gulf Cities since 2000

As the various chapters in this volume demonstrate, since the late 1990s and the early 2000s the cities of the Gulf region have been competing against one another through modern approaches to urbanization in order to attract global awareness and to remake their images. Most Gulf states have utilized the concept of the city to align their images with modernity and internationalization. This largely symbolic approach has utilized enormous finances to deliver new cities with different and often spectacular designs to distinguish them from others in the region. Top-down governance has pushed for rapid, high-quality urban development, which has been possible due to direct final transfers from the monarchies to city developers and consumers. In turn, the cities of the Gulf have recently been distinguished by increased tourism, investments by multinational corporations, and extensive (and expensive) real estate development. Decision-makers have delivered these developments in accordance with various development plans, national visions, and mega events that required

7 "World DataBank," 30 April 2015, http://databank.worldbank.org/data/databases. aspx, last accessed 26 May 2016.
8 Stephen Wilkins, "Higher education in the United Arab Emirates: an analysis of the outcomes of significant increases in supply and competition," *Journal of Higher Education Policy and Management*, Vol. 32, No. 4 (2010), pp. 389–400.

fast-paced urbanization. While effective in realizing projected outcomes, decision-making processes have lacked bottom-up social participation, like that typically seen by grass-roots social organizations elsewhere, and socio-political components, such as political and cultural decision-making. Nevertheless, populations of the Gulf's cities (except for low-paid expatriates) enjoy economic stability, given the huge economic boosts from infrastructure investment and real estate development.

Notably, due to the absence of social participation in decision-making, much development in emerging Gulf cities tends to produce isolated urban pockets that lack optimal connections to the city cores. For instance, between the years 2000 and 2010, Dubai introduced Jumeirah Beach Residence on the peripheries of the city, a project that is similar to Lusail City, currently being constructed north of Doha, Qatar. The peripheral Lusail City is being rapidly developed to host the World Cup in 2022. This massive, modern urban expansion, which is meant to signify Qatari progress, has required many market-oriented policies at the expense of bureaucracy to increase the speed of development and deliver outcomes according to new strategic attitudes toward competition among neighbors and the countries beyond. The outcomes so far—in line with those seen in other Gulf cities—have included the importation of global architectural trends, inadvertently introducing the major challenge of distortion of the local urban identity. In other words, with the key outputs being the growing number of tall and sophisticated buildings—Dubai has built the tallest building in the world, the Burj Khalifa, and some cities aspire to build similarly tall skyscrapers—Gulf cities have worked with pride and passion toward their achievements, but they have done so by breaking from their heritage. Moreover, this architectural shift has compromised many sustainability measures, as it has required the high consumption of energy and other resources.

The populations of most Gulf cities have been challenged by two other major issues. First, new cultures that have recently been incorporated into their cities, resulting in cultural diversity but causing cultural tensions. Yasser Elsheshtawy defined the emerging Arab city as a "place of unprecedented development, rising skyscrapers, modern shopping malls, unabashed consumerism. Most importantly it is a setting where one can observe the tensions of modernity and tradition; religiosity and secularism; exhibitionism and veiling; in short a place of contradictions and paradoxes."[9] These contradictions

[9] Yasser Elsheshtawy, *The Evolving Arab City: Tradition, Modernity and Urban Development* (New York: Routledge, 2008), p. 3.

and paradoxes are due to states seeking to make a statement with rapid urbanization and growth but only being able to do so by attracting large numbers of low-paid expatriates, which lead to situations of increased socio-economic competition and segregation, given wealth and income disparities between local residents and expatriates. Indeed, in the cases of Kuwait City and Doha, where local citizens reside away from expatriates to avoid cultural infringements, ideological competition and urban segregation are evident.

The related second challenge is the extensive use of migrant labor in urban expansions. Unavailability and high costs of skilled labor have caused an increase in the number of migrant worker settlements, with less attention or experience by authorities leading to urban poverty and inhumane living conditions for migrant workers. These challenges have raised the question of why neoliberalism has not fulfilled its major goal of achieving economic and social sustainability. Accordingly, some Gulf cities recently revisited their approaches and explored new urban developments with more sustainable philosophies and outputs.

The emergence of smart cities in the Gulf region should be investigated within this context. Technological advancements may provide the ideas, solutions, and methods that can decrease the use of exhaustible national resources and improve sustainability outcomes. In tandem with adopting new technologies, Gulf societies need to change current lifestyles by being open to new possibilities and methods. For instance, smart cities involve the accommodation of larger numbers of residents with various interconnected functions and responsibilities without relying on the use of automobiles, by increasing use of solar energy and producing food in local urban settings to fulfill immediate needs. Smart cities adopt compatible living arrangements, wherein the public sector, the private sector, civil society and other members of the population can meaningfully contribute to a city's livelihood and dynamics.

Investments in urban expansion—whether they are investments in infrastructure, transportation, or utilities—require pragmatic approaches based on informed and unbiased research, which should be the key prerequisite for action. The GCC's decision-makers need to envision smart cities not as buildings for business and profit turnovers, but rather as living organisms in which every entity is a driving factor and an indicator. Smart cities should introduce systems where resources are recirculated, including human, energy, and waste resources. Such systems differ greatly from current cities, which are considered consumption machines. The keystone of smart cities in the Gulf is a system that meets the needs of residents with less importation and transportation, which will improve sustainability outcomes.

The core idea of the Gulf smart cities is to secure healthy environments not only by decreasing pollution and carbon use, but also by encouraging residents to adopt healthier, more socially sustainable lifestyles. The realization of this idea requires a high degree of awareness and developed educational systems. Knowledge-based economies are better equipped to solve environmental and social dilemmas. However, the idea of Gulf smart cities requires acceptance by, not co-option of, populations. Admittedly, such criteria make the acceptance of architectural designs, in terms of aesthetics and function, a challenge in cities with culturally diverse populations, but social participation is indeed possible, such as through popular polls, which are conducted elsewhere in the world.

Emerging forms of urbanization in Gulf cities are in dire need of new designs, including vibrant open public spaces. Such spaces have been found to promote healthier lifestyles.[10] Eventually, people may develop a preference for walking and, in turn, give up their cars. With reductions in automobile use, Gulf smart cities would likely restructure functional zoning and advocate less centralization. In addition, communities will cluster upon multi-passenger transportation lines and service areas. It is hoped that there would develop more respect for the rights of pedestrians and cyclists, to increase the uptake of healthier lifestyles. Overall, how people live in smart cities will go through tremendous changes—people will discover how intensive community life can be.

Another major factor within smart cities is types of housing arrangements and their designs. Housing should be arranged in groups both to enable livable population densities within close proximities and to decrease external envelope exposure, thereby avoiding uncontrolled losses or gains in temperature. Given new technologies in zero-carbon constructions, new smart cities can be built with efficient and sustainable materials that do not consume non-renewable energy and do not emit carbon. Decision-makers need to think about how to use new technologies and especially incentives to shape smart cities into vibrant, dynamic, and holistic organisms. The way that a city is perceived is what promotes holism in particular. The populations of new smart cities need to acknowledge humanity and the environment as complementary, relegating individual preferences to the background.

The architecture of smart cities needs to be widely accepted by populations to minimize feelings of alienation and have a similar value to heritage buildings, which reflect the identities of populations. Such architecture could come

---

[10] George Cristian Lazaroiu and Mariacristina Roscia, "Definition methodology for the smart cities model," *Energy*, Vol. 47, No. 1 (November 2012), pp. 326–32.

in many forms and styles that are grounded in the history of the Middle East. Another crucial factor is that core buildings, such as government buildings, need to be connected with other entities to improve the ease of commuting, moving away from current urban designs that prioritize image and single entity identification. This approach to connectivity would enable a dense but efficient transportation network that provides a sense of urban identification and belonging to members of the population living in all parts of a city. Importantly, such connections would increase interactions between the center and peripheries. Smart cities that adopt conservative approaches to energy consumption in urban design may help instill in populations a respect for nature and revive values such as sensitivity to the environment.

The Case of Masdar City

When the UAE officially declared itself an independent federation of seven emirates in 1971, Abu Dhabi was the natural choice for the capital of the new country due to its wealth, its undisputed political clout, as well as the strength of its leaders' local and foreign alliances.[11] Although economic development is ongoing in all emirates, most of the major infrastructure projects are concentrated in two—Dubai and Abu Dhabi. The UAE has started the process of "transforming oil wealth into renewable energy leadership, and has set the long-term goal of a transition from a 20th Century, carbon-based economy into a 21st Century sustainable economy."[12] Three years before the UAE's announcement of its first renewable energy policy in 2009, Abu Dhabi made the decision to initiate the Masdar Initiative.[13]

To implement the initiative, Abu Dhabi created the Abu Dhabi Future Energy Company, which would later be called Masdar in 2006.[14] Masdar City

[11] Rasha Nasra and M. Tina Dacin, "Institutional Arrangements and International Entrepreneurship: The State as Institutional Entrepreneur," *Entrepreneurship Theory and Practice*, Vol. 34, No. 3 (2010), pp. 583–609.

[12] Daniel Reiche, "Renewable Energy Policies in the Gulf countries: A case study of the carbon-neutral Masdar City in Abu Dhabi," *Energy Policy*, Vol. 38 (2010), pp. 378–82.

[13] Toufic Mezher and Jacob Park, "Meeting the Renewable Energy and Sustainability Challenges in GCC Economies: Masdar Initiative Case Study," in Mohamed A. Ramday, ed., *The GCC Economies: Stepping Up to Future Challenges* (New York: Springer, 2012), pp. 69–84.

[14] Mezher and Park, "Meeting the Renewable Energy and Sustainability Challenges in GCC Economies," pp. 74–6.

was established by Mubadala Development Company, a public joint stock company founded by the Abu Dhabi government[15] and designed by Foster and Partners, a British architectural firm.[16] The city, described as an emerging global renewable energy and clean technology cluster that is populated by thousands of residents and hundreds of renewable energy companies, is "presented as a solution to the equally pressing current problems of resource depletion and climate change."[17] It is a US$ 22 billion carbon-neutral zone located seventeen kilometers from Abu Dhabi's downtown.[18] The city is built to achieve various objectives, such as contributing to sustainable human development and economic diversification, situating the UAE as a technology developer and producer, and expanding Abu Dhabi's role in the global energy market.[19]

Discussions on neoliberalism must be contextualized within local realities to fully appreciate the changes and developments in a country. In other words, neoliberalism in one country may look significantly different from neoliberalism in another. Within the context of Masdar City, the degree of openness (that is, neoliberalism) is expressed in the following ways:

• Inputs: Openness to global markets
• Outputs: Capacity-building, development and diffusion of skills, and commercialization of new technologies
• Influence on future direction and priorities: Contributions to policy-making within Abu Dhabi and beyond

Masdar City (*masdar* is Arabic for "source") represents a significant departure from the status quo—not only in the UAE, but the rest of the world—by recognizing the unsustainable impacts that humans are having on the environment and acting to effect change. Sustainable development has been extensively discussed for several decades, particularly as the impact of industrialization on the world's ecosystems has increased. The 1987 Brundtland Report, formally

---

[15] John Perkins, "The Role of Masdar Initiative and Masdar Institute of Science and Technology in Developing and Deploying Renewable Technologies in Emerging Economies," *ATDF Journal*, Vol. 5, Nos. 1/2 (2009), pp. 10–15.

[16] Nicolai Ouroussoff, "In Arabian Desert, A Sustainable City Rises," *New York Times*, 25 September 2010.

[17] Lindsey Snyder, "Masdar City: The Source of Inspiration or Uneconomical Spending?" *International Environmental Issues* (2009).

[18] Mezher and Park, "Meeting the Renewable Energy and Sustainability Challenges in GCC Economies," p. 74.

[19] Ibid., p. 76.

known as the *Report of the World Commission on Environment and Development: Our Common Future*, was a watershed moment that reflected an increasing concern about negative ecological impacts resulting from decades of industrialized economic development.[20] The report, which defined sustainable development as "development that meets the needs of the present without compromising the ability of future generations to meet their own needs," sought to change perceptions about progress by highlighting the following:

- Sustainability should be considered "distributional equity" between present and future generations.
- Economic and social development must be defined in terms of sustainability, not resource extraction and consumption. Also, at a minimum, sustainable development must not endanger natural life support systems (such as the atmosphere, soil, water).
- Institutions are critical in helping ensure that both economic and environmental perspectives are part of decision-making processes.
- Environmental costs should be internalized in order to address the challenges of sustainability. This involves creating and leveraging "intersectoral linkages" (government institutions, civil society organizations, private firms, other key institutions) so that more sustainable outcomes can be achieved.
- Re-orienting and mobilizing institutions, technology and investments so that they work together to achieve sustainable development.

Despite the thoroughness of the report, the challenge according to the vast majority of economists has always been how to balance being more sustainable with the threat that doing so would have serious economic repercussions. Typically, the mere thought of an economic slowdown in most countries has been enough to allow the status quo to persist.

Masdar City does not claim to be the panacea of sustainability, but it is a manifestation of an acknowledgement that change can only come through a clear commitment to action. At its core, Masdar City represents a paradigm shift away from the oil-based economy of the UAE toward a knowledge-based economy that is powered by renewable energy. With an initial commitment of US$ 15 billion from the Abu Dhabi government, the company Masdar's mission is to invest in, incubate, and formally establish commercially viable renewable energy and clean technology industries in Abu Dhabi and around

---

[20] Gro Harlem Brundtland, *Report of the World Commission on Environment and Development: Our Common Future* (Oslo: United Nations, 2009).

the world, thereby contributing to the *Abu Dhabi Economic Vision 2030*.[21] Masdar is comprised of four separate but integrated business units: Masdar Capital, an investment arm; Masdar Clean Energy, a renewable energy power generation and operation unit; Masdar Institute, an independent research-driven graduate university; and Masdar City, "a cutting-edge urban complex where innovative technologies can be tested and implemented in a real-life context of residences and workplaces."[22] Masdar City is designed to operate as a hub for innovation by bringing together knowledgeable actors (e.g. government officials, researchers, investors and entrepreneurs, representatives of small and medium-sized enterprises and established firms), emerging technologies and key institutions to facilitate knowledge creation, knowledge transfer, innovation, and commercialization of new technologies.

The Masdar model hinges on openness, specifically creating strategic partnerships that foster collaboration and attract highly skilled expatriates from all over the world. Such openness is an essential part of Masdar City's success within Abu Dhabi and beyond. This openness to global markets is evidenced by the fact that Masdar City is currently home to 198 companies and institutions, many of which are foreign. Key examples include the International Renewable Energy Association (IRENA)[23] and Massachusetts Institute of Technology (MIT).[24] Another indicator of openness to global markets is Masdar Capital's investment in and incubation of renewable energy and clean technologies. Projects within the UAE and elsewhere in the world are managed by two investment funds. The Masdar Clean Tech Fund is a US$ 250

---

[21] "Masdar Economic Vision 2030," https://www.ecouncil.ae/PublicationsEn/economic-vision-2030-full-versionEn.pdf, last accessed 26 May 2016.

[22] Emirates Competitiveness Council, *Policy in Action; Masdar: Powering UAE's Competitiveness with Clean Energy* (Dubai: Emirates Competitiveness Council, 2013).

[23] IRENA, which is now headquartered in Masdar City, is the world's leading organization to support the transition to renewable energy usage by developing new synergies, facilitating dialogue, and sharing information and best practices with various public and private sector institutions. IRENA's presence not only brings world-renowned expertise and credibility to the renewable energy vision of the UAE, but also much-needed data and policy advice on renewable energy policy to the GCC.

[24] MIT's role relates to the initial establishment of the Masdar Institute (the world's first graduate-level university dedicated to sustainability-related issues) and, since then, conducting collaborative research projects and educational exchanges with doctoral candidates from the Masdar Institute. Anchor corporate tenants include Siemens, Mitsubishi Heavy Industries, General Electric and others.

million venture-capital vehicle that invests in the development and commercialization of renewable energy, energy efficiency, and water desalination technologies. The DB Masdar Clean Tech Fund, a US$ 290 million fund co-managed by Deutsche Bank Climate Change Advisors, invests in clean energy, energy efficiency, and environmental resources projects across Asia, Europe, and North America. Furthermore, Masdar Clean Energy has committed over US$ 1.7 billion and funded utility-scale renewable energy projects that have produced nearly 1.5 gigawatts of energy, with 92 per cent of the capacity produced outside the UAE.[25] These projects, which are co-funded and involve collaboration with some of the most established companies in the world, reflect Masdar's approach to risk management and financing.

Masdar's partnerships, its investments in emerging technologies, and the growing portfolio of its projects represent a clear commitment to action, given the technical and financial feasibility of renewable energy as a viable alternative to fossil fuels. This paradigm shift is even more astounding given that Abu Dhabi generates 57 per cent of its gross domestic product from the sale of oil and gas,[26] with reserves expected to last another 150 years.[27] The Abu Dhabi government increasingly sees renewable energy as a significant market opportunity as new technologies improve while oil and gas reserves decline. Having said that, further investigation is required to determine the extent to which Masdar's partnerships, investments, and projects foster good corporate governance and accountability outside the company within the broader landscape of Abu Dhabi's institutions and companies.

Capacity-building, economic diversification, and moving toward knowledge-based economies remain priorities for many GCC states, which include these in their national development strategies. In the case of Abu Dhabi, vast oil and gas resources provide the financial stability and freedom necessary to make long-term investments that support the *Abu Dhabi Economic Vision 2030*.[28] Masdar is one actor helping to realize this vision. There is evidently a degree of openness regarding Masdar's investments in projects and new tech-

[25] "Masdar Fact Sheet," http://www.masdar.ae/en/assets/detail/masdar-fact-sheet-ver-1-jan-2013, last accessed 26 May 2016.

[26] Department of Economic Development, *Economic Report of the Emirate of Abu Dhabi 2013* (Abu Dhabi: Department of Economic Development, 2014).

[27] "Isthmus Partners Publications," http://www.isthmuspartners.ae/Publications.html, last accessed 26 May 2016.

[28] "Abu Dhabi Economic Vision 2030," https://www.adced.ae/sites/En/ev/SitePages/ev.aspx, last accessed 26 May 2016.

nologies, with an apparent preference for investing outside the UAE. The majority of Masdar Capital and Masdar Clean Energy projects appear to be outside the UAE. This outward orientation is counterbalanced in part by local solar projects in Abu Dhabi (Masdar City and Shams 1 are relatively small in comparison to the other projects, particularly those in the United Kingdom and Spain), and by contributions to capacity-building via the Masdar Institute. Masdar's outward orientation poses an interesting question. To what degree can a renewable energy and clean technology cluster develop in Abu Dhabi when significant investments are made outside the UAE? Innovation theory indicates that close physical proximity is a key enabler of innovation and commercialization, because capturing and transmitting tacit knowledge, which is so critical to the innovation process, works best with close human interaction and personal relationships.[29] Given that Masdar City is composed of actors both inside and outside Abu Dhabi, the critical question is: does this mix hinder or strengthen capacity-building, innovation, and commercialization processes?

The answer would be within the scope of this chapter, but more time is required for disaggregated data and evidence-based studies on outcomes to become available, given that Masdar was established in 2006 and the UAE's national innovation system is still developing—the system has made exceptional progress in a relatively short period of time but evidence-based studies were unavailable at the time of writing. For the purposes of this chapter, the focus will be on what capacity-building and commercialization activities have taken place thus far, rather than attempting to answer the above question, which is an avenue for future study.

Capacity-building and commercialization within the context of Masdar City will be examined from the perspectives of the Masdar Institute and Masdar's contribution to local events that promote sustainability. The Masdar Institute, the world's first graduate-level university focusing on providing solutions to sustainability-related issues, represents a significant investment in capacity-building, knowledge transfer, technology-based innovation, and eventual commercialization of new technologies in the UAE. Established in 2007, the institute's focus is exclusively on engineering, with eight masters programs in engineering and one doctoral program in interdisciplinary engineering. The institute has enjoyed a strong relationship with MIT since its

29 Jon-Arild Johannessen, Bjorn Olsen, Johan Olaisen, "Aspects of innovation theory based on knowledge-management," *International Journal of Information Management*, Vol. 19 (1999), pp. 121–39.

197

establishment and collaborates via student/faculty exchanges, research facilities, and funding of joint research projects. In terms of research, there are five sponsored research centers focusing on areas of interest to industry and government, as well as five additional Institute Research Centers—iCenters—that complement the sponsored centers.[30]

In terms of faculty and students, the Masdar Institute currently has eighty-one faculty members from thirty countries, with a faculty/student ratio of 1:5. Despite the global diversity of faculty and students, strong local participation by Emirati students is critical for building local capacity in a part of the world that widely relies on expatriates who often remain in a country for only a few years. The inaugural intake consisted of 89 students from 79 countries. As of 2014, there was a total of 491 students, of which 189 were new that year, with 88 Emiratis. Just under half, or 44 per cent, of the student population were female; and of those, 44 per cent were Emiratis. A total of 307 students have graduated to date, with an additional 38 expected to graduate as the class of 2014.[31]

It is essential for institutions, companies, and individuals in Masdar City to champion the cause of sustainability, but populations must also be empowered to participate in the cause. Masdar's mission is to demonstrate to the UAE and the world via its projects that living in a more sustainable way is not only achievable, but also economically prosperous for those on the leading edge of innovation. Sustainability must not be seen as a challenge or threat. Rather, it should be considered an opportunity for populations to be active parts of solutions. Masdar's recognition of the importance of social engagement is clear, evident from the myriad of initiatives that it leads in collaboration with other institutions in the UAE, including the Zayed Future Energy Prize, Sustainability Week, and World Water Forum. The increasing awareness and importance of these annual events help to institutionalize the principles of sustainability across communities and empower local populations to participate in the cause of sustainability. One of the most significant contributions that the Abu Dhabi government and Masdar have made, this empowerment is increasingly becoming institutionalized across the UAE and other GCC states.

As capacity-building continues, the focus of the public and private sectors will naturally shift to the commercialization of new technologies. Assessing Masdar's contribution to commercialization is a complex undertaking because

[30] "Masdar Institute, Research Centers," http://www.masdar.ac.ae/research/research-centers/icenters-research, last accessed 26 May 2016.
[31] Ibid.

commercialization involves many actors and it is often difficult to ascribe causality in cases of success and failure without disaggregated data and evidence-based studies. According to the Masdar Institute, sixty-eight invention disclosures have been received, forty-four patent applications are pending and, three patents have been approved so far.[32] Further in-depth analysis is required to go beyond the numbers and determine the nature of the commercialization support programs at the institute and their interaction with other institutions and companies around the world. The challenge of commercialization is multifaceted, and thus further examination is required to assess other contributing factors, such as the strength of the intellectual property regime in the emirate; policies that promote corporate innovation and university-industry collaboration; the degree of knowledge sharing and transfer among all actors within Masdar City; funding programs for the creation of prototypes and other activities prior to commercialization; and access to private equity to fund commercialization and economic development (one of the seven policy priorities in the *Abu Dhabi Economic Vision 2030*).

Policy-making is an essential role for states, which is particularly relevant in the context of sustainability, simply because shifts toward more sustainable societies will only come via deliberate government intervention. It is increasingly evident that profit-seeking companies are largely unwilling to act voluntarily to achieve (sometimes costly) sustainability outcomes unless prompted by state regulations and incentives. Although market forces are an essential part of addressing sustainable energy challenges, market forces will not trigger such shifts—only state action and social pressure can do this.

As a state-led initiative, Masdar plays an important role in influencing the policy agenda through its legitimacy and its leadership in addressing sustainable energy challenges. Data, which must be gathered, and institutions are critical in this regard. Data gathered by various think tanks and other key institutions, such as Masdar business units and IRENA, can be used to identify challenges, define the policy agenda and direct policy-making, a process known as evidence-based policy making. In April 2015, Masdar, IRENA, and the UAE Ministry of Foreign Affairs issued a joint report entitled *Renewable Energy Prospects: United Arab Emirates*,[33] which leverages local resource

---

[32] "Masdar Institute," http://www.masdar.ac.ae/, last accessed 26 May 2016.

[33] Masdar, International Renewable Energy Agency, and United Arab Emirates Ministry of Foreign Affairs, *Renewable Energy Prospects: United Arab Emirates* (Abu Dhabi: International Renewable Energy Agency, 2015).

expertise to create a portfolio of renewable energy options and outline the associated costs for the UAE. This collaboration with the UAE Ministry of Foreign Affairs exemplifies the multi-stakeholder approach that is needed to succeed when data are initially unavailable. Furthermore, new innovations in sustainable energy technologies are emerging through the Masdar Institute, sponsored research centers and iCenters and are being validated for commercial potential. Masdar-funded projects across the globe are implementing these new technologies and gathering vital data on the feasibility of these innovations through large-scale renewable energy projects.

Abu Dhabi's commitment to Masdar City, and the conviction that renewable energy and clean technology will play a key role in sustaining Abu Dhabi's economic prosperity, represent a significant paradigm shift, especially in an emirate that is endowed with vast oil and gas resources. Masdar City's achievements in catalyzing synergies have been possible due to strategic partnerships. Yet, more needs to be done, especially with regard to data in line with the data revolution being proposed to accompany the country's development agenda. Masdar must continue to lead and engage broader populations by bringing together states, industries, civil society and academia, and by devising solutions that address environmental concerns and reward innovation. This is not an easy task, as evidenced by the many developed countries that lack a clear strategy on the use of renewable energy sources. The challenge is not a technological one, as economically viable solutions exist. Rather, the central challenge is managing the often-conflicting interests of states, industries, and populations, as seen in experiences with the Kyoto Protocol and United Nations climate change negotiations. Credible institutions such as Masdar City have the potential to push sustainability agendas forward and enable robust national innovation systems whereby achieving greater sustainability is not only a social imperative, but also a significant untapped economic opportunity.

Conclusions

The globalization of neoliberal ideals and practices is manifest in the development of new markets across the world, with much convergence and divergence being evident. In the Gulf region and elsewhere, one product of such globalization is the "smart city." As people and capital move more freely around the world, people increasingly have the option to choose where they want to live. Such new-found choice has sparked competition among global cities. The case of Masdar City demonstrates that smart cities have been designed in accordance with that competition to attract knowledge-rich and entrepreneurial people, who are assumed to benefit the state's economy through their ideas and their goods and services. The neoliberal market mentality is imbedded in the development of smart cities because of the competition for global talent, but not necessarily due to the absence of state intervention.

In the Gulf, state-owned enterprises have played a critical role in state-building and economic development. It is essential to realize that within the Gulf context, market mechanisms have not been completely free. Monarchies of the Gulf region have used a brand of state-managed capitalism that includes cooperation between the public and private sectors to conceptualize and implement national policy programs and initiatives such as the Masdar Initiative. Neoliberal market theory promotes minimizing state intervention in business and economic affairs. Yet, states in the Gulf often use their state-owned enterprises or solicit the business expertise of multinational corporations to implement policy programs. The point is that the framework of economic competition, efficiency, and incentives is associated with neoliberal free market theory, but the reality is that development projects such as smart cities are not likely to come to fruition without interventions by states.

The qualities and outcomes of Masdar City described in this chapter are not necessarily typical of a smart city, nor are they the natural products of a free market economy. But they can be promoted through policy processes put forth and executed by states. The construction of smart cities in the Gulf is a progressive idea that has the potential to meet many of the goals of states in the region and address problems that tend to emerge with the rapidly growing populations in the urban areas, such as poor sustainability outcomes as well as deep-rooted challenges such as diversification of natural resource-dependent economies.

9

URBAN DYNAMICS IN IRANIAN PORT CITIES

GROWTH, INFORMALITY, AND DECAY IN BANDAR ABBAS

Pooya Alaedini and Mehrdad Javaheripour

Bandar Abbas, the capital of Hormozgan Province, is Iran's largest port, with a long history of trade and fishing activities. It is located at the entrance of the Persian Gulf on the northern side of the Strait of Hormuz, and is strategically important to the country in both a commercial and military sense. Bandar Abbas's natives mostly speak a dialect of Persian and adhere to either Sunni or Shi'a Islam. There are Arab, Baluchi, and African as well as earlier South Asian and perhaps European influences on the population of the city. Named after the Safavid monarch Shah Abbas the Great, Bandar Abbas was in the past also known as Gumbarun (or a similar variation). Despite its importance as a trading port, it had a population of no more than 10,000 before the modern era,[1] owing to its relatively inhospitable climate and the scarcity of water in the area. While modern municipal activities and town improvements were initi-

---

[1] Willem Floor, *Bandar Abbas: The Natural Trade Gateway of Southeast Iran* (Washington, DC: Mage, 2011), pp. 16–17.

ated in Bandar Abbas in the 1920s,[2] the city's development was delayed as it was bypassed by the Trans-Iranian Railways, inaugurated in the 1930s. Yet, its rapid expansion in the late 1960s in terms of population and area was facilitated by the construction of new deep water port facilities, and it has been enhanced ever since by further economic investment and migration.[3]

To a large extent, Bandar Abbas' rapid growth in the last four decades reflects general urbanization trends in Iran. According to figures from the Statistical Center of Iran,[4] the total population of the country grew at an average annual rate of 2.32 per cent, from 33.7 million persons in 1976–7 to 75.1 million 2011–12. Iran's urban population grew at an average rate of 3.54 per cent from 15.85 million to 53.65 million (71.4 per cent of total) in this 35-year period. Population densities (averaging about 45 persons per square kilometer) and urbanization (size and number of urban settlements) are much lower in the south and east as compared to the north and west of Iran, due to differences in precipitation rates between the two halves of the country. Bandar Abbas has nonetheless grown rapidly in the past few decades to rank among the top 20 of around 80 Iranian cities that have more than 100,000 inhabitants.[5]

As in many other developing countries, a byproduct of rapid urbanization in Iran has been the proliferation of unplanned, under-serviced, and poverty-stricken neighborhoods often referred to as slums. There is evidence for informal shelter in Bandar Abbas going back several decades. An informative study conducted in the early 1970s on the housing situation on the city's fringes recorded tents and date-palm huts as well as other traditional makeshift dwellings still existing in Bandar Abbas.[6] Yet, the proliferation of informal, decaying, under-serviced, and/or poverty-stricken neighborhoods in Bandar Abbas is related to the city's rapid growth in the last four decades.

Although similar macro circumstances and urban regulatory regimes affect Iranian cities, their spatial and socio-economic outcomes have certain distinct characters in each case. This is arguably more true for Bandar Abbas, taking into account its unique location, its economic potential, and the regional and

---

[2] Ibid., pp. 220–27.

[3] X. De Planhol, "Bandar-e Abbas," in *Encyclopaedia Iranica*, www.iranicaonline.org

[4] Statistical Center of Iran, Excel file on Iran's population, http://amar.org.ir

[5] Ibid.

[6] H. Nirumand and M. Ahsan, "Hashiyih-neshinan-i Bandar Abbas" (Squatter settlers of Bandar Abbas), Institute for Social Studies and Research, University of Tehran (1972).

exogenous forces by which it is influenced. In this chapter, we probe the dynamics of urban growth, informality, and decay in Bandar Abbas as well as public sector initiatives addressing the latter two issues. We discuss some of the general factors that influence informality and decay in Iranian cities in the next section: in particular, inflation and unemployment, income stagnation and inequality, and speculative land markets and restrictive land-use regulations. We then suggest that though Bandar Abbas has become Iran's main cargo transit port, receiving manufacturing investment as well as migrants from outside the province, its economy is polarized into traditional and modern parts, neither of which produces adequate employment and income for the city's poor households more or less native to the region.

After examining the spatial dimensions of this polarization in Bandar Abbas, we turn to the socio-economic and physical characteristics of the city's low-income and under-serviced neighborhoods categorized as informal settlements in the government's recent initiatives. In the last section before our conclusion, we examine the outcome of earlier informal settlement pilot upgrading projects in Bandar Abbas as well as recommendations of more recent initiatives aimed at providing a citywide plan for the city's low-income neighborhoods. We further speculate on the future of the low-income and under-serviced settlements in Bandar Abbas and express optimism about current initiatives that are supposed to take a holistic and regional approach to addressing urban polarization in Bandar Abbas and the plight of unplanned, poverty-stricken, and under-serviced settlements. Much of our analysis in this chapter is based on published and unpublished reports prepared for the Iranian government.[7] We also make extensive use of data from the Statistical Center of Iran and other official sources, complemented by findings from recent field inquiries and communication with public sector authorities.[8]

---

[7] The present authors were involved in three of the earlier studies cited in this chapter. These studies benefited from extensive field research, including quantitative surveys, facility surveys, observations, and/or individual and group interviews with local residents in target neighborhoods of Bandar Abbas, as well as with public sector officials and other stakeholders.

[8] To address information gaps, a short trip was made to Bandar Abbas in February 2014 by one of the authors. Additional information was collected through communication with officers of the Urban Development and Revitalization Organization and Bandar Abbas Municipality.

Informality and Decay in Iranian Cities: Circumstances, Influencing Factors, and Public Policy Responses

While the slum situation in Iran is not as dire as is depicted in some of the alarmist literature on Third World urbanization,[9] almost all Iranian cities have settlements exhibiting a combination of informal tenure, low-quality construction, lack of spatial organization, inadequate urban services, and poverty in economic, social, and cultural terms. Overall, most Iranian cities have been facing difficulty in dealing with rapid growth, fostering a dynamic economy, or adequately addressing informality and decay.[10] A number of factors have influenced these circumstances in Iran—some more or less distinct and others rather typical of developing countries.

In the past few decades, the Iranian economy and by extension Iranian cities have been subjected to a number of structural problems ironically caused by significant oil revenues.[11] Some of these include economic volatility and high or extremely high inflation rates,[12] capital-intensive production together with double-digit unemployment rates,[13] and import-based commercial activities against a background of highly unequal income-generating opportunities. Despite the existence of significant oil revenues, per capita income has not risen above its peak figure of 1976 in real terms.[14] Whereas inequality is believed to have decreased after the 1979 Revolution, as evidenced by improvements in the Gini coefficient,[15] the average annual expenditure figure

[9] For example, see Mike Davis, *Planet of Slums* (London: Verso, 2006).

[10] Descriptions of this situation may be found in S. M. Kamrava, *Shahr-sazi-i mu'asir dar Iran* (Contemporary Urban Development in Iran), 4th edn (Tehran: University of Tehran Press, 2012), as well as in M. Ghomami, *Barrasi-i vaz'iyat-i shahr-sazi va barnamih-rizi-i shahri va mantaqih-i dar Iran-i mu'aser* (Analysis of Urban Development and Urban and Regional Planning in Contemporary Iran) (Tehran: Afrand, 2013).

[11] See M. Karshenas, *Oil, State, and Industrialization in Iran* (Cambridge: Cambridge University Press, 1990); Hadi Salehi Esfahani, et al., "An Empirical Growth Model for Major Oil Exporters," Cesifo Working Paper No. 3780 (March 2012).

[12] Central Bank of Iran, "Economic Indicators" (various years, www.cbi.ir, last accessed 23 March 2014).

[13] Ibid.

[14] World Bank economic data on Iran, www.worldbank.org, last accessed 18 March 2014).

[15] Statistical Center of Iran, "Tawzi'-i daramad dar khanevarha-i shahri, rustai, va kolli keshvar, 1380–1391" (Income distribution for urban, rural, and all families of the country), http://amar.org.ir

of 81,289,000 rials for urban households in 2007–8 still fell between the averages of the 7th and 8th highest deciles—that is, expenditure for around 70 per cent of urban households was below the average figure.[16]

Rising oil prices in certain periods, as in the last few years, can also cause sharp increases in the price of non-tradables—in particular, real estate—with detrimental impacts on the production of tradables as well as on the overall inflation rate.[17] This in turn results in land speculation and housing shortages and, by extension, the growth of unplanned and under-serviced settlements that house low-income groups. For example, according to the 2006–7 census,[18] there were 1.5 million more households than housing units in the country, while 500,000 housing units were vacant. Furthermore, based on the studies conducted for the revision of the Comprehensive Housing Plan,[19] urban households' ability to purchase homes has continuously decreased in the past decade and a half, with a more severe decline experienced among lower-income groups. This is also reflected by the drop in the proportion of urban households owning their dwellings, which fell from 67 per cent in 1996–7 to 56.6 per cent in 2011–12.[20] Indeed, with the scarcity of alternative investment opportunities against a background of rising prices, the real estate market has acted as a positive feedback loop through which home values have increased faster than the general inflation rate. Under these circumstances, informal housing where official planning and regulations are absent has become the only affordable option for many low-income households.[21]

---

[16] Statistical Center of Iran, "Natayiji-i tarh-i amargiri-i hazinih va daramad-i khani-varha-i shahri va rustai, 1386" (Results of statistical survey of expenditure and income of urban and rural families), http://amar.org.ir

[17] This is referred to as the "Dutch disease," on which see, for example, J. P. Neary and S. J. G. van Wijnbergen, *Natural Resources and the Macroeconomy* (Cambridge, MA: MIT Press, 1986).

[18] Statistical Center of Iran, *Salnamih-i amari-i Iran, 1386* (Statistical Yearbook of Iran) (2008).

[19] Ministry of Housing and Urban Development, "Motaliat-i baznigari-i tarh-i jami'-i maskan" (Studies for revision of comprehensive housing plan), internal report (2014).

[20] Ibid. (based on figures from the Statistical Center of Iran).

[21] See P. Baross, "Sequencing Land Development: The Price Implications of Legal and Illegal Settlement Growth," in P. Baross and J. Linden, eds, *The Transformation of Land Supply Systems in Third World Cities* (Aldershot, Hants: Avebury, 1990), pp. 57–82; D. E. Dowall, "Comparing Karachi's Informal and Formal Housing Delivery System," *Cities*, Vol. 8, No. 3 (1991), pp. 217–27.

Master plans—a combination of comprehensive and detailed plans for each municipality of significant size—are prepared for Iranian cities on a regular basis, determining official municipal boundaries, land-use patterns, and circulation. While master plans are also supposed to link to the urban economy on the one hand and to financial resources of the municipalities on the other, they have been criticized for erroneous forecasts as well as for being no more than a wish list prepared in the form of maps.[22] Indeed, many of the plans' details never materialize, due partly to the fact that they are prepared under the auspices of the central government without taking into account the realities and finances of the municipalities and urban line agencies.

More importantly, the formal planning process has been criticized for short-changing low-income households in its downstream urban land-use designs, for not reaching its intended beneficiaries with its subsidies, and for failing to supply adequate land, thus severely limiting the "right to the city" for low-income households.[23] Each city in Iran has an official boundary outside which urban services are not supposed to be provided. Additional land may be brought within this boundary when a new master plan is prepared based on future demand estimates, through political pressure, and/or in acceptance of realities—for example, once the presence of a new informal settlement outside the city boundary becomes imposing enough. Furthermore, the government holds vast land properties in and around cities which it releases only gradually. In fact, in the past decades, the government has taken over much more land than it has released.[24] Public sector land allocations for housing in the last three decades have been mostly achieved through housing cooperatives, which do not serve those included in the informal economy and by extension a large portion of low-income households. Finally, urban land-use plans set minimum lot sizes that are for the most part outside the affordability range of low-income households. Thus, informality is at least partially produced by public sector planning itself,[25] although it is ironically a target of its intervention as well.

[22] Sharmand Consulting Engineers, *Shiviha-i tahaqquq-i tarhha-i tawsi'ih-i shahri* (Methods of Researching Urban Development) (Tehran: Municipalities Organization, 2000).

[23] E. Zebardast, "Marginalization of the Urban Poor and the Expansion of the Spontaneous Settlements on the Tehran Metropolitan Fringe," *Cities*, Vol. 23, No. 6 (2006) pp. 439–54; the concept of the "right to the city" is advanced in H. Lefebvre, *The Production of Space* (Oxford: Blackwell, 1974).

[24] F. Fardanesh, "Housing Profile of Iran," prepared for Urban Development and Revitalization Organization (2013).

[25] As suggested for example by A. Soliman, "Tilting at Sphinxes: Locating Urban

All of the above factors point to the reasons behind the proliferation of unplanned, poverty-stricken, and under-serviced settlements in Iran, which are recognized by the government in two categories: a decaying fabric or physically-stressed zone (*baft-i farsudih*) and an informal settlement (*sukunat-gah-i ghayr-i rasmi*). According to the official definition,[26] decaying fabric is characterized by micro land divisions (less than 200 square meters for more than 50 per cent of the lots), impenetrability (less than 6 meter wide alleys in 50 per cent of cases), and lack of sustainability (lack of structural integrity in more than 50 per cent of buildings). Depending on the existence of one or more of these conditions, an area is considered relatively stressed, highly stressed, or extremely stressed. Furthermore, the national document on "Strategies for Enabling and Regularizing Informal Settlements" addresses urban areas with the following features: "Hastily constructed housing often built by their eventual occupants, mostly without permit to construct ... outside existing formal planning ... Concentration of lower income groups ... with functional linkages to the main city... [and] low quality of life and desperately low urban services ... and high population density."[27]

According to the figures provided by the Urban Development and Revitalization Organization (UDRO) on twenty major Iranian cities,[28] informal settlements on average cover around 8 per cent of urban areas, 93 per cent of which are found within the official municipal boundaries. Needless to say, there are significant differences from one city to the next. For example, in Bandar Abbas about 30 per cent of the land area is taken by the government to comprise informal settlements, whereas the corresponding figure for Zanjan is less than 1 per cent. Furthermore, it is estimated that 9–10 per cent of Iranian urban areas constitute decaying fabric.[29]

Informality in Egyptian Cities," in A. Roy and N. Al Sayyad, eds, *Urban Informality: Transnational Perspectives from the Middle East, South Asia and Latin America* (Lanham, MD: Lexington Books, 2004), pp. 171–207.

[26] Urban Development and Revitalization Organization, www.udro.org.ir, last accessed 26 May 2016.

[27] Urban Development and Revitalization Organization, "Strategies for Enabling and Regularizing Informal Settlements," brochure (2004).

[28] Headed by a deputy minister of roads and urban development and in charge of addressing informal settlements and decaying fabric.

[29] Pajuheshkadih-i Towsi'ih-i Kalbadi, "Samandihi-i va tavanmandsazi-i sukunatgahha-i nabisaman" (Settlement and empowerment of squatter settlers), unpublished report prepared for Urban Development and Revitalization Organization (2011);

In practice, there is a great deal of overlap between informal settlements and decaying fabrics. Yet, decaying fabrics more often than not are located in the historical/central parts of Iranian cities that have been experiencing steady physical, economic, and social decline. With better-off households moving to the more modern parts of the cities, these areas have become low-income neighborhoods that further attract poor migrants. Such neighborhoods are usually under-serviced, due partly to their physical attributes. Yet their lands, located within the central zones of the cities, are often valuable and may potentially be leveraged in urban renewal programs—this perhaps being the most important criterion by which decaying fabrics are designated as such by the public sector.

By contrast, informal settlements usually develop outside official city boundaries in their initial phases, attracting migrants (often from rural areas) as well as poor households already in the city, who cannot afford regular types of housing offered in the formal market. A great amount of unused land around Iranian cities outside official city boundaries is privately owned and may be sold informally to poor households demanding it. Furthermore, due to droughts as well as opportunity costs (affected also by rising wages), agricultural land in the vicinity of cities may also be destined for low-income housing through informal transactions. What makes these types of land attractive is exactly the fact that they do not have proper lot divisions or construction permits and are thus much cheaper than land inside the official city boundaries. Some documentation is usually provided for the transaction, such as a promissory note (*qawlnamih* or *patih*), which means that buyers are more or less legal owners, although they may lack construction permits and full titles. Construction on such sites therefore tends to take place at night and illegally. While these settlements are not recognized by the municipal authorities, they often get some urban services. New low-income developments formed in villages located just outside city boundaries, as well as squatter settlements which are becoming rarer in Iran in recent years, may be considered special cases of such settlements. Over time, settlements formed outside city boundaries are likely to get incorporated into the municipal areas under pressure, as a way to provide them with basic services. Yet, considering how such neighborhoods start, even when they are incorporated into municipal areas,

Abbas Mokhber and Pooya Alaedini, "Urban Informal Settlements in Iran: Contributing Factors and Population Estimates," *Tashakkol*, Vol. 6 (2011), pp. ii-iv.

they retain much of their slum characteristics, that is, low level of social services, improper lot divisions, poor quality housing stock, narrow alleys difficult to service, or illegal water and electricity connections.

There is always a complex background of property interests against which formalization in informal settlements must take place.[30] In the Iranian context, many of the residents already have some degree of security against eviction, and possessing a full title does not necessarily translate into a collateral— for entrepreneurial purposes, for instance. Thus, titling in such neighborhoods, as suggested by De Soto,[31] is certainly not a panacea. Indeed, many opulent homes in Iran lack full titles and we should therefore be careful when treating lack of title as equal to poverty.[32] Furthermore, formalization under certain circumstances, especially in the absence of other programs, can actually push poorer households out of a neighborhood by making the market less affordable,[33] or through replacement of low-income households by more affluent ones.[34] In practice, formalization is a slow and lengthy process in Iran and has not been taken up by the government as a specific program in the informal neighborhoods, most likely due to the fear of attracting more rural migrants to these settlements.

A major initiative focussed on upgrading Iran's informal settlements was undertaken through the Urban Upgrading and Housing Reform Project (UUHRP). It was implemented by UDRO with the assistance of the World Bank in the period 2004–9.[35] A main purpose of UUHRP was to pilot-test and refine an integrated approach to upgrading under-serviced neighborhoods in five Iranian cities—Bandar Abbas, Kirmanshah, Sanandaj, Tabriz, and Zahidan—ultimately improving living conditions based on community priori-

---

[30] O. Razzaz, "Legality and Stability in Land and Housing Markets," *Land Lines*, Vol. 9, No. 3 (1997), pp. 1–4.

[31] H. De Soto, *The Mystery of Capital: Why Capitalism Triumphs in the West and Fails Everywhere Else* (New York: Basic Books, 2000).

[32] A. Roy "Urban Informality: Toward an Epistemology of Planning," *Journal of the American Planning Association*, Vol. 71, No. 2 (2005), pp. 147–58.

[33] G. Payne, *Land, Rights, and Innovation: Improving Tenure Security for the Urban Poor* (London: ITDG Publishing, 2002).

[34] R. Burgess, "Self-help Housing Advocacy: A Curious Form of Radicalism: A Critique of the Work of John F. C. Turner," in P. Ward, ed., *Self-help Housing: A Critique* (London: Mansell, 1982), pp. 55–79.

[35] World Bank, UUHRP Project Document, 2004, www.worldbank.org, last accessed 19 January 2008.

ties, helping indigenize an urban upgrading model for Iran, and providing feedback for the institutionalization of an upgrading structure at the national, provincial, and urban levels. Whereas the project faced many difficulties and could not undertake all its activities by its completion date, it succeeded in bringing about a new public sector direction in dealing with informal settlements in Iran.[36] Bandar Abbas's low-income and under-serviced neighborhoods have continued to remain a target of national government initiatives.

Concerning decaying fabric, the government has in the past few years adopted a new "participatory" approach, which entails facilitating renovation of decaying fabric through the activities of local agents, municipalities, the private sector, banks, local cooperatives, and charity foundations. A renovation incentive package is provided to qualifying residents, which includes discounts on taxes, provision of inexpensive bank facilities, and addressing the cost of temporary relocation during reconstruction or retro-fitting of buildings in zones considered to be decaying. In Tehran, renovation of stressed fabric is being promoted through neighborhood-based facilitation offices by a powerful municipal organization. In Bandar Abbas and other mid-size Iranian cities, however, there are only decaying fabric designations with no proactive program, which enables owners of certain lots to benefit from the facilities and discounts mentioned above, if they so choose. Furthermore, in Bandar Abbas, parts of the decaying fabric have been lumped together with informal settlements as the target of public sector activities—discussed in more detail below—meaning that certain areas in the city may be both targeted for upgrading and qualify for a decaying fabric renovation package of incentives. This double designation in Bandar Abbas may also reflect the government's evolving—although not yet settled—approach to low-income and under-serviced urban areas.[37]

In the Comprehensive Housing Plan prepared in 2005–6 for the Fourth National Development Plan,[38] certain strategies were formulated to lower the cost of land and the price of housing. While the Comprehensive Housing

---

[36] Pooya Alaedini, et al., "Erteqa'-i vaz'iyat-i rifahi-i ahali-i sokunatgahha-i ghayr-i rasmi dar Iran" (Upgrading welfare status of the informal settlements in Iran), *Rifah-i Ijtima'Ie*, Vol. 41 (2011), pp. 69–92.

[37] Based on personal communication with UDRO authorities, a new document addressing informal settlements and decaying fabric together has been prepared and is currently undergoing the government's approval process.

[38] Ministry of Housing and Urban Development, "Tarh-i jami'-i maskan," (Comprehensive housing plan), internal report (2006).

Plan was abandoned by the Ahmadinejad administration, one of its strategies was turned into a program called Mihr Housing Plan (MHP) and was given full public sector support after 2007–8 as the main low-income housing initiative.[39] The plan entails constructing medium- to high-rise buildings on publicly-owned lands and exempting them from construction taxes and fees. In this way, only the price of construction is reflected in each housing unit, making it affordable for low-income households. To qualify for MHP, applicants must show that they do not own any house or urban land, have used no government housing credit previously, have lived in the city for five years, and are heads of households or older than a certain age. Around one third of the cost of housing must be covered by the applicant—usually in installments that may take between a few months and a couple of years—before keys are handed over to the applicants. The rest is covered by a government-subsidized bank loan. MHP's activities are relevant to the discussion of informality and decay in Bandar Abbas and will be described later in the chapter.

The Economy of Bandar Abbas

By the early 1960s, Bandar Abbas had only a few workshops, an under-utilized fish-canning plant, and port facilities that handled an insignificant amount of cargo.[40] Yet, it received a serious boost when a large deep water port was constructed to the south-west of the city in the mid-1960s, and Iranian naval headquarters were moved nearby in the mid-1970s. Major highways that connected Bandar Abbas to other areas of the country were also constructed in this period. The city grew rapidly after the mid-1970s, owing to the expansion of commercial, transport, and to some extent manufacturing activities. Furthermore, the Iran–Iraq War, which was intensely fought close to the western ports of Iran in the Persian Gulf during the 1980s, ironically had a positive impact on the growth of Bandar Abbas.

The first comprehensive plan for the city of Bandar Abbas was approved in 1967,[41] which reported that due to the scarcity of water, manpower, and access

[39] M. Rashid-Nahal, et al., *Ta'avuniha-i maskan-i mehr: anchih mutaqaziyan va a'za' bayad bidanand* (Mehr Housing Cooperatives: What Applicants and Members Should Know) (Tehran: Paygan, 2009).

[40] X. De Planhol, "Bandar-e Abbas," in *Encyclopaedia Iranica*, www.iranicaonline.org (1998), last accessed 13 December 2013.

[41] Ministry of Housing and Urban Development, [First] Comprehensive Plan of Bandar Abbas, prepared by A. Adibi Consulting Engineers (1967).

to connecting highways, Hormozgan Province generally and Bandar Abbas County specifically hosted a limited number of industries, comprising some small workshops as well as larger canning, food-processing, and construction material plants mostly located in the general area of Bandar Abbas. In the 1970s, the government's vision for Bandar Abbas was to develop it into a commercial pole with a major military component. Redevelopment of port facilities and the establishment of related industries in Bandar Abbas quickly added to the population of the city. Housing for the workers was accordingly planned in the western part of the city, as Shishsad Dastgah (600 unit complex) and Duhizar (2,000 unit complex) developments. Another comprehensive plan for the city was drafted prior to the 1979 Revolution, but was subsequently abandoned due to post-revolutionary events. It envisioned the following: further development of the port facilities as well as fishing and canning industries; construction of major metal smelting, chemical, petrochemical, and nuclear plants; establishment of major shipyards; further development of military facilities; and the construction of new housing units for 60,000 personnel over a ten-year period.[42] Despite long periods of delay in the completion of the above initiatives due to post-revolutionary uncertainties and funding shortages during the Iran–Iraq War, many were eventually realized.

The port and customs facilities of Shahid Rajai, which are located just outside the western municipal boundary of Bandar Abbas, processed 10.991 million metric tons of imported cargo in 2012–13 worth US$ 18.887 billion, which constituted 37.84 per cent of national imports in terms of value and 35.34 per cent of national imports in terms of weight.[43] In the same fiscal year, the port also processed 2.62 million tons of exported cargo worth US$ 505.15 million, comprising 36.61 per cent of the total national non-oil exports in terms of weight and 16.16 per cent of the total national non-oil exports in terms of value.[44] The much smaller Shahid Bahunar port of Bandar Abbas— previously known as Suru and dating back to the late 1960s—is nevertheless the eighth largest port in the country. In the Iranian fiscal year 2012–13, it processed more than 555 thousand metric tons of export cargo worth upward of US$ 120 million, comprising 7.76 per cent of the total national non-oil

---

[42] Ministry of Housing and Urban Development, [Unapproved Second] Comprehensive Plan of Bandar Abbas, prepared by A. Adibi Consulting Engineers (1979).

[43] Customs Organization of Iran, *Salnamih-i tejarat-i khariji-i Jumuhi-i Islami-i Iran, 1391* (Yearbook of Foreign Trade of the Islamic Republic of Iran) (2013).

[44] Ibid.

exports in terms of weight and 3.87 per cent of the total national non-oil exports in terms of value.[45] Due to the international sanctions in place against Iran, a significant part of imports processed through both ports comes from the United Arab Emirates as re-exported goods.

The largest sectors of employment in 2011/12 were secondly transport and warehousing, employing 24 per cent of the 128,339 workers in the County of Bandar Abbas; but the largest employer was the government/ public sector, accounting for 25 per cent of total employment.[46] A large number of those employed in the public sector may not be from the province itself, their residence in Bandar Abbas often being of a temporary nature. By comparison, agriculture, including fishing, employed only 3.6 per cent of the total number of workers; while around 10 per cent of employment was attributed to manufacturing.[47]

The development of government-supported industrial estates in Hormozgan to help the manufacturing sector began in the 1980s. By the mid-2000s, thirteen such estates were established in the province, including three in the vicinity of Bandar Abbas. Bandar Abbas I and Bandar Abbas II, located north of the city, and Marine Industries (*Sanayi'-i daryai*) located west of the city, have been planned for around 220 plants. Yet, the latter really consists of two large plants, while Bandar Abbas I and II have not been fully occupied due to transport problems, high cost of inputs, scarcity of skilled labor,[48] and, apparently, water shortages.

The statistics for size of workshops paint an interesting picture. The entire province of Hormozgan had 180 workshops with 10 or more workers in 2011–12,[49] down from 198 units in 2010–11,[50] 35 of which employed 50 or more

[45] Ibid.

[46] Statistical Center of Iran, Excel file on employment in the counties of Hormozgan, 2011, www.amar.org.ir (accessed 26 March 2014).

[47] Ibid.

[48] Ministry of Economy and Finance, "Barrasi-i amalkard-i shahrakha-i san'ati-i ustan-i hurmuzgan" (Performance analysis of the industrial estates of Hormozgan Province), internal report prepared by Bahram Bahrami, et al. (2004).

[49] These 35 workshops employed 13,240 persons and produced 1.96 per cent of the national value-added for such establishments; Statistical Center of Iran, "Natayij-i amargiri-i kargahha-i san'ati-i 10 nafar karkun ya bishtar, 1390" (Survey results of workshops with 10 employees or more) (2012).

[50] Statistical Center of Iran, *Salnamih-i amari-i ustan-i hurmuzgan, 1389* (Statistical Yearbook of Hormuzgan Province) (2011).

workers,[51] down from 40 in 2010/11.[52] In the County of Bandar Abbas, the number of workshops with 10 or more employees was recorded as 64 in 2010/11, of which 7 were publicly owned, and 6 of these had more than 100 employees.[53] Of the 40 workshops in Hormozgan employing more than 50 persons in 2009–10, 24 were located in the County of Bandar Abbas, with 7 employing 50–99 workers and 16 employing over 100 workers.[54] Furthermore, workshops with more than 10 workers in the Country of Bandar Abbas employed 7,682 persons in 2010/11, with 6,352 employees in the 100+ person establishments, 422 employees in the 50–99 person establishments, and 908 employees in the 10–49 person establishments.[55] With only around 13,000 persons working in manufacturing (of the approximate total employment of 130,000), manufacturing employment in the county not only has a relatively small impact in terms of creating opportunity for labor, but is also highly polarized. It is concentrated at two extremes: in the 16 plants with 100+ workers, and in the establishments employing fewer than 10 workers. These two types to a large degree employ different types of workers—skilled versus unskilled, high-wage versus low-wage, and migrants from outside the province versus natives of the province—as observed through our recent field inquiries.

Retail and wholesale activities, including repair, represented 11 per cent of total employment in the County of Bandar Abbas in 2011–12.[56] Many of the small- and medium-size stores are located around the Old Bazaar, while since the 1990s new commercial centers have also appeared in their vicinity. The Zeytun Commercial Complex was the first modern shopping center established in Bandar Abbas. It was soon followed by other shopping centers such as South Star (*Sitarih-i janub*) built next to the older shopping areas such as the Municipal Bazaar (*Bazar-i shahrdari*) and Day Bazaar (*Bazar-i ruz*). These centers specialize in the sale of clothes and household appliances and have provided some limited employment in the city. In the 1990s, these shop-

[51] In comparison, the corresponding nationwide figure was 4,481 units; Statistical Center of Iran, "Natayij-i amargiri-i kargahha-i san'ati-i 50 nafar karkun ya bishtar, 1390" (Survey results of workshops with 50 employees or more) (2012).

[52] Statistical Center of Iran, *Salnamih-i amari-i ustan-i hurmuzgan, 1389* (Statistical Yearbook of Hormozgan Province) (2011).

[53] Ibid.

[54] Ibid.

[55] Ibid.

[56] Statistical Center of Iran, Excel file on employment in the counties of Hormozgan, 2011, http://amar.org.ir

ping centers gained duty exemption benefits from their connection to the Qeshm Island Free Zone, which possibly even trickled down to low-income groups or at least to small-time players. However, these exemptions are no longer available. Currently, there is little evidence of economic synergy between Bandar Abbas and Qeshm Island Free Zone, and Bandar Abbas' shopping centers are less than booming. Bandar Abbas has not been able to leverage its seaside to attract visitors and tourists either: although located next to some shopping areas and the Ghadir Boulevard, it attracts a rather limited number of tourists from outside the province for a few months and is not active during the rest of the year.[57]

It may thus be argued that Bandar Abbas's economic and employment structure is of a polarized nature. The city's traditional economy is based on old-style trading and fishing activities, which are not in a booming state and can hardly provide new employment. Yet, the modern urban economy, which is based on international commerce and modern industrial activities, is strongly influenced by exogenous forces, in particular national-level policies, investment, and relations with other countries. Furthermore, the effect of modern economic activities on employment and investment in the city are limited, or at least lopsided. A large number of those employed in international transport, large manufacturing plants, and high-end commerce are most likely migrants from other cities, as evidenced by the fact that more than 38 per cent of the city's residents were born elsewhere.[58] By contrast, residents of low-income settlements, who are for the most part from either the city or the province, have difficulty securing work in these modern economic activities, as evidenced by the high unemployment rates in such settlements, which will be discussed in a later section. The locals are nonetheless affected by rising prices, including those in the real estate market, as well as environmental pollution caused by industrial and shipping activities. Furthermore, as much of the modern shipping and manufacturing activities takes place outside the municipal boundaries, their positive impact on the city's tax base is rather small.

Urban Growth Dynamics in Bandar Abbas

Based on successive census results, Bandar Abbas' small population of 17,710 persons in 1956–7 grew to 87,981 by 1976–7; 273,578 by 1996–7; 379,301

---

[57] Ibid.

[58] Statistical Center of Iran, *Salnamih-i amari-i ustan-i hurmuzgan, 1387* (Statistical Yearbook of Hormuzgan Province) (2009).

by 2006–7; and 448,861 by 2011–12.[59] The population of Bandar Abbas represents one third of the total for Hormozgan, and completely dwarfs the population of the province's second largest city, Minab. Furthermore, the majority of the residents of the County of Bandar Abbas, 558,258 persons in 2011–12,[60] live in the city itself.

In the early twentieth century, the town was limited by the sea to the south, the village of Nayband to the east, the village of Suru to the west, and hilly terrain to the north.[61] With the rapid growth of its population, Bandar Abbas's land area has significantly expanded over time. In particular, since the mid-1960s, each successive comprehensive plan prepared for Bandar Abbas has expanded the city's official boundaries. Its area of 5,323 hectares has recently been expanded to 7,113 hectares, based on the revision of the city's latest comprehensive plan.[62] The old airport was at one point the eastern boundary of Bandar Abbas, whereas its site, now occupied by a hospital, is located between the North Nayband neighborhood and the bus terminal, while the villages of Nakhl-i Nakhuda and Damahi have also been incorporated into the eastern part of the city.[63]

Although industrial and port-related activities have expanded in the west since the 1990s, they are mostly located outside the official city boundaries. Bandar Abbas's main area of formal growth since the 1980s has been in the east. By the end of the Iran–Iraq War, the south-eastern part of the city, close to the new airport, had been taken up for military purposes. Furthermore, public-sector housing cooperatives have built homes in the vicinity of this area, while middle- and upper-middle-income families have also found homes in the eastern part of the city. In fact, at least nine neighborhoods have been

[59] Statistical Center of Iran, Excel file on the population of Iran, http://amar.org.ir
[60] Ibid.
[61] Floor, *Bandar Abbas*, p. 3.
[62] Ministry of Housing and Urban Development, "[Approved Third] Comprehensive Plan of Bandar Abbas," prepared by Sharmand Consultants and subsequently revised (2008).
[63] M. Javaheripour, Background social study of Amayish and Towsi'ih-i Alborz Consultants, "Tahiyyih-i barnamih-i samandihi-i sukunatgahha-i ghayr-i rasmi va iqdamat-i tavandmand-sazi-i ijtima'at-i anha ba ta'kid bar bihsazi-i Bandar Abbas ba didgah-i shahr-nigar: kamarbandi, Bihisht-i Zahra, Allahu Akbar, va Duhizar" (Preparation of plan for upgrading informal settlements and their social empowerment within the context of Bandar Abbas: Beltway, Bihisht-i Zahra, Allahu Akbar, and Duhizar), prepared for Urban Development and Revitalization Organization (2012).

added to the city in the east, including the upscale North Gulshahr. Many public and private offices have moved from the inner city to the new areas in the east as well. Indeed, a number of office buildings, commercial centers, and housing units have been built in the east, although some newly constructed buildings remain vacant due to the lack of demand. Furthermore, some building projects started in recent years have remained unfinished as a result of rising costs.[64]

Developments in the western, and especially the north-western, areas of the city have been of a different nature, resulting in the expansion of informal settlements. Based on the recommendations of the first comprehensive plan for Bandar Abbas in the late 1960s, the beltway (*kamarbandi*), which is now called the Jumhuri-i Islami Boulevard, was constructed as the outer limit of the city to the north-west; whereas Shahid Rajai Highway is now considered the beltway. While some industrial workshops, including those producing construction materials, were located outside the ring, this artificial boundary in fact gave impetus to the formation of informal settlements in its vicinity and to the west of the road terminating at the Isini Village. This said, until 1985 when the second comprehensive plan of the city was approved,[65] not counting the unapproved second comprehensive plan mentioned above, few people lived above the old beltway. Yet, the area attracted a large number of informal settlers relatively quickly after this period.[66]

As mentioned earlier, Duhizar and Shishsad Dastgah neighborhoods were originally formed in connection with the development of port facilities starting in the 1970s to house white- and blue-collar workers. Yet, Duhizar has become a low-income neighborhood and has been informally expanding. While some formal housing developments have appeared in the west, mostly to house port-related workers, Allahu Akbar Hill and Bihisht-i Zahra, next to the cemetery, have also morphed into informal settlements. During the Iran–

[64] Ibid.
[65] Ministry of Housing and Urban Development, "[Approved Second] Comprehensive Plan of Bandar Abbas", prepared by Sharistan Consultants, 1986.
[66] Tarh and Mi'mari Consulting Engineers, Combined Report of "Tahiyyih-i bar-namih-i samandihi-i sukunatgahha-i ghayr-i rasmi va iqdamat-i tavandmand-sazi-i ijtima'at-i anha ba ta'kid bar bihsazi-i Bandar Abbas ba didgah-i shahr-nigar" (Preparation of plan for upgrading informal settlements and their social empowerment within the context of Bandar Abbas: Beltway, Bihisht-i Zahra, Allahu Akbar, and Duhizar), prepared for Urban Development and Revitalization Organization (2012).

Iraq War, Bandar Abbas replaced Khurramshahr near the border with Iraq as the main Iranian transit port. Coupled with population increases in Hormozgan's rural areas against the background of scarce economic opportunities and recurring droughts, this most likely acted as a population pull factor from the villages to Bandar Abbas. Unable to afford residence in the city proper, many of the rural migrants found home in the expanding informal settlements, including Bihisht-i Zahra, Allahu Akbar Hill, and Duhizar as well as north of Shishsad Dastgah. Furthermore, some of the residents of the old area south of the Chahistani neighborhood migrated to the west and north of Kamarbandi. Others ended up in the twenty-two Bahman sub-neighborhood, south of Duhizar, which has housed a number of war-displaced families since the 1980s as well. When the Imam Husayn Boulevard was being constructed, some homes were demolished and many of their residents also ended up in the Kamarbandi and Duhizar neighborhoods.[67]

The Duhizar and Shishsad Dastgah neighborhoods have grown to their limits in the north and west to meet the highlands. Furthermore, the area directly facing the informal settlements of Kamarbandi has been taken up for MHP and is thus limiting further growth of the neighborhood. Apparently due to the limitations of Kamarbandi, Duhizar, and Shishsad Dastgah neighborhoods, since the early 2000s Shahrak-i Tawhid has steadily attracted both poor migrants and low-income households pushed out of the main areas of the city. Yet, North Nayband and South Nayband as well as perhaps the Chahistani neighborhood are likely destined for renovation through market forces or even gentrification, since land in the center east of the city is becoming valuable, which is evidenced by the renovation plans drawn up by the municipality as noted in our field inquiries.

Thus, Shahrak-i Tawhid in the west notwithstanding, Bandar Abbas has been assuming a bipolar character (see Figure 9.1). It may be divided into an eastern part growing as a new formal development; and a western part which comprises informal settlements as well as the core of the city, including the old bazaar and its surrounding neighborhoods with some traditional character. The old city core, its surrounding military and naval facilities notwithstanding, can more or less be categorized as decaying fabric if the official definition is used.[68] Based on the recommendations of the latest comprehensive plan, around 1,000 hectares of mostly vacant land with no infrastructure is now

[67] M. Javaheripour, Background social study (2012).
[68] Ibid.

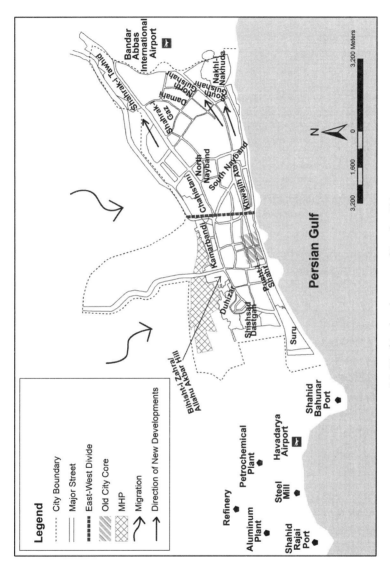

9.1: The bipolar character of Bandar Abbas

incorporated within the official city boundaries in the north along the Sirjan Highway and above the informal settlements.[69] Yet, it is difficult to foresee this as bringing about any change in the east–west polarization of the city.

Characteristics of Low-Income Settlements in Bandar Abbas

As part of UUHRP, mentioned earlier, a relatively large social assessment was conducted in several low-income settlements of Bandar Abbas in 2006, that is, before the start of the upgrading activities.[70] The study focused on five settlements, namely, Duhizar, North Nayband, Kamarbandi, Nakhl-i Nakhuda, and Suru. Although the old neighborhood of Suru as well as the old villages of Nayband and Nakhl-i Nakhuda have more in common with decaying fabric elsewhere in the city, since they were poverty-stricken and to some extent under-serviced they were included in the social assessment. In the study, most residents were found to have been born in the city itself, since the population was also found to be quite young, or to have migrated to the city from within Hormozgan Province. High rates of unemployment, underemployment, and employment in the informal economy were observed in the neighborhoods. An examination of household consumption levels in the surveyed settlements revealed a high incidence of poverty. Households fell within the lowest consumption brackets among all urban households in Bandar Abbas. There was almost a complete absence of social, cultural, and sports centers in the neighborhoods. The local arms of the Ministry of Energy had been able to provide water and electricity to the overwhelming majority of the households in the settlements, but the municipality often lacked adequate funds or enough capacity to improve street conditions or deliver other services. The residents in turn were more or less estranged from the urban management and were not in reality full citizens. Security issues faced by informal settlement residents, in particular women and girls, were found to be partially related to the unsatisfactory street conditions as well as the limitations of security forces. Houses in the studied settlements were found to have been constructed using relatively durable materials in the Iranian context, but

[69] Ministry of Housing and Urban Development, "[Approved Third] Comprehensive Plan of Bandar Abbas," prepared by Sharmand Consultants and subsequently revised (2008).

[70] Pooya Alaedini, et al., "Land Markets and Housing Dynamics in Low Income Settlements in Iran Examining Data from Three Cities," presented at the World Bank Urban Research Symposium (2007).

they had not been built to official standards. Most houses did have some form of kitchen and toilet as well as shower facilities in a relatively large number of cases, but their overall situation was less than desirable. Furthermore, some water discharge from homes flowed into the streets and canals, depending on the settlement. There were few sources of housing finance other than the households' own funds. While a large percentage of households did have bank accounts, they had not been able to benefit from the housing loan system. A relatively large number of households were found to own their homes, but a significant number of owners did not have full titles. This said, since there was little threat of eviction made against those households who did not have titles for their homes, lack of full title only affected the price of homes.

Another study of the low-income neighborhoods of Bandar Abbas was commissioned in 2012–13 by UDRO, with the aim of recommending a city-wide action plan for its upgrading.[71] It designated twelve neighborhoods as informal settlements, including Duhizar, Kamarbandi, Bihisht-i Zahra/Allahu Akbar Hill, Shahrak-i Tawhid, Shishsad Dastgah, and Chahistani, as well as North Nayband, South Nayband, Khwajih Ata, Pusht-i Shahr, Suru, and Nakhl-i Nakhuda, which should be more appropriately called decaying fabric. In fact, as Figure 9.2 shows, there is some overlap between these twelve neighborhoods and the municipality-designated decaying fabric. This means that some residents in Suru, Khwajih Ata, and Nakhl-i Nakhuda may be able to apply for the decaying fabric renovation facilities and tax exemptions. However, based on personal communication with the municipal authorities, very few households have actually benefited from the incentive package to this day, apparently since there is no proactive facilitation program and the price of land and construction in many areas may not make renovation financially feasible despite the incentive package. Yet, as mentioned, North Nayband and South Nayband as well as perhaps the Chahistani neighborhood, which are located in the center east of the city, are likely to be renovated through market forces or even gentrified due to the potential value of their lands.

---

[71] This study was conducted by four consulting firms (Tarh & Mi'mari, Amayish & Towsi'ih-i Alborz, Pardaraz, and Tadbirshahr) and summarized in Tarh & Mi'mari Consulting Engineers, Combined Report of "Tahiyyih-i barnamih-i samandihi-i sukunatgahha-i ghayr-i rasmi va iqdamat-i tavandmand-sazi-i ijtima'at-i anha ba ta'kid bar bihsazi-i Bandar Abbas ba didgah-i shahr-nigar" (Preparation of plan for upgrading informal settlements and their social empowerment within the context of Bandar Abbas), prepared for Urban Development and Revitalization Organization (2012).

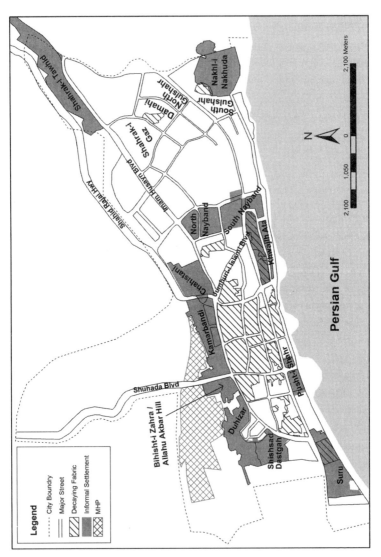

9.2: Twelve neighborhoods considered informal settlements in Bandar Abbas

Findings of the above study on the characteristics of the twelve designated informal settlements may be summarized as follows. The twelve settlements house about 30 per cent of the population of the city. The rate of migration to these neighborhoods from outside Bandar Abbas is lower than the citywide figure as most new settlers have moved from another location in the city itself. Furthermore, home ownership rate in the settlements at 78 per cent of households is higher than the corresponding figure of 70 per cent for the city as a whole. However, many homes lack official titles, although they are considered "regular housing" in official statistics. Labor force participation rate is in the order of 30–40 per cent in the twelve settlements, which is lower than the corresponding citywide figure. Participation rate appears to have increased in recent years, resulting in a higher unemployment rate. Whereas the unemployment rate in Bandar Abbas was officially put at 11 per cent when the study was conducted, Nakhl-i Nakhuda, Suru, and Shahrak-i Tawhid were found to have rates of unemployment in the order of 30–40 per cent. Women's participation rate is quite low and their unemployment rate is around 50 per cent. Furthermore, employment opportunities in the settlements lack diversity, and most workers are employed as unskilled labor or are working with very small amounts of capital. Around 0.3 per cent of those with an occupation are employers of others. Finally, average monthly household income is 4,000,000–4,500,000 rials versus the average figure of 7,500,000 rials for the city.

State Initiatives in Bandar Abbas

As mentioned in the previous section, UUHRP specifically targeted five low-income settlements of Bandar Abbas for upgrading in the period 2005–9. In a rapid evaluation conducted at the end of UUHRP activities,[72] project initiatives were found to have shown some success with regard to beneficiary satisfaction, participation, and sustainability. Sustainability and participation had been enhanced in areas where interactions between the municipality and the people had been high. Many of the resident priorities had materialized, including better street conditions, surface water drainage, canal rehabilitation, access to transport services, garbage collection, and demarcation of green spaces for families in which to spend their leisure time. The project had ended

---

[72] Pooya Alaedini, et al., "Erteqa-i vaz'iya-i rifahi-i ahali-i sokunatgahha-i ghayr-i rasmi dar Iran" (Measuring the conditions of informal settlers in Iran), *Rifah-i Ijtima'I*, Vol. 41 (2011), pp. 69–92.

the isolation of the neighborhoods and had increased their security. However, the scale as well as the geographic and substantive scope of the initiatives had been limited. The neighborhoods were still found to need a range of services. Community mobilization activities, interactions between the community and service agencies, and other enabling initiatives, such as municipality–resident interactions, a neighborhood mayor, and microfinance groups, were found to be promising. However, these enabling activities did not create the desired synergy with the physical improvement initiatives, and had not been adequate in number or coverage to leave a lasting impact. Furthermore, the increased focus of urban management appeared to have stopped short of being institutionalized in an inter-agency sense or possibly in dealing with any other/future informal settlements.

The detailed study mentioned in the previous section on the twelve designated informal settlements of Bandar Abbas has been the government's follow-up initiative to UUHRP activities in the city.[73] It was carried out by a team of four consulting firms in 2012–13 with the specific aim of formulating a set of sub-projects for upgrading each settlement. The detailed lists of sub-projects have been prepared, and if they are implemented will certainly have a significant positive impact on the settlements. However, the proposed activities formulated for the twelve designated informal settlements of Bandar Abbas are yet to receive funding. This obviously pivotal issue notwithstanding, most sub-projects are physical in nature, giving inadequate attention to socio-economic, including enabling, activities. Yet, as discussed earlier, the appearance and expansion of informal settlements in Iranian cities generally and in Bandar Abbas specifically are a reflection of a number of related issues, including inadequate urban service provision, restrictive land use and municipal regulations, and failure of the urban economy to provide adequate employment and income. It is not expected that any plan addressing the plight of informal settlement residents will solve all these problems, especially those stemming from the macro environment. However, it is hoped that such plans pay serious attention to the socio-economic issues afflicting informal settlements and are at least cognizant of any future impetus for the

---

[73] Summarized in Tarh & Mi'mari Consulting Engineers, Combined Report of "Tahiyyih-i barnamih-i samandihi-i sukunatgahha-i ghayr-i rasmi va iqdamat-i tavandmand-sazi-i ijtima'at-i anha ba ta'kid bar bihsazi-i Bandar Abbas ba didgah-i shahr-nigar" (Preparation of plan for upgrading informal settlements and their social empowerment within the context of Bandar Abbas), prepared for Urban Development and Revitalization Organization (2012).

proliferation of urban informality and decay, including that caused by the upgrading initiative itself.

The plan formulated by the consulting firms also includes resettlement for some households when located in hazard-prone areas and when conflicting with major land-use regulations or imminent domain. These include a very large number of lots, involving more than 5,000 households. One option for housing this relatively large number of households would be through MHP, which has been building homes in a 260 hectare area next to the informal settlements of northern Bandar Abbas.[74] The price of MHP apartment units was originally 3,400,000 rials per sq m, excluding the cost of major appliances such as water heater, elevator, etc.[75] This price has been out of the affordability range of the residents of Duhizar or Bihisht-i Zahra/Allahu Akbar neighborhoods as well as other poverty-stricken households in the rest of the designated informal settlements. Furthermore, due to inflation, new applicants must pay higher prices for MHP apartments now. In fact, based on our field inquiries, many of the 3,600 finished MHP units have gone to the low end of middle-income households—for example, members of company-based cooperatives—rather than low-income households.[76] Thus, while certain residents of the older target settlements with decaying fabric characteristics may be able to afford MHP apartments, although not many have benefited from them to this day, they will most likely not be among those who are resettled. Additionally, whereas some residents of these neighborhoods can benefit from the decaying fabric home renovation facilities, and therefore do not need to move, the resettlement compensation that many others are supposed to receive in exchange for their low-priced land will probably not be adequate to buy MHP apartments.

While a number of low-income families remain in the old low-income neighborhoods of Bandar Abbas, many among the next generation as well as new migrants from inside the province may end up in the informal settlements

---

[74] Based on personal communication with MHP authorities.

[75] Ibid.

[76] It should also be mentioned that, according to the Deputy Minister of Energy, completing the water, sewerage, and electricity components of MHP in the Hormozgan Province will require an additional 550 billion rials (http://www.mehrnews.com/TextVersionDetail/2307307, last accessed 26 May 2016). Since the Rouhani administration appears less than interested in MHP as it is reviving "social housing" through a revised Comprehensive Housing Plan, this large sum is unlikely to be allocated any time in the foreseeable future.

in the city's north-west. Furthermore, Bandar Abbas will need unskilled and semi-skilled labor for its service and construction activities. These are people who are likely to be attracted to the informal settlements in the absence of any plan to house them otherwise. At the same time, uniquely in Bandar Abbas, 350 hectares of land was allocated to UDRO by order of the Ahmadinejad administration as "capital" whose proceeds are supposed to be used for informal settlement upgrading in the city.[77] This land cannot really be sold in its present condition or developed in partnership with the private sector. Using it to house low-income families or even to develop as a site and services project will also require significant investment, which should nonetheless be considered by UDRO.

To end this section on an optimistic note, it is worth mentioning that at the time of writing, following the Minister of Roads and Urban Development's recent visit to the city, UDRO is working on a request for proposals for an "Urban and Regional Spatial Strategy" or an "Urban and Regional Development Strategy" uniquely for Bandar Abbas.[78] Some of the questions this strategy is to answer include: How can the public sector connect the modern and traditional parts of the urban and regional economy and reduce socio-economic and, by extension, spatial polarization? Through what job creation, equal opportunity, service provision or other enabling programs can urban poverty in Bandar Abbas be reduced? What infrastructure and social service projects are the priority for upgrading informal settlements and decaying fabric, as well as reducing spatial isolation and social exclusion? What are the capacity-building needs of the urban and regional management for an integrated approach to revitalizing the city and the region? How can the public sector facilitate the participation of various stakeholders in urban and regional revitalization? How can the public sector ensure financial sustainability of the revitalization efforts?

The strategy, if developed, is supposed to leverage the results and recommendations (sub-project list) of the earlier study of the twelve designated informal settlements of Bandar Abbas. The strategy will also attempt to improve on renovation activities in designated decaying fabrics and check any possible gentrification that may result in the proliferation of informal settlements.

---

[77] Based on personal communication with UDRO management.
[78] Ibid.

Conclusion

A by-product of rapid urbanization in Iran, as in many other developing countries, has been the proliferation of unplanned, under-serviced, and poverty-stricken neighborhoods. Influenced by macro circumstances such as inflation and unemployment, income stagnation and inequality, and speculative land markets and restrictive land-use regulations, Bandar Abbas has its share of such neighborhoods. Although residents in these settlements usually have access to piped water and electricity and their housing stocks are of relatively durable construction materials—yet built using substandard construction methods—they suffer from a host of deficiencies in their built environments, as well as from highly inadequate access to most socio-economic services. We suggested that the polarized economic structure and the concentration of informal settlements in the North-West of Bandar Abbas are creating an East–West divide. We further argued that whereas Bandar Abbas is Iran's largest port and has also received some major manufacturing investment as well as migrants from outside the province, the city's modern economic activities have not produced adequate employment and income for the more or less native residents of low-income settlements. The government has implemented a pilot upgrading project in a few low-income settlements of Bandar Abbas, helping to reduce the isolation of target neighborhoods by having the urban management recognize residents' rights to urban services, attempting to engage them and improve their subsistence through a few socio-economic activities, and delivering a set of important physical upgrading sub-projects in priority areas. The unaddressed challenges of this initiative notwithstanding, it has encouraged the government to commission a study aimed at preparing a plan with a list of sub-projects, until now unfunded, for the upgrading of twelve designated informal settlements in Bandar Abbas— some of which are or should be designated as decaying fabric. We argued that the upgrading plan for the twelve neighborhoods paid inadequate attention to the need for enabling and other socio-economic activities as well as for addressing future expansion of the informal settlements, which may also be caused by the initiative's own resettlement recommendations. Yet, we suggested there were signs that the plan might be reworked through a more holistic and participatory initiative, taking a regional approach to reducing economic, social, and spatial polarization of the city and delivering a set of programs for physical and environmental improvement, enabling, job creation, equal opportunities, and service provision for the benefit of informal settlement residents. While such a reworked participatory plan is likely to be formulated, we would particularly recommend that funding and careful managing of the implementation are also prioritized.

10

RESIDENTIAL SATISFACTION AND PLACE IDENTITY IN A TRADITIONAL NEIGHBORHOOD

THE CASE OF MUTRAH, OMAN

Marike Bontenbal

The Sultanate of Oman is undergoing significant change as a result of rapid urban development and population growth. Urbanization rates have increased from 11 per cent in 1970 to 84 per cent in 2009.[1] Oman's urbanization follows a pattern that is common for Gulf states and is largely the result of welfare poli-

[1] The author would like to thank students from the BSc programmes "Sustainable Tourism and Regional Development" and "Urban Planning and Architectural Design" of the German University of Technology in Oman who participated in March 2011, January 2012, and January 2013 in the field research in Mutrah and shared their observations and pictures. Also thanks to Adrijana Car for the provision of the Mutrah maps. Mohammad Abdul Hamid Al Laithi, Mohammad Al Hindawi, Mohammad Al Khandouri, Faraj Al Jabri, and Ahmed Almip, *Population Distribution, Migration and Urbanization in Oman* (Muscat: Ministry of National Economy, 2010).

cies, which provide free access to a number of services and assets, including land. Experts in the field claim that the granting of land to citizens has been a major factor in shaping Gulf cities.[2] In Oman, this has resulted in vast urban areas of "land grant neighborhoods,"[3] which are of relatively low density and are often located on the urban fringe, where Omani families construct a home on a granted plot of land that meets today's comfort standards.

Within these urban dynamics, the meaning of traditional "old" neighborhoods and inner-city districts as residential areas has shifted considerably. In an era of globalization and modernization, where private vehicles dominate and the significance of distance diminishes, the historical residential urban areas in Gulf cities seem to have lost their residential appeal to many of their traditional urban dwellers,[4] who now prefer a higher level of comfort, larger houses, more space and privacy, and less congestion.

This chapter is based on a neighborhood study that addresses how its inhabitants view the meaning of Mutrah as a place of residence—one of Muscat's oldest neighborhoods. The study examines the identification that residents experience with their neighborhood and community, and their level of appreciation of the neighborhood. Drawing from the literature on place identity, sense of community, and residential satisfaction, as well as how these are all interlinked,[5] this study demonstrates that appreciation of the neighborhood in Mutrah is largely a function of the inhabitants' sense of identification with their neighborhood and the social groups to which they belong. I argue that in Mutrah, the residential *experience* appears to be far more positive than the actual physical housing and neighborhood conditions would predict, which can be explained by a strong place attachment and sense of community among Mutrah residents.

The research for this study comprises both quantitative and qualitative methods. A survey was conducted among 260 Mutrah residents to assess

[2] Mustapha Ben Hamouche, "The Changing Morphology of the Gulf Cities in the Age of Globalisation: The Case of Bahrain," *Habitat International*, Vol. 28, No. 4 (2004), pp. 521–40.

[3] Sharon Nagy, "Making Room for Migrants, Making Sense of Difference: Spatial and Ideological Expressions of Social Diversity in Urban Qatar," *Urban Studies*, Vol. 43, No. 1 (2006), pp. 119–37.

[4] Ibid.

[5] See, for example, Gustavo S. Mesch and Orit Manor, "Social Ties, Environmental Perception, and Local Attachment," *Environment and Behavior*, Vol. 30 (1998), pp. 504–19.

demographic and socio-economic characteristics, housing characteristics, and opinions of dwellings and neighborhood facilities. Interviews with random Mutrah residents were then conducted to examine the quality of the relationship they have with their neighborhood, and how the self is situated in the socio-spatial environment.

The chapter starts with an overview of urbanization patterns in the Gulf and Oman, primarily from a population and housing perspective, and the changing meaning of traditional neighborhoods in these urban dynamics. Then, drawing from geography and environmental psychology discourses, a number of concepts are discussed relating to neighborhoods and place identity, followed by a description of the methodology. The findings are then presented from the empirical study in the Mutrah neighborhood, with an introduction of the study area, and an exploration of three place identity components: place attachment, sense of community, and place dependence. The chapter concludes with a discussion on the findings in the context of Gulf cities. Policy options are explored to identify how place identity as a precursor to residential appreciation can inform urban planning decision-making and future redevelopment of traditional residential neighborhoods in Gulf cities.

Traditional Neighborhoods in the Urbanizing Gulf

Gulf cities have been characterized by ongoing and unlimited sprawl and growth during recent decades. Today, the Gulf region is among the most rapidly urbanizing regions in the world, where the sudden wealth and construction boom resulting from the exploitation of oil resources have affected the rate and nature of urbanization.[6] The Arab region is now more urbanized than developing countries as a whole (50 per cent compared to 45 per cent), and is projected to see its urban population more than double by 2050.[7] The two main factors—in both the present and recent past—that have contributed to

---

[6] Hassan Hakimian, "From Demographic Transition to Fertility Boom and Bust: Iran in the 1980s and 1990s," *Development and Change*, Vol. 37, No. 3 (2006), pp. 571–97; Salih A. El-Arifi, "The Nature of Urbanization in the Gulf Countries," *Geojournal*, Vol. 13, No. 3 (1986), pp. 223–35; Edward J. Malecki and Michael C. Ewers, "Labor Migration to World Cities: With a Research Agenda for the Arab Gulf," *Progress in Human Geography*, Vol. 31, No. 4 (2007), pp. 467–84; Barry Mirkin, *Population Levels, Trends and Policies in the Arab Region: Challenges and Opportunities, Arab Human Development Report Research Paper Series* (UNDP, 2010).

[7] Mirkin, *Population Levels, Trends and Policies in the Arab Region*.

rapid urbanization in the Gulf region, at least from a population perspective, include a high natural increase of the population and the massive in-migration of foreign labor to support the region's booming economies. Both trends have predominantly affected urban areas, which absorb the majority of natural increase and migration influx. Indeed, it has been predicted that virtually all population growth in the next thirty years in the region will be concentrated in cities.[8]

High population concentration has always characterized the spatial pattern of Omani society, due to the limited availability of natural resources. However, the nature and degree of urban growth in the country has changed rapidly in the past three decades. Whereas in 1975 an estimated 15 per cent of the Omani population was living in urban areas,[9] today this level has increased to more than 70 per cent.[10] The recent change has in general been more significant than in other countries in the Gulf, which had already achieved fairly high urbanization rates by 1980 (Kuwait 98 per cent, UAE 81 per cent, Bahrain 81 per cent) when 78 per cent of the Omani population was still residing in rural areas.[11] Census data show that the total number of housing units in Oman had increased from 344,846 in 1993 to 430,996 in 2003—a 25 per cent increase in dwellings over ten years, the majority of which are in urban areas. In 2010, the total number of housing units had further grown to 551,058, an additional increase of 28 per cent in seven years (2003–10).[12]

Urbanization is intrinsically linked to the socio-economic transformation of Oman, which started in the 1970s under the current ruler Sultan Qaboos and was backed by massive oil revenues; it has led the country into an era of rapid progress—modernization, development, and an increasingly diversified economy. Oman's recent economic development has brought wealth, a higher national income, construction and economic expansion, and changing lifestyles and consumption patterns. Within this context of rapid socio-economic transformation, the demand and supply of housing for urban residents has changed drastically. The dynamics of Muscat's relentless urbanization process

[8] Barney Cohen, "Urban Growth in Developing Countries: A Review of Current Trends and a Caution Regarding Existing Forecasts," *World Development*, Vol. 32, No. 1 (2004), pp. 23–51.
[9] El-Arifi, *The Nature of Urbanization in the Gulf Countries*.
[10] Laithi et al., *Population Distribution, Migration and Urbanization in Oman*.
[11] El-Arifi, *The Nature of Urbanization in the Gulf Countries*.
[12] Ministry of National Economy Census, *Final results of the Oman 2010 Census* (Muscat: Ministry of National Economy, 2010).

have been fueled by different population movements, including rural–urban migration, international migration, and outmigration from traditional urban settlements to new suburban areas. New residential neighborhoods have been planned since the first residential development of Madinat Sultan Qaboos was created in the 1970s.[13] While aspirations for more modern and spacious homes were rising, reflecting the increasing standard of living in the country, new residential settlements have been continuously developing.

Within these urban dynamics, the meaning of traditional "old" neighborhoods and inner-city districts as residential areas has shifted considerably. Traditional residential urban settlements in Gulf cities from before the oil boom seem to have lost their residential appeal to many of the original inhabitants.[14] As a result of dissolving tribal residential spatial patterns and the new emerging spatial mixing of national households from various tribal backgrounds as well as expatriates, space and privacy have become key elements of today's residential preferences of urban Gulf residents, which is reflected in the low-density set-up of the suburbs and land-grant neighborhoods.

The original settlements and small towns from which Gulf cities developed, and which once operated as singular, functional urban units, have become absorbed into wider urban structures and their infrastructure, services, amenities, and dynamic economic and residential landscapes. Some traditional neighborhoods, such as Al Shindagha near Dubai Creek, have lost their residential function and have been preserved as visitor destinations and proposed heritage sites. Some areas have lost residential appeal due to physical decay and lack of renovation, and have been turned into cheap housing areas for expatriates, while original inhabitants have moved to newer residential areas. Other areas, such as Muharraq in Bahrain and Mutrah in Oman, have preserved their traditional residential and commercial functions. In many cases, the meaning of historical city districts in contemporary Gulf society is often primarily interpreted as a locational display of cultural heritage and national identity, and as an asset to attract tourists and entertain visitors. However, this one-sided understanding tends to obscure the residential significance that many of these historical areas still possess. This is especially true for Mutrah, which continues to be densely populated with both newcomers and families who have lived there for generations.

---

[13] J. E. Peterson, *Historical Muscat: An Illustrated Guide and Gazetteer* (Leiden: Brill, 2007).

[14] Nagy, *Making Room for Migrants*.

Neighborhoods and Place Identity

Places are more than merely physical settings. They are produced and maintained through an array of social and cultural mechanisms that ascribe meaning or values to them. The psychological dimension of experiencing place, person–place relationships, and the "spatialization of identity"[15] have been subjects of study within the realm of environmental psychology. Sense of place goes beyond understanding place as merely a location; rather it addresses the relationship people have with that place, and the involvement between people within that place.

The meaning of neighborhoods as places is a social and cultural construct, and different groups give different meanings to these places. Place can be described by multidimensional physical, social, and psychological environmental attributes that are the result of human activity carried out there.[16]

As bounded locales imbued with personal, social, and cultural meanings, places become central to identity.[17] The social processes, symbols, and values deriving from places inform the identity formation of people. Hence, place is important in the social construction of the self. Place identity can be described as an interpretation of self that uses environmental meaning to symbolize or define identity.[18]

Place attachment, sense of community, and place dependence are further sub-concepts of place identity, which to a certain extent overlap in the literature in defining and containing elements of emotional ties, affiliation, behav-

---

[15] Ghozlane Fleury-Bahi, Marie-Line Félonneau, and Dorothée Marchand, "Processes of Place Identification and Residential Satisfaction," *Environment and Behavior*, Vol. 40 (2008), pp. 669–82.

[16] Grace H. Pretty, Heather M. Chipuer, and Paul Bramston, "Sense of Place Amongst Adolescents and Adults in Two Rural Australian Towns: The Discriminating Features of Place Attachment, Sense of Community and Place Dependence in Relation to Place Identity," *Journal of Environmental Psychology*, Vol. 23, No. 3 (2003), pp. 273–87; Kaylene A. Sampson and Colin G. Goodrich, "Making Place: Identity Construction and Community Formation through 'Sense of Place' in Westland, New Zealand," *Society and Natural Resources*, Vol. 22 (2009), pp. 901–15.

[17] Setha M. Low and Irwin Altman, *Place Attachment* (New York: Plenum, 1992); Sampson and Goodrich, *Making Place*; Lee Cuba and David M. Hummon, "A Place to Call Home: Identification with Dwelling, Community, and Region," *The Sociological Quarterly*, Vol. 34, No. 1 (1993), pp. 111–31.

[18] Cuba and Hummon, "A Place to Call Home."

ioral commitment, satisfaction, and belonging.[19] Place attachment is described by Low as the "symbolic relationship formed by people giving culturally shared emotional and affective meanings to a particular space [...] that provides the basis for the individual's or group's understanding of, and relation to, the environment."[20] Place attachment is not only expressed in terms of the subjective feeling toward a geographical location, but also as a behavior of commitment towards the community, personal assets (such as homes and businesses) in the location, and social involvement and neighboring. Sampson and Goodrich argue that attachment to place affects place identity because the symbolic meaning of place generated through place attachment processes gives meaning and identity to oneself.[21]

Communities are central in attachment to place, belonging, and identity. Communities, as symbolically constructed social places, provide the medium through which individuals develop identity and belonging. Human interaction and shared community practices provide the social context in which individuals can articulate who they are.[22] The role of belonging to community through local social involvement in place identification has received ample empirical support.[23]

Place dependence considers the goal-oriented behavioral component of residents' sense of place. It expresses the value attributed to place in supporting activities and sustaining daily needs; or, in other words, how residents compare the quality of life, facilities, community, and opportunities in their area with the perceived quality of life and community in alternative places of residence, taking into account their activities and behavior. Place dependence relates to identity, as the latter can be constructed and maintained through engaging in practices and behaviors that connect individuals to particular places.[24]

[19] Pretty et al., *Sense of Place Amongst Adolescents and Adults in Two Rural Australian Towns*; M. Carmen Hidalgo and Bernardo Hernandez, "Place Attachment: Conceptual and Empirical Questions," *Journal of Environmental Psychology*, Vol. 21 (2001), pp. 273–81.
[20] Setha M. Low, "Symbolic Ties that Bind," *Human Behavior and Environment*, Vol. 12 (1992), pp. 165–85.
[21] Sampson and Goodrich, *Making Place*.
[22] Ibid.
[23] Cuba and Hummon, "A Place to Call Home."
[24] Pretty et al., *Sense of Place Amongst Adolescents and Adults in Two Rural Australian Towns*.

Methodology

Fieldwork was carried out in Mutrah in March 2011, January 2012, and January 2013, to gather data on demographic and socio-economic character-istics of residents, housing characteristics, and perceived quality of dwellings and neighborhood facilities. Moreover, the subjective evaluation of residents' attachment to place, sense of community, and place dependence were assessed.

A survey was carried out among 268 Mutrah residents during the first field visit. An eight-page questionnaire was developed in both Arabic and English that served to measure the following indicators: residence location, demo-graphic characteristics, employment, education, characteristics and condition of the dwelling, residential mobility, neighborhood attributes, sense of secu-rity, and neighborhood challenges. The research area was divided into eleven sub-areas for which a sample target was set. Such a stratified sampling tech-nique assured a geographically and demographically representative distribu-tion of residents over eighteen years of age from all parts of Mutrah. Of the 268 filled questionnaires, 264 were deemed as valid entries for analysis.

Quantitative data were supplemented with a qualitative assessment of the place identity and neighborhood attachment of Mutrah's residents in two of the eleven sampling areas during the second and third field visits. Short interviews with local residents—both nationals and expatriates—were conducted on the streets in the neighborhood in January 2012 and January 2013. The qualitative research was performed to acquire a more detailed understanding of the rela-tionship between residents' appreciation of the neighborhood and to what extent they identified with Mutrah, which the quantitative survey had insuffi-ciently managed to capture. The qualitative data serve to examine in more depth the quality of the relationship residents have with their neighborhoods.

The 2012 fieldwork focused on assessing neighborhood appreciation among residents, and interview questions addressed the following items: level of satisfaction with 1) the home (dwelling), 2) the neighborhood (physical and social aspects), and 3) facilities and services such as utilities, parking, recreational space, shops, health and educational services. It furthermore addressed questions on residential origin and history, intentions to move, perception of safety, and neighborhood problems.

During the 2013 fieldwork, place attachment, sense of community, and place dependence were the main concepts approached during the interviews, and questions asked related to residents' relationships with neighbors, the presence of family and friends nearby, level of attachment to the home and the neighborhood, reasons for attachment, duration of residence, sense of belonging and community, moving intentions and underlying reasons, values ascribed to Mutrah neighborhood as a place of residence, engagement in local activities such as community work and neighborhood social life, and economic dependency on the neighborhood (such as local employment and businesses). Besides interviews, observations in the area and photographic documentation provided additional evidence to demonstrate the mixed variety of housing quality and visual interpretations of sense of community in the neighborhood.[25]

Place Identity in the Mutrah Neighborhood

This section presents the findings of the research, and starts with an introduction to the neighborhood and an overview of housing and population characteristics in Mutrah. Place identity in Mutrah is then discussed, based on three components: place attachment, sense of community, and place dependence.

The greater Muscat Capital area has developed from a number of small-sized settlements along the coast. Mutrah, one of such settlements, has traditionally held the position of a trade and commercial node in the region. Around 1900, Mutrah was considered the largest town of the sultanate. Historical accounts of Mutrah describe its famous *souq* (market) and the town's key position as the "loading and unloading place of all caravans for and from the interior."[26] Mutrah is now a main tourist destination in greater Muscat and a port of call for cruise ships. The town is located in Wilayat Mutrah (see Map 10.1), west of adjacent Muscat town, north of Ruwi and the

---

[25] Working with undergraduate students in the field had both its advantages and limitations. The fact that the large majority of students were Omani nationals and all of them spoke Arabic greatly facilitated interaction with local residents, broke down language barriers, and helped gain trust among the interviewees. Some students even spoke additional languages, like Balushi and Hindi, and were very familiar with the area. Challenges on the other hand were observed with the fact that working with students meant an additional step in the process from raw field data (interview quotes, observations) to research findings, where knowledge was unavoidably transformed, lost, or compromised due to the generalization of findings, translation from Arabic to English, and the fact that qualitative data collection is sensitive to context and often takes an unstructured approach to data collection. See Alan Bryman, *Social Research Methods*, 4th edn (Oxford: Oxford University Press, 2012).

[26] John George Lorimer, *Gazetteer of the Persian Gulf, Oman, and Central Arabia*, 2 vols. (Calcutta: Superintendent of Government Printing, 1908–1915; reprinted by Archive Editions, 1986).

Central Business District, and east of the newer residential and expansion areas of the greater capital area. Due to its surrounding mountains and hills, the town has long maintained its unique character and size. Today's dominant economic activities continue to be commerce and retail, mainly in the *souq* area, as well as fishing, transport, and logistics via Port Sultan Qaboos, located in Mutrah bay (see Map 10.2). Mutrah's urban structure and character differ in many aspects from other parts of the urban agglomeration. Not only do they differ dramatically from the newer low-density residential areas, but are also distinct from its "twin town," Muscat. While nearby Muscat has lost its traditional set-up to urban redevelopment, which started in the 1970s to make room for a new financial and administrative center, Mutrah continues to be a typical port settlement, with its original urban structure partly intact, an irregular street pattern, a high population and housing density, a mixture of residential and commercial land use, and the typical lively and bustling atmosphere of trade hubs. Skeet's description of Mutrah in the 1970s is still largely valid today:

> The narrow alleys of the suq are crowded with bedu, with Batina Baluch, with sweating porters; there is a constant clack of coffee cups, a babble of bargaining ... [In Mutrah] the simple necessities of life are bought and sold; cloth, rice, coffee versus dates and limes ... Mutrah pulsates with life, with commerce, with activities of one sort or another.[27]

Mutrah currently has approximately 47,000 inhabitants and has become absorbed into the greater urban Muscat region.[28] Its population is heterogeneous, with a roughly equal number of Omani and expatriates. Mutrah is a traditional place of residence for Omani from various ethnic and tribal origins who have lived in the neighborhood for generations, as well as an area that absorbs migrant labor, particularly those of low-skilled and low-paid status. Due to its function as a trade and commerce hub, Mutrah has always been inhabited by a variety of population groups. In the *Gazetteer of the Persian Gulf, Oman and Central Arabia*, published c.1900, the multi-ethnic and heterogeneous composition of the population was described by J. G. Lorimer, who witnessed the presence of "Khojhas, Baluchis, Jadgals, Hindus, negroes, Bayasirah, Anadharah, Arabs of mixed tribes, and Persians."

[27] Ian Skeet, *Oman Before 1970: The end of an era* (London: Faber and Faber, 1974).
[28] Oman 2010 Census, http://85.154.248.117/MONE2010/#view=viewCensusSummary&selectedWafers=0&selectedColumns=1,2,3&selectedRows=2,5,7,8,9.

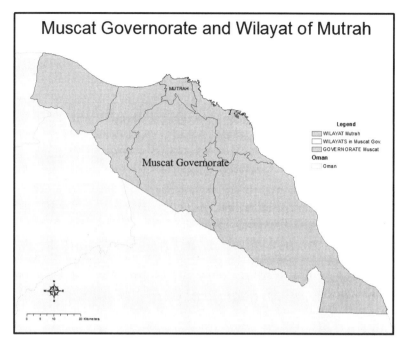

10.1: The Muscat Governate and Wilayat of Mutrah. Map courtesy of Adrijana Car

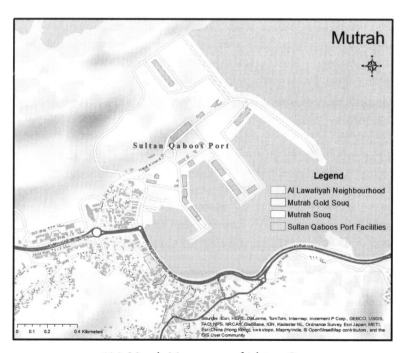

10.2: Mutrah. Map courtesy of Adrijana Car

It is useful to describe briefly the cultural and ethnic composition of the Mutrah population in more detail here. As Peterson notes, contemporary Mutrah has retained a large proportion of its original residents who have lived there for generations.[29] Although Mutrah was originally occupied by an Omani Arab tribe, already by the turn of the twentieth century they no longer comprised the majority of residents. With its history of maritime trade and seaward orientation, Mutrah has always attracted a range of outside population groups, mainly from other areas than present Oman. Peterson further estimates that during the last century, Arabs were only a minority of the mixed population. Baluch, originally from Baluchistan, situated in Pakistan and Iran, formed the largest share, followed by people of sub-Saharan African descent. In addition, 'Ajam, or Persians, and various families of Arab Shi'ah, known as Al-Baharinah, have been among the traditional groups of the area. Mutrah has furthermore been home to the Lawatiyyah, or Khojas, who are Ja'fari Shi'ah of Indian origin. These merchant families have traditionally occupied a walled quarter of Mutrah known as Sur al-Lawatiyyah, overlooking the harbor and corniche, which still exists today.'[30] Common family names in Mutrah are Al Balushi, Al Lawati, and Al Zadjali, the latter deriving from the *jadgals*, who are considered a subdivision of the Baluch. Baluchi, Lawati, and Zadjali are commonly spoken languages in Mutrah, in addition to Arabic. Peterson further observes that Baluch residents still predominate in Mutrah today.[31] Mutrah possesses both a Harat al-Balush (Baluch quarter) and Harat al-Zadjal (Zadjali quarter). It is important to note here, however, that the large majority of these ethnic groups now have Omani citizenship and fully participate in the nation society that Oman has built since the 1970s.

Demographic and socio-economic characteristics of neighborhood residents are not fixed in time, and survey data provide a snapshot of the status of Mutrah's residents in March 2011. The survey data confirm census data that Mutrah is home to expatriates and Omani alike. Half of the respondents are Omani, while the expat population comprises mainly Indians (one-third of the entire population), Bengali (9 per cent), and Pakistani (6 per cent).[32] Two-

---

[29] Peterson, *Historical Muscat*.
[30] Ibid.
[31] J. E. Peterson, "Oman's Diverse Society: Northern Oman," *Middle East Journal*, Vol. 58, No. 1 (2004), pp. 31–51.
[32] The spatial mixing of Omanis and expatriates is not unique to Mutrah: Peterson notes in *Historical Muscat* that nowhere in the Muscat region can a clear residen-

thirds of the respondents indicated that they were married, but this does not necessarily reflect household composition, as many expatriates live without their families. The low-income migrant status that many expatriate residents hold in Mutrah prevents them from bringing their families to Oman, due both to a lack of financial and accommodation means to support their families in Oman and to the restrictions of their sponsorship arrangements which exclude family residence in the country. The age structure demonstrates that the majority of residents are between twenty and forty years of age, reflecting a relatively young population of working age.[33] The young demographic profile of the national population as well as the dominant age cohorts of 25–29, 30–34 and 35–39 for the migrant population explain these trends.[34]

A wide variety of dwelling types exist in Mutrah. Detached houses, or villas, and apartments are the dominant dwelling types, although (shared) rooms and semi-detached (terraced) houses also contribute to the mix of dwellings. The traditional houses that have remained from the pre-oil era are mainly courtyard stone houses, usually one-storey high. Courtyard houses have commonly been split into smaller dwellings, each occupying one side of the original house. According to survey data, clear differences exist between the Omani and expat population and the dwelling types in which they reside. According to survey findings, while the majority of Omanis live in detached houses, most expats reside in apartments. In addition, it can be observed that Mutrah residents tend to rent rather than own a dwelling: 63 per cent of the respondents rent their residence against 37 per cent who own. Given the legal restrictions on expats owning property in Oman, it is evident that most of the house owners are Omani (95 per cent), whereas expats dominate the group that rents (78 per cent). Rents tend to be low compared to the general trend in the wider Muscat area, in the range of 50–150 Omani rial (OMR) per month. None of the renters pay more than 900 OMR per month for their dwelling in Mutrah, which is an amount more common in the more affluent neighborhoods of Qurum, Madinat Al Ilam, and Madinat Al Qaboos. On average, seven people reside in a single dwelling in Mutrah, with 4.9 adults and

---

tial segregation of Omani and expatriates be observed, a pattern that appears to have developed naturally.

[33] Observe that the data exclude the population younger than 18, since the target sample population constituted adult residents only.

[34] National Center for Statistics and Information, "Population", *Statistical Yearbook 2013* (Muscat: NCSI, 2013).

two children per household. Households on average consist of one kitchen, one bathroom/toilet, and 3.3 rooms.

As described above, the expatriates residing in Mutrah mainly come from the Indian subcontinent and can be characterized as low-income migrants. Since many expatriates are employed in the numerous shops in Mutrah's commercial area, many houses in Mutrah have been divided into apartments and rooms and are rented to large groups of foreign workers.[35]

Throughout its history, Mutrah has been known as a poor, low-quality neighborhood with cheap housing. Despite the presence of a number of wealthy merchant families in the area, Skeet described Mutrah around the 1970s as "a dirty town with pools or rivulets of filth all about it; unhealthy from too many people, no sanitation, too little water, too much poverty."[36] The survey data on resident and housing characteristics confirm that to this day Mutrah cannot be considered a wealthy neighborhood. The predominance of small-sized accommodation and relatively numerous households of seven members on average suggest situations of domestic overcrowding. The predominance of rent over ownership, and in particular the low monthly rental fees, reflect cheap housing and are a further indication that many Mutrah residents belong to the lower-income groups. Level of education, another proxy of socio-economic class, was also found to have a relatively low average in the neighborhood: secondary school was the highest level of education completed for 74 per cent of the respondents.

In the analysis of place identity in the Mutrah neighborhood, it is important to take into account this qualification of the area as a low-quality neighborhood in terms of physical attributes and socio-economic composition. A number of studies have demonstrated that residents of poor neighborhoods with a low socio-economic status tend to have a lower appreciation of their neighborhood than residents with a high socio-economic status.[37] Other studies have demonstrated that the low-quality status of an area can lead to a stronger intention to leave the neighborhood and lower levels of place attachment.[38] With

[35] Peterson, *Historical Muscat.*

[36] Skeet, *Oman Before 1970.*

[37] Alison Parkes, Ade Kearns, and Rowland Atkinson, "What Makes People Dissatisfied with their Neighbourhoods?" *Urban Studies*, Vol. 39, No. 13 (2002), pp. 2413–38; Victoria Basolo and Denise Strong, "Understanding the Neighbourhood: From Residents' Perception and Needs to Action," *Housing Policy Debate*, Vol. 13, No. 1 (2002), pp. 83–105.

[38] Ade Kearns and Alison Parkes, "Living in and Leaving Poor Neighbourhood

the understanding that Mutrah can be considered a poor-quality neighborhood, I will now explore to what extent this affects levels of place attachment
among Mutrah residents.

Below, I argue that despite the low quality of housing and neighborhood
facilities in Mutrah, and contrary to earlier studies that have demonstrated
that residents of low-quality neighbourhoods are more likely to leave, Mutrah
residents express a strong attachment to their homes and neighborhood. In
other words, the physical characteristics of housing and neighborhood conditions are not the key precursors that explain why residents appreciate living in
the neighborhood. I will first present the values and opinions that Mutrah
residents ascribe to the physical quality of their houses and neighborhood
conditions. Then I will demonstrate how attachment to place is of far greater
importance to the residential experience of Mutrah residents than the mere
physical attributes of the area. Finally I will discuss further the specific characteristics of length of residence, residential origin, and moving intentions of
residents and how they explain place attachment in Mutrah.

How do Mutrah residents value the physical quality of their housing situation? Survey data reveal that the general housing condition in Mutrah can be
considered substandard. While survey respondents perceived the physical
condition of the dwelling as acceptable with regard to water and electricity
services (78 per cent and 93 per cent, respectively), the majority (61 per cent)
also stated that their dwelling is in need of modification or renovation and
that substantial improvements are needed to make their dwelling a more
acceptable place to live. Moreover, about one-third (35 per cent) perceived
their dwelling to be overcrowded, and one-third (34 per cent) experienced
outside noise to be a nuisance to their living and comfort. In-depth interviews
with Mutrah residents further shed light on the quality of housing in the
neighborhood. Many respondents ascribed the poor and overcrowded conditions to the expanding household sizes. One Omani woman explained that as
her family expanded, her house had become increasingly overcrowded, with
each son living in the house with his wife and children. The increasing size of
the household had compromised her personal space, privacy, and ability to

---

Conditions in England," *Housing Studies*, Vol. 18, No. 6 (2003), pp. 827–52; Hans
Skifter Andersen, "Why Do Residents Want to Leave Deprived Neighbourhoods?
The Importance of Residents' Subjective Evaluations of their Neighbourhood and
its Reputation," *Journal of Housing and the Built Environment*, Vol. 23 (2008),
pp. 79–101.

manage the household chores. A thirty-two-year-old Omani male respondent illustrated how his family of twenty-five members lived in a six-room house and how all family members were disturbed by the overcrowding.

Respondents were furthermore asked how they valued the various neighborhood services and facilities in their area of residence. A high level of satisfaction is reported for police protection (88 per cent of respondents found this service adequate), the availability and vicinity of mosques or other places of worship (87 per cent), and the municipal services of street lighting (80 per cent) and garbage collection (76 per cent). Respondents were least satisfied with the availability and vicinity of parks, green spaces, and playgrounds (13 per cent), indoor recreational facilities (19 per cent), and social meeting places (32 per cent). In-depth interviews with residents produced the picture of a neighborhood lacking recreational space, especially for children who are constrained to playing in the alleys and streets of the neighborhoods. The nearest playground and parks, such as Riyam Park, are located on the fringes of Mutrah and are not within walking distance. Youngsters in particular mentioned the need for football pitches. Noise pollution and traffic congestion were also mentioned as elements that further negatively affect the level of comfort in the neighborhood.

Some additional, open-ended survey questions were posed to assess the most commonly reported problems occurring in the neighborhood (Figure 10.3). The open-ended character of the questions allowed respondents to prioritize the main issues as they saw them. These issues were mainly related to parking, which was mentioned by 56 respondents (21 per cent), followed by drainage and sewerage (mentioned 43 times, or 16 per cent of respondents). Parking is a main concern in the area, and both commercial and residential areas of Mutrah face a shortage of parking spaces. Narrow streets, sidewalks, and empty land are often blocked by parked vehicles, hindering the flow of traffic and pedestrian passage, and affecting the visual appearance of the area. Residents complained that the number of cars had increased during recent years. Residents further expressed their frustration with the drainage and sewerage problems in the area. Whenever it rains, the entire area is covered in overflowing sewage, which floods streets and homes, as well as the *souq*.[39]

However, despite substandard housing conditions, many residents would not consider moving from their homes. The above-mentioned Omani male respondent explained that it was not only the financial constraint that hindered him

[39] *Muscat Daily*, "Mutrah suq shop owners want permanent solution to flooding" (19 December 2012).

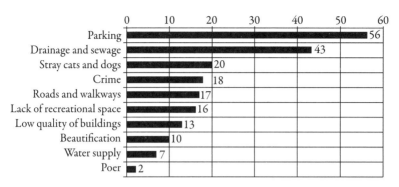

10.3: Neighborhood problems according to respondents (number of times mentioned)

from moving to a larger house in a less congested area, but also the strong attachment he and his family felt toward the neighborhood. A 39-year-old Omani female respondent described the poor condition and modest size of her house, which consisted of two rooms and a kitchen, and how this affected the living standards of her family of nine (Figure 10.4). Lack of finance and government support prevented the family from renovating. At the same time, the woman would not consider moving house even if she had the financial means. Another Omani respondent depicted how his extended family of seventeen members lived in a five-room dwelling that belonged to his grandmother. However, he did not report his home to be overcrowded. An Omani female respondent also stated that she felt comfortable in her house of four rooms occupied by ten persons. Hence, the housing *experience* appears to be far more positive than the actual physical housing condition would predict.

As regards their appreciation of the neighborhood, Mutrah residents pointed out a number of problems with the physical condition and facilities in the area. While some basic services such as water supply and electricity prove to be adequate, others such as sewerage, recreational space, and greenery were not. Overcrowding and general poor maintenance and condition of dwellings are of major concern. Parking and traffic congestion were often mentioned as key neighborhood problems. However, despite compromising housing and neighborhood standards, there is no overwhelming evidence that residents are highly unsatisfied with their neighborhood. While houses were overpopulated, respondents said they were content with their homes and would not consider moving.

It seems that physical dwelling and neighborhood conditions are not the key determinants that define how Mutrah residents value their neighborhood. In earlier studies, appreciation of the neighborhood (neighborhood satisfaction) determinants have often been classified into a physical and a social component,[40] or, in the words of Johnston,[41] the *impersonal* environment versus the *interpersonal* environment. Interaction with neighbors, such as talking with neighbors and having friends and relatives living in the neighborhood, has been found to have a strong positive effect on neighborhood appreciation.[42]

Below, I argue how place identity and its elements of place attachment, sense of community, and place dependence largely define and explain the residential experience and appreciation of the neighborhood among Mutrah residents.

The relationships between appreciation of the neighborhood, length of residence, the intention to move, home ownership, and place identity have been addressed in earlier studies.[43] Length of residence has been found to have a positive effect on neighborhood appreciation and place attachment, resulting from the social and psychological ties to a place that increase over time, from the duration of home ownership, and from social interaction and psychological dynamics among residents.[44] As Mesch and Manor observe,[45] home ownership is instrumental to developing social involvement and place attachment. Moreover, they note that as the development of sentiments toward

---

[40] Misun Hur and Hazel Morrow-Jones, "Factors that Influence Residents' Satisfaction with Neighborhoods," *Environmental Behavior*, Vol. 40, No. 5 (2008), pp. 619–35.

[41] R. J. Johnston, "Spatial Patterns in Suburban Evaluations," *Environment and Planning*, Vol. 5 (1973), pp. 385–95.

[42] Hur and Morrow-Jones, "Factors that Influence Residents' Satisfaction with Neighborhoods"; Johan Mohan and Liz Twigg, "Sense of Place, Quality of Life and Local Socioeconomic Context: Evidence from the Survey of English Housing, 2002/03," *Urban Studies*, Vol. 44, No. 10 (2007), pp. 2029–45.

[43] See for example Mesch and Manor, "Social Ties, Environmental Perception, and Local Attachment"; Fleury-Bahi et al., "Processes of Place Identification and Residential Satisfaction"; Ondřej Špaček, "Meaning of Place in Neighbourhoods of Prague," presented at the Sustainable Cities and Regions conference, Örebro University, Sweden, 11–13 March 2009; Robert J. Sampson, "Local Friendship Ties and Community Attachment in Mass Society: A Multilevel Systemic Model," *American Sociological Review*, Vol. 53 (1988), pp. 766–79.

[44] Špaček, "Meaning of Place in Neighbourhoods of Prague"; Hur and Morrow-Jones, "Factors that Influence Residents' Satisfaction with Neighborhoods".

[45] Mesch and Manor, "Social Ties, Environmental Perception, and Local Attachment."

10.4: Poor housing conditions in Mutrah (field visit January 2012), Photo courtesy of: Maryal Al Farsi and Fathiya Al Kindy

place is a temporal process, length of residence tends to have a positive effect on place attachment. Duration of residence has been found to provide an important temporal context for imbuing place with personal meanings,[46] and is shown to be a factor that reduces moving intentions.[47] Hence length of residence, residential origin, and moving intentions are considered key factors explaining place attachment. In order to assess place attachment among Mutrah residents, this section describes where Mutrah residents originally come from, how long they have lived in the neighborhood, and to what extent they consider moving.

Survey data demonstrate that most Mutrah residents have lived in their current dwellings for a considerable time: more than eighteen years. The difference between the expatriate and Omani population is logical yet striking: whereas most expatriates have resided in Mutrah for five years or less, with 73 per cent coming directly to Mutrah from another country, the overwhelm-

---

[46] Cuba and Hummon, "A Place to Call Home".
[47] Skifter Andersen, "Why Do Residents Want to Leave Deprived Neighbourhoods?"

ing majority of Omani residents have lived in the neighborhood for more than twenty years (Figure 10.5). Moreover, most Omani Mutrah residents are originally from Mutrah (65 per cent). The majority of Omani residents in Mutrah were thus born in the area and grew up there. In addition, one-third of them are still living in the house they were born in: this was the case for 33 per cent of respondents.

Would Mutrah residents prefer to leave their neighborhood? Thanks to land grant schemes and social welfare policies that allow all citizens to obtain land for residential purposes, the detached villa on a walled plot in one of the new residential neighborhoods has become the new residential aspiration for Omani families. Does this pull Omani residents away from high-density and overcrowded Mutrah? Survey data on residents' moving intentions reveal that Mutrah residents in general are not likely to leave their dwelling. For Omanis and expats alike, the majority of respondents (58 per cent and 72 per cent respectively) did not plan to move in the next three years. Of those who did plan to move, the Omani residents tend to have a stronger preference to move outside Mutrah, whereas the expats lean more strongly to moving within the Mutrah area.[48] While Omani residents may look for a more modern residential setting in one of the land grant neighborhoods where a detached home on a walled plot is within their reach, migrants expressed the desire to live near their work in the Mutrah area.

It is interesting to note here that residents who aspire to more modern housing do not necessarily leave the neighborhood. In addition to traditional, pre-oil houses, Mutrah has a wide range of new or renovated "modern" homes, defined by the National Center for Statistics and Information as "modern housing units," which tend to be more spacious, meet today's comfort standards, and are comparable to dwellings in the new residential areas of the city (Figure 10.6). In Mutrah, one finds modern homes mingling with "old" and damaged homes (Figure 10.7A). Modern housing units have replaced a number of traditional homes, and renovation and construction of new homes was also witnessed at the time of research (Figure 10.7B). Investment and renovation of dwellings are

---

[48] In-depth interviews with expatriates showed that many of them are less than satisfied with their current dwelling, which could explain the expressed desire to move house. Many expatriates described the poor housing conditions and overcrowding they were facing. Sharing a room with six to twenty roommates is not uncommon. At the same time, budget constraints as well as the fact that housing is organized by their sponsor limits their decision-making abilities toward finding better housing.

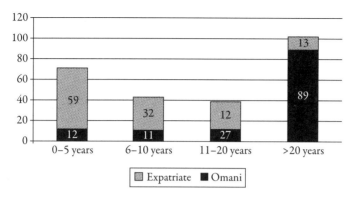

10.5: Omani and expatriate residents: number of years lived in Mutrah

symbolic signs of the intention to stay in the neighborhood. Data on building permits[49] in the area for the years 2006–11 confirm that renovation and construction of residential homes is common in the Mutrah area, and that Muscat Municipality has been supportive in this regard. More than half the permits were allocated to residential space, while commercial and mixed-use buildings accounted for the bulk of the remainder of permits.

Interview data reveal that Omani Mutrah residents feel strongly attached to their neighborhood and share a common discourse that refers to Mutrah as the place where they were born and have their family roots. This process of giving symbolic meaning to place which is created and maintained by means of a continued connection to place through birth, history, marriage, and family lineage has been described by Low as "genealogical attachment."[50] Many respondents said they would never want to leave Mutrah; some even said that it was impossible to imagine. In particular, but by no means exclusively, elderly interviewees expressed a strong emotional attachment to their neighborhood. They grew up in the neighborhood, have childhood memories of their place of living, and many live in homes that have been in the family for generations. They explained how their fathers, grandfathers, and great-grandfathers had lived in Mutrah, and how they will continue to do so. While such rooted, localized residential history was customary in the pre-oil tribal society of Oman, this has become more of an exception in the modern Muscat capital

[49] Norplan, *Mutrah Redevelopment Master Plan Working Paper 18: Private Sector Investment*, December 2011.
[50] Low, "Symbolic Ties that Bind."

10.6: Modern housing units in Mutrah (field visit January 2013)

10.7: Old versus new: mixed quality of housing in Mutrah (top); Investments and renovation in the neighborhood symbolize the intention to stay (bottom)

area, with the arrival of urbanization, new white-collar employment opportunities, land grant neighbourhoods that have destabilized spatial–tribal patterns, and car mobility.

An elderly woman said that her house was largely destroyed during cyclone Gonu in 2007,[51] which rendered the majority of rooms uninhabitable. But she was adamant about not moving out, as she claimed her parents and grandparents also used to live in the house and therefore she did not want to leave. A Baluch trader and shop owner explained that even though he now owned houses in two other areas of the city, he preferred to be in Mutrah "as this is the area [he] was raised in and where [he felt] comfortable."

Inheritance of homes and businesses strongly affects the people–place dynamics of the neighborhood, as it provides a physical as well as an emotional component for why Omani residents in Mutrah tend to have lived in the neighborhood for a long number of years, are reluctant to move, and feel attached to their neighborhood. Many homes of Omani residents have been passed on from generation to generation. Moreover, a considerable number of the small-scale businesses and shops in the area—in particular the *souq*—have been in the family for generations. One shopkeeper at the vegetable *souq* said that he had been selling fruit and vegetables since he was a young boy. He had been working in his shop, which once belonged to his great-grandfather, for more than thirty years. The shared family history of Mutrah residents generates a strong sense of affiliation and emotional bonding with the neighborhood.

This case study will now turn to assessing the sense of community as a second component of place identity in Mutrah, drawing primarily from the qualitative data gathered in the neighborhood. Sense of community should not be considered as a stand-alone element of place identity, separate from place attachment. On the contrary, place attachment and sense of community are largely intertwined, and the indicators of place attachment, such as length of residence and residential origin, are not only a function of place but also a function of community.

Meanings and experiences of place usually involve relationships with other people.[52] It has been found that a high sense of community increases the appreciation of the neighborhood and place attachment.[53] Skifter Andersen

<hr>

51 Cyclone Gonu, the strongest tropical cyclone in the Arabian Sea ever recorded, left massive damage to many coastal regions in Oman, including Muscat.

52 Mesch and Manor, "Social Ties, Environmental Perception, and Local Attachment."

53 Ibid.; Fleury-Bahi et al., "Processes of Place Identification and Residential Satisfaction."

found that the stronger the sense of community in a neighborhood, the lower the intention to move.[54] He considers the affiliation with a neighborhood, having friends and family in the area, and good relations with neighbors as strong elements of a sense of community. Mohan and Twigg argue that such correlations would imply that as long as residents are able to establish good social networks over time, they are not necessarily dissatisfied with their neighborhood, even if they are living in relatively poor, crowded, rundown, or polluted locations.[55] Social support in the community and the presence of family and friends nearby lead to higher neighborhood appreciation and place attachment. How do these factors relate to the case of Mutrah?

Interview findings confirmed the historical ties of Mutrah residents with the neighborhood and the social and ethnic groups that have traditionally lived here. Many Omani respondents confirmed that they had a strong social network of relatives and extended families living in their direct vicinity. One respondent from the Al-Lawatiyyah quarter explained that members of the Al Lawati who no longer live in Mutrah usually return to the quarter on religious occasions and other celebrations. The quarter maintains an important socio-spatial function of group identity, and puts the notion of place central to the socialization process of the Al Lawatiyyah.

In Mutrah, residents frequently mentioned how important the presence of family and friends was in their direct area of residence, and how much it meant to them to have a positive and active relationship with their neighbors. One respondent stated: "If I moved away from Mutrah, the neighbors [in the new place of residence] would not ask after each other and they would not visit each other." Many residents have relatives living nearby. Often, a cluster of houses is occupied by different members of one extended family, hence neighbors and relatives occupy the same position and role in the social fabric of the direct residential area. A study by Logan and Spitze confirms the importance of the role of family to social interaction,[56] as they found that the number of family neighbors is the best predictor of neighborhood social interaction.[57] The meaning of Mutrah as a place to interact with relatives and

---

[54] Skifter Andersen, "Why Do Residents Want to Leave Deprived Neighbourhoods?"

[55] Mohan and Twigg, "Sense of Place, Quality of Life and Local Socioeconomic Context."

[56] John R. Logan and Glenna D. Spitze, "Family Neighbors," *American Journal of Sociology*, Vol. 100, No. 2 (1994), pp. 453–76.

[57] It should be noted here that expatriates also felt positive about their relationship

neighbors leads to a strong sense of place, a feeling of belonging. As such, Mutrah serves as a symbol of self or group identity, mediated through both place and community.

Friendly neighborhood relations contribute to the sense of security among residents. Survey data reveal that Mutrah residents tend to have a high sense of security in their area of residence: 88 per cent of the respondents felt safe in public areas in Mutrah. Respondents stated that knowing their neighbors and being surrounded by family and friends contributed greatly to their feeling of safety. Both Omani and expatriates, as well as male and female, said that they felt safe and secure at all times of day in the neighborhood. It was also observed that many homes in Mutrah with direct access to the street have their doors open all day long, allowing free passage for inhabitants and visitors, blurring the boundaries between the public and private sphere.

In the context of neighborhoods as place, place dependence addresses residents' perception of the quality and assets of their neighborhood by comparison with other, alternative neighborhoods; or, in other words, how residents compare the quality of life, facilities, community, and opportunities in their area with the perceived quality of life and community in alternative places of residence. Place dependence thus expresses the value attributed to place in supporting activities and sustaining daily needs.

One expression of place dependence in Mutrah is the strong economic ties that residents have with their neighborhood. The majority of respondents are employed (61 per cent) and further analysis on the employed population reveals that three out of four employed respondents work in the Mutrah area proper (75 per cent).[58] Working in Mutrah was especially significant for the male expat population, of which 93 per cent were employed in the area. These findings suggest that a large number of residents work in the relatively extensive retail

---

with neighbours. Clashes between people from different nationalities or ethnic groups were hardly reported. Both Omanis and expatriates perceived their neighbors to be "friendly and hospitable," as one respondent put it. One Pakistani respondent explained how he feels comfortable with his Omani neighbors and that he has befriended both Omani and expatriate neighbors.

[58] More than half of employed Mutrah residents are male expats (57 per cent), whereas Omani males constitute about one-third (32 per cent) of the employed respondents. The traditional activities of trade and commerce in Mutrah are reflected in the survey data: the dominant sector of employment for Mutrah residents is the trade and retail sector (55 per cent).

sector in Mutrah,[59] characterized by the many small-scale shops and businesses, including the *souq*. Overall, Mutrah is a place for both living and working, and the Mutrah population tends to live and work in the same area. Low found that economic connections to place reinforce place attachment and place identity.[60] Galster et al. found the extent of local business and employment in the area to be an important indicator of neighborhood appreciation.[61]

The findings thus reveal that the large majority of employed residents work in Mutrah, primarily in the area's extensive retail sector. Respondents considered these economic ties and the economic, business, and employment opportunities of the commercial area of Mutrah to be unique neighborhood features, and irreplaceable in alternative locations. For many Omani residents of Mutrah, the small-scale shops which they own have economic significance (providing an income) as well as emotional significance (these shops have been passed on by family lineage). Residents valued the fact that they live close to their work, making it easy to move between their professional and social lives, and allowing a mingling of the two spheres. This has become a rather unique setting within the context of the greater Muscat capital area, which since the 1990s was subject to urban master planning based on functional segregation and zoning, resulting in new residential areas segregated from employment and recreation and requiring car mobility. Shopkeepers also mentioned the added value of having long-lasting relations with the large, local neighborhood customer base.[62] This further created a sense of pride based on their ability to satisfy local shopping needs and meet customers' expectations.

It appears that Mutrah offers residents a certain lifestyle that is highly valued by its residents and would not easily be found in different areas of the city. This

---

[59] The results show that of those respondents working in Mutrah, 66 per cent work in retail. Of the respondents who work outside Mutrah, only one was said to be employed in the retail sector.

[60] Low, "Symbolic Ties that Bind."

[61] George Galster, Chris Hayes, and Jennifer Johnston, "Identifying Robust, Parsimonious Indicators of Neighbourhood Quality of Life," *Journal of Planning Education and Research*, Vol. 24, No. 3 (2005), pp. 265–80.

[62] Despite lower levels of appreciation with their individual dwelling, expatriates said they were content living in Mutrah. An important factor in Mutrah's residential attractiveness for expatriates is providing proximity of residence to place of work, and hence reduced commuting time and cost. As demonstrated above, the majority of Mutrah residents work in the neighborhood, especially expatriates. Also, for survey respondents who were not originally from the area, the main reason to move to Mutrah was to be near their work.

lifestyle comprises "rootedness"[63] in the neighborhood; the proximity and presence of relatives, extended family, and social and ethnic group members; reduced barriers between public and private space and the blurred separation of professional and private activities; easy interaction with neighbors; a sense of security; and the physical characteristics of the neighborhood. Residents described how comfortable they feel living in Mutrah, how they do their shopping in the local retail outlets and corner shops, and how they walk to work, to do their groceries, to go to school instead of having to rely on motorized transport. The respondents also frequently reiterated that the neighborhood features that define their quality of life would not be available in alternative areas of residence. Some of the specific neighborhood features mentioned that were unique to the area include: the general atmosphere in the public domains of the streets and *souq*, the specific small-scale shopping and trading activities of the area, and the liveliness and specific physical amenities of the area such as the corniche and *souq*. Economic and social participation of residents in the Mutrah neighborhood increases the overall level of neighborhood activity. This constant involvement in activities develops feelings of familiarity, belonging, and attachment. Mutrah as a neighborhood appears to provide residents with ample opportunities to engage and participate, which subsequently intensifies identity formation with the place in which these activities occur.

Obviously, there were differences in opinion as well. Some (often younger) residents expressed mixed feelings about the quality of life in Mutrah and the extent to which they could identify with their neighborhood. Some said they would like to move out if they could. A single male Omani said he would like to move because of the small size of the houses and the "village" feel of the neighborhood. For a number of Omani respondents, the disadvantages of the neighborhood were taking their toll and they considered seeking a higher standard of living outside the neighborhood. As reasons to move out of Mutrah, some respondents mentioned in particular the overcrowding and growing population in the area; poor neighborhood facilities, such as the sewerage system; and small and poorly maintained homes as against their need for large houses to accommodate expanding families. Indeed, the survey results indicated that while the majority of Omani respondents have the intention of staying in Mutrah, more than one in four respondents intend to move outside the area. One young Omani woman residing in Sur-al-Lawatiyyah explained how she would prefer to move to a place that was less "traditional."

---

[63] Robert Hay, "A Rooted Sense of Place in Cross-Cultural Perspective," *Canadian Geographer*, Vol. 42, No. 4 (1998), pp. 245–66.

She preferred to be near entertainment facilities in other parts of the city that contained malls, bowling centers, and cinemas, rather than the more traditional shopping and leisure offered by Mutrah's *souq*. Also other young residents thought that they could obtain a different lifestyle outside Mutrah, arguing that "life is different now than before." Apparently, Mutrah not only represents a place of residence; it also represents a way of life that remains attractive to many of its residents, but not to everyone.

Discussion and Conclusions

This neighborhood study has examined aspects of place identity, community, and belonging, and the interrelationships of these notions, as well as how place is constructed and practiced in Mutrah, Oman. The study has demonstrated that appreciation of the neighborhood, despite the substandard quality of housing conditions and neighborhood attributes, tends to be relatively high in Mutrah, which is mainly the result of the strong sense of identity that residents feel toward their neighborhood. Both length of residence and residential origin are important factors for understanding sense of place and the level of identification with the neighborhood. To many of its residents, Mutrah serves as a strong symbol of self or group identity. It is a place of childhood memories and of rootedness, and it generates a sense of belonging and economic subsistence. Unlike other residential areas of the Greater Muscat region, Mutrah is still occupied by citizen groups who have resided there for generations. This partly explains the strong sense of community and interaction with neighbors, who are often part of the same family or social/tribal group. Furthermore, Mutrah provides economic opportunities for the majority of employed residents, and a way of life that is perceived to be unique to the area. For expatriates, proximity to work (place dependence) and social acceptance explain a certain level of neighborhood appreciation, despite their poor housing conditions. Even though new housing and new land is now accessible to many Omanis, thanks to land grant schemes and social welfare policies, many of the Mutrah residents prefer to stay in the area.

What can the case of Mutrah tell us about neighborhood planning in Oman and in the Gulf? As Hur and Morrow-Jones observed, the neighborhood remains the most basic environmental unit in which social life occurs, and it unavoidably affects residents' quality of life.[64] While new residential areas in the

---

[64] Hur and Morrow-Jones, "Factors that Influence Residents' Satisfaction with Neighborhoods."

Greater Muscat region provide better infrastructure and sanitation, and generally more modern housing with more space and privacy than older districts such as Mutrah, it also diminishes residents' sense of community and identification with their area of residence. For the majority of urban dwellers in Gulf cities, the role of neighborhoods appears to have become less significant.

The rapid urban development and the urban design initiatives in contemporary urban planning in the Gulf may cause the weakening of place identity. Gulf cities have witnessed a process where traditional and original urban structures have been replaced by modern ones, leading to a strong homogenization and standardization of Gulf cities' character and image. In many cases, this standardization has led to loss of local context and culture, and localized practices of traditional economic activities, ways of life, and the historically intrinsic connections between place and community. Whereas some urban renovation or rehabilitation initiatives have been successful in maintaining or strengthening the original character and function of historical districts, such as Souk Al-Mubarakiya in Kuwait City and Muharraq district in Bahrain, for other historical urban districts such initiatives have come too late. These neighborhoods have followed the typical stages of neighborhood transition in the Gulf: urban degeneration and decay, loss of residential quality, outflow of original residents, transition of dwellings into cheap housing, and the concomitant influx of low-income migrant labor.

While comparing Mutrah with other historical districts in the Gulf, it stands out because it has been continuously occupied by a large Omani population; the economic vitality of the area discourages original residents from moving out; and the fact that Oman, among the poorer nations of the GCC, has lower levels of inequality, also between residential areas. These aspects may have prevented Mutrah from entering the downward spiral of Gulf neighborhood transition as described above. While the strong sense of community in Mutrah may be explained by the presence of family and tribe members in the neighborhood, it is unclear whether there is also a strong inter-ethnic and inter-cultural interaction among the different population groups (citizens and non-citizens) within Mutrah or whether tensions exist between Omani residents and the low-income migrants that have arrived in more recent times. Future research could address this in more detail, and focus in particular on the diverse ethnic heritage and self-identity of the originally non-Arab overseas population groups in Mutrah who are Omani citizens today but were once migrants themselves. Some urban design projects aiming to reconstruct and rehabilitate traditional neighborhoods have begun in many Gulf cities, where not only physical structures and buildings are being demolished and replaced, but also new identity and meaning are recreated and imbued. One example is Msheireb in the old district of Doha, which according to the project developer is envisioned to "bring people back to their roots ... and rediscover a sense of community and togetherness."[65] The commercial project of neighborhood design emphasizes the qualities of neighborhood identity and community, and as such place attachment, identity, and sense of community become commoditized features of new urban design. In the practice of placemaking, place meaning is often created in a reduced kind of physical appearance and image, but not with the meaning of place held by the residents.

The weakening of place identity can thus be witnessed across Gulf cities. However, identification with place is important as it fosters social and political cohesion and the preservation of the physical and social assets that characterize neighborhoods and ensure social stability.[66] Urban planning and neighborhood design too often address only the physical facilities and appearance of neighborhoods, despite the fact that neighborhood appreciation is often primarily a socio-emotional function of residents' sense of identification with their neighborhood.

Quality of life is an important precondition for people to stay in their neighborhood, and place identity and sense of community have a positive impact on quality of life. Maintaining a thriving community spirit is not only relevant in the light of quality of life for its residents, but also for reasons of tourism and cultural heritage preservation. The plethora of urban functions that Mutrah offers—commerce and tourism, display of history, national identity, and cultural heritage—easily obscures the significance of the area as a place to live. To maintain its livelihood, it is important to retain the current residents, and make the place attractive to prospective middle-class residents; also, to make it attractive to tourism—*souq* shops run by Omani locals, a neighborhood life in which everyone participates—which may offer a welcoming change to many of the Disneyfied tourist experiences in Gulf cities where many places have been stripped down from their original character and repackaged in an artificial manner. Notions of new urbanism—including

---

[65] Msheireb Properties, "Msheireb Downtown Doha", http://www.msheireb.com/en-us/projects/msheirebdowntowndoha.aspx#sthash.pGuDLqjP.dpufv, last accessed 26 May 2016.

[66] Mesch and Manor, "Social Ties, Environmental Perception, and Local Attachment"; Skifter Andersen, "Why Do Residents Want to Leave Deprived Neighbourhoods?"

walkable neighborhoods, a functional mixture of jobs and housing, high-density development, and public space that encourages social interaction—apply to the urban vitality of Mutrah and constitute a unique selling point to attract outside visitors.

The case of Mutrah may provide a meaningful insight into understanding place identity in other historical city areas in the Gulf that are still populated by their original residents. Even though many of these areas may face low standards of living and poor housing conditions, quality of life may be perceived to be high by their residents, based on their emotional attachment and sense of belonging to the neighborhood. The role of place identity in quality of life challenges certain urban redevelopment decisions, such as the planned demolition of the historical Hafah district in Salalah in Oman's Dhofar region to make way for a new tourist area. Future research could look into comparing in more detail the historical districts in Gulf cities, and their meaning to residents. Recognizing that place identity is an important precondition to neighborhood appreciation and quality of life in urban planning may help us maintain livable and vibrant communities within sustainable Gulf cities.

INDEX

INDEX

INDEX

green field sites 37
Green Island, Kuwait 63
grid-pattern roads 52, 60
Guggenheim, Abu Dhabi 69–7, 129, 151, *152*
Gulf Air 172
'Gulf Cities Emerge as New Centers of Arab World' (al-Qassemi) 103, 105–6, 109
'Gulf Cities: Space, Society, Culture' 108–9, 111
Gulf Cooperation Council (GCC) 45–6, 98, 114, 127, 130, 175, 180–1, 184, 188, 198, 260
    and Arab Spring 180
    competition within 46
    Dubai as regional hub 39
    economic diversification in 181, 184, 188, 196
    and globalization 45, 181
    infrastructure in 59
    Iran and 114
    Iraq and 114
    real estate market in 175
    regulations in 65
    smart cities in 190
    taxation in 98
    urbanization of 112
    Yemen and 114
Gulshahr, Bandar Abbas 219

Hadid, Zaha 108, 147, 151
Hafah, Oman 262
Hall, Stewart 139–40
Hamad bin Isa, King of Bahrain 173
Hamad bin Khalifa University, Doha 143, 153
Harat al-Balush, Mutrah 242
Harat al-Zadjal, Mutrah 242
harbors 4, 26, 33, 60, 64–5, 127–9, 204, 213

Harris, John 163
Harvey, David 102, 107, 113, 119
Hay, Rupert 83, 85
Heard-Bey, Frauke 86
Heart of Europe Island, Dubai 132
Hein, Carola 22
heritage 10, 13, 44, 65, 72–3, 113–4, 117, 141, 155, 189, 191, 235, 260, 261
    museums 44, 61, 68–9, 77, 129, 149–52
high-rise towers 9, 46, 53, 60–2, 70, 72–4, 111, 118, 121, 134, 147, 164, 167, 189
highways *see under* roads
Hijaz, Saudi Arabia 33
Hilling, David 36
hinterlands 6, 21, 22, 23, 26, 32, 81, 89, 91, 159
Hong Kong 77, 125
honor and shame 88
Hormozgan Province, Iran 203, 214, 215, 216, 218, 220, 222
Hormuz Straits 26, 31, 203
hotels 59, 60, 61, 68, 73, 77, 128–9, 165
housing *see under* residential areas
Hoyle, Brian 36
Huffington Post 103
Hur, Misun 259
hydrocarbons 46
hydroelectricity 126
hyper-urbanism 115, 18, 116
Ideascapes 124
identity 10, 12, 14, 17, 28, 53, 61, 66–8, 70, 110, 121, 137–56, 189
    and architecture 10, 15, 61, 67–8, 121, 137–56, 189
    place identity 17, 236–62
illicit trade 39, 51–6, 55–6
Imam Husayn Boulevard, Bandar Abbas 220

INDEX

Isozaki, Arata 153
Istanbul, Turkey 8, 32

Jacobsson, Staffan 187
Japan 5, 125, 186
Javaheripour, Mehrdad 16
al-Jazeera 124
al-Jazira Tourism Company 172
Jebel Ali Port, Dubai 37, 39, 64–5, 96,
    98–9, 124, 128, 158, 164, 169–70,
    179
Jeddah, Saudi Arabia 123, 125, 147
Johnston, R. J. 248
Juffair District, Manama 175, 177, *178*
Jumeirah, Dubai 132, 141, *142*, 166,
    167
Jumhuri-i Islami Boulevard, Bandar
    Abbas 219

Kaaba, Mecca 73
Kamarbandi, Bandar Abbas 220, 222,
    223
Kanna, Ahmed 12, 15, 38
Karachi, Pakistan 31
Karwa 136
Katara Cultural Village, Doha 61
Keshavarzian, Arang 14, 44
Khalaf, Sulayman 1, 76
Khalifa, Emir of Abu Dhabi 70
Khalifa, Ali Mohammed 87, 97–8
Khobar, Saudi Arabia 47
Khojas 242
Khor Abdullah waterway 34
Khor Azzubeir, Basra 57
Khor Fakkan, Sharjah 92
Khorramshahr, Iran 53, 220
Khuzestan, Iran 48, 49
Khwajih Ata, Bandar Abbas 223
King Faisal Highway, Bahrain 134, 177
Kingdom Tower, Jeddah 147
kinship 23, 28, 30

Kirmanshah, Iran 211
Knowledge City, Dubai 124
knowledge economy 6, 16, 46, 115,
    125, 127, 154–5, 188, 194, 196
knowledge production 6, 101–2, 104,
    107–8, 118–20, 154
Kobe, Japan 5
Koolhaas, Rem 108
Kuwait
    Ahmadi 47
    American University of Kuwait
        (AUK) 108–9, 111–12
    architecture 57, 66, 68
    British protectorate 33
    Bubiyan Island 33–4
    Burj Mubarak Al Kabir 72
    Central Bank 68
    city v. state 35
    City of Silk 72–3, 137
    development plan (2010–14) 12
    free trade zones 128
    global aspirations 5, 9, 13, 15, 20,
        43–4, 46–7, 59, 123, 125
    Green Island 63
    Gulf War (1990–77) 34, 45, 68, 171
    Iraqi–Kuwait border skirmish
        (1972) 34
    Madinat Al Hareer 72–3, 137
    master plan 65
    migration/segregation 38, 75, 190
    National Museum 69
    oil 37, 47, 62, 84, 162
    pearling 27, 28, 30–1, 62, 90
    port facilities 34
    service hub 154–5
    Shuaiba Port 37
    Souk Al-Mubarakiya 260
    unrest 11, 173
    Warba Island 33–4
    Water Towers 68
Kyoto Protocol 200

273

informal settlements 220–2, 225
and identity 50, 53
place identity 234–5, 238, 240,
242–4, 249–51, 255–7, 259
and segregation 37–8, 39, 41,
49–52, 74–7, 121, 132, 134–7,
161, 189
temporary society 129–30
Mihr Housing Plan (MHP) 213, 227
Mina Al Salam, Dubai 141, *142*
Mina Salman, Manama 164
Minab, Iran 218
Ministry of Electricity and Water,
Bahrain 174
Ministry of Energy, Iran 222
Ministry of Foreign Affairs, Kuwait 68
Ministry of Housing, Bahrain 173–4
Ministry of Municipalities and Agricultural Affairs, Bahrain 174
Ministry of the Interior, Bahrain 147
Ministry of Works and Housing,
Bahrain 174
Mitchell, Timothy 116
Mitsubishi Heavy Industries 195
modernity 9–10, 59, 65, 70, 73–4, 82,
92, 99, 112, 117, 123, 137–56, 162,
189, 232, 234
architecture and 141, 145
cities and 59, 188
gift of 109
in Iran 51
port cities and 4, 73
real estate development and 13
urban planning/urbanization and 9,
18, 109
Mohammed bin Rashid, Emir of Dubai
165, 169
Mohan, John 255
Mojtahed-Zadeh, Pirouz 83
Mokka, Yemen 30
Molotch, Harvey 159

Moore, Amelia 117, 119
Morocco 124
Morrow-Jones, Hazel 259
Mossessian and Partners 145, 147
Msheireb Downtown Doha 126, 145,
146, 147, 261
Mubadala Development Company
188, 193
Muharraq, Bahrain 175, 235, 260
multicultural cities 28–9, 30, 77
multiple modernities 15, 17, 121,
137–56
Municipal Bazaar, Bandar Abbas 216
Munif, Abdelrahman 66
Muscat, Oman 14, 17, 18, 26, 30, 31,
93, 123, 125, 232–62
Museum of Islamic Art, Doha 61, 68,
69, 150, *150*
museums 44, 61, 68, 69, 77, 129,
149–52
Mussadiq, Muhammad 51
Mutrah, Muscat 17, 18, 232–62
MZ Architects 110

al-Naim, Mashary 67
naïve realism 15, 103–4
Nakheel 166–70
Nakhl-i Nakhuda, Bandar Abbas 218,
222, 223, 225
al-Nakib, Farah 62
nation-building 14, 82, 86
National Museum, Doha 68, 69, 151
National Museum, Manama 69
nationalism 41, 51
natural harbors 26
Nayband, Bandar Abbas 218, 220, 222,
223
neo-traditional architecture 67–8,
140–47
neoliberalism 102, 106, 108, 117, 118,
183–201